Neoliberal Spatial Gov

Neoliberal Spatial Governance explores the changing nature of English town and city planning as it has slowly but clearly transformed. Once a system for regulating and balancing change in the built and natural environments in the public interest, planning now finds itself facilitating development and economic growth for narrow sectional interests.

While lip service is paid towards traditional values, the progressive aims and inclusivity that provided planning's legitimacy and broad support have now largely disappeared. The result is a growing backlash of distrust and discontent as planning has evolved into neoliberal spatial governance. The tragedy of this change is that at a time when planning has a critical role in tackling major issues such as housing affordability and climate change, it finds itself poorly resourced, plagued by low professional morale, lacking legitimacy and support from local communities, accused of bureaucracy and excessive 'red tape' from businesses and ministers and subject to regular, disruptive reforms. Yet all is not lost. There is still demand and support for more comprehensive and progressive planning, that is not driven purely by the needs of developers and investors. Resistance is growing against the idea that planning exists to help roll out development.

Neoliberal Spatial Governance explores the background and implications of the changes in planning under the governments of the past four decades and the ways in which we might think about halting and reversing this shift.

Phil Allmendinger is Professor of Land Economy at the University of Cambridge, a Fellow of Clare College and Head of the School of Humanities and the Social Sciences.

Routledge Research in Planning and Urban Design

Series editor:
Peter Ache
Radboud University, Nijmegen, Netherlands

Routledge Research in Planning and Urban Design is a series of academic monographs for scholars working in these disciplines and the overlaps between them. Building on Routledge's history of academic rigour and cutting-edge research, the series contributes to the rapidly expanding literature in all areas of planning and urban design.

Neoliberal Spatial Governance

Phil Allmendinger

Routledge
Taylor & Francis Group

LONDON AND NEW YORK

First published 2016
by Routledge
2 Park Square, Milton Park, Abingdon, Oxon OX14 4RN

and by Routledge
711 Third Avenue, New York, NY 10017

First issued in paperback 2017

Routledge is an imprint of the Taylor & Francis Group, an informa business

British Library Cataloguing in Publication Data
A catalogue record for this book is available from the British Library

Library of Congress Cataloging in Publication Data
Names: Allmendinger, Philip, 1968- author.
Title: Neoliberal spatial governance / Philip Allmendinger.
Description: Abingdon, Oxon ; New York, NY : Routledge, 2016. |
Series: Routledge research in planning and urban design | Includes index.
Identifiers: LCCN 2015040385| ISBN 9781138936751 (hardback : alk. paper) |
ISBN 9781315676647 (ebook)
Subjects: LCSH: City planning--Great Britain. | Land use--Great
Britain--Planning. | Open spaces--Great Britain--Planning. | Regional
planning--Great Britain. | Neoliberalism--Great Britain.
Classification: LCC HT169.G7 A653 2016 | DDC 307.1/2160941--dc23
LC record available at http://lccn.loc.gov/2015040385

ISBN 13: 978-1-138-49034-5 (pbk)
ISBN 13: 978-1-138-93675-1 (hbk)

Typeset in Sabon
by Taylor & Francis Books

For Claudia, Hannah, Lucia and Eleanor

Contents

Illustrations

Acronyms

Terms

BPZ	Business Planning Zone
EZ	Enterprise Zone
LAA	Local Area Agreement
LDF	Local Development Framework
LDO	Local Development Orders
LEP	Local Enterprise Partnership
LLPA	Local Planning Authority
MAA	Multi-area Agreement
NPM	New Public Management
PDG	Planning Delivery Grant
PPG	Planning Policy Guidance Notes
PPS	Planning Policy Statement
RDA	Regional Development Agencies
RSS	Regional Spatial Strategies
SPZ	Simplified Planning Zone
SCS	Sustainable Community Strategy
UCD	Urban Development Corporation

Organizations, governmental bodies and departments

BPF	British Property Federation
CPRE	Campaign to Protect Rural England
CBI	Confederation of British Institutes
DEFRA	Department for Environment, Food and Rural Affairs
DCLG	Department of Communities and Local Government
DoE	Department of the Environment
DETR	Department of the Environment, Transport and the Regions
DTI	Department of Trade and Industry
HMG	Her Majesty's Government
HMT	Her Majesty's Treasury
HBF	Home Builders Federation

HoC	House of Commons
HoC ODPM	House of Commons (Office of the Deputy Prime Minister) Housing, Planning, Local Government and the Regions Committee
HoC CLG	House of Commons Communities and Local Government Committee
HoC EAC	House of Commons Environmental Audit Committee
HoC TLGR	House of Commons Transport, Local Government and the Regions Committee
NAO	National Audit Office
NHPAU	National Housing and Planning and Advice Unit
ODPM	Office of the Deputy Prime Minister
PAG	Planning Advisory Group
RTPI	Royal Town Planning Institute
TCPA	Town and Country Planning Association
TPI	Town Planning Institute

1 Change and planning

The beginning of wisdom is in the discovery that there exist contradictions of permanent tension with which it is necessary to live and that it is above all not necessary to seek to resolve.

André Gorz, *Farewell to the Working Class: An Essay on Post-industrial Socialism*. Pluto Press, 1994: 19 (original, Editions Galilee, Paris, 1980)

Introduction

The contemporary history of English planning is characterized by instability and change. Reform has been driven by a ceaseless search for an ideal system, one that reconciles apparently irreconcilable tensions, seeking to provide certainty as well as flexibility and speed as well as coordination and comprehensiveness. That such tensions are played out against a backdrop of short-termism in political timescales and a lack of collective memory about previous rounds of reform at the national level and a growing demand for involvement if not autonomy at the local level produces a consistent and constant pressure for change. Underpinning the restlessness is a desire to reconcile another set of tensions which are more familiar to planning and planners. The desire for economic and physical growth, particularly since the late 2000s, has sat alongside the aspiration to protect the environment and tackle the drivers and effects of climate change, factors that question the simple 'growth model' of planning.

While change is a relatively new phenomenon for planning it is not just change and the resolution of tensions that is the issue. A certain bias, or movement, has influenced reforms. In short, planning has shifted incrementally but perceptibly away from an area of public policy that was an arena where such issues could be determined in the public interest to one that legitimizes state-led facilitation of growth and development by superficially involving a wide range of interests and issues. This book is about how and why planning has changed, the implications of this and what the future might hold. Underpinning the book is the understanding that land use planning is inherently contentious. Its disputatious nature derives from a range of characteristics and factors though the main reason is that those involved in the planning process largely seek different and irreconcilable objectives. For the environmentalist, planning exists to promote a particular form of sustainability related to protecting environmental assets and mitigating the impacts of climate change. For the developer or landowner, planning exists to manage change and provide information to help markets and reduce uncertainty. For the financier, planning helps to reduce risk by limiting and managing changes in the supply of land for development. For the local community, planning provides a way of ensuring that valued places are protected and that development proceeds in a sustained and coordinated way alongside infrastructure. Neighbours tend to see planning as a way of ensuring that their investment in a property is not reduced by inappropriate development and that their enjoyment of their home is not affected.

Land use planning is the arena in which these sometimes competing and sometimes overlapping interests come to be played out and ideally resolved in a transparent, democratic and rational way. Of course, these different views on the purpose of planning are not mutually exclusive or fixed – an environmentalist needs to live somewhere and a developer may value open countryside, for example. Nor do different interests and actors necessarily or even ordinarily 'play fair' when it comes to determining outcomes. Like other areas of public policy, planning is subject to ideological scuffles and the system is regularly reorientated and reformed to meet the expectations and agendas of different interests. In the 1980s business interests held sway while the 1990s were characterized more by what planning could do to help to protect the environment as well as to mitigate and adapt to growing concerns over climate change. In other words there is a struggle over the objectives of planning as well as the outcomes. The restless and regular reform of planning as it is pulled in different directions is partly a function of such tensions around the system's purpose and priorities: developers claiming that the system is inhibiting development and environmentalists claiming that it is creating unsustainable development. Yet experience shows that simply reorienting planning to new national objectives and regulatory forms is not so simple – 'fixing' planning is never as easy as the advocates for reform assume. On the one hand there is a cognitive dissonance over interests: an ideologically libertarian landowner might agree that planning is necessary to protect the countryside, as long as it is not the area of countryside that he or she wishes to develop. Similarly, there is near universal agreement that the UK needs to build more housing; the questions arising are where, what kind of housing, and who will pay for the infrastructure? Answers to these questions impinge upon sectoral, personal as well as spatial interests. Sectorally, for example, landowners and developers have successfully resisted repeated forms of land taxation necessary for the provision of infrastructure (see Allmendinger, 2011, ch. 7). Spatially and personally there is a growing resistance to certain types of new development: private (rather than social) residential is the most desired form of development by housebuilders though it is also the most actively opposed at the local level (Saint UK Index, 2012). This contradiction – recognizing the need for more housing 'but not in my backyard' (NIMBY) – can be partly understood by the difference between homeowners and non-home-owners: the former are nearly twice as likely as the latter to oppose new residential development (NHPAU, 2009: 8).

On the other hand if planning is national in its orientation then it is largely local in its implementation. As protests against wind farms and high-speed rail routes reveal, consensus over nationally determined objectives can fall apart once the local consequences become clear. Discretion within the political space of local planning can mean that national policy objectives may be derailed and even subverted when local material considerations are factored in: what makes sense in Whitehall may not appear quite so clear in Whitehaven.

So not only is planning contentious but it is necessarily and rightly so. National planning objectives need to be both general and aspirational in order to cover the wide variety of local circumstances in which issues such as 'sustainable develop-ment' are made sense of. There are fundamental issues tied up in the different positions and attitudes towards planning around the nature of the state and the role of the market. There are also significant questions that are difficult if not impossible to address objectively, e.g. does planning inhibit economic growth; should we trade environmental for economic objectives in times of recession; should the national interest prevail over local considerations? A narrow view, such as that taken by the McKinsey Global Institute in its study of UK competitiveness, would argue 'yes' to the first question. This now infamous analysis, commissioned by the Treasury following the 1997 general election, argued that planning and other regulations were the root of the UK's competiveness problem. Down-playing, if not ignoring, the beneficial role of planning when addressing market failure, facilitating social inclusion and wider, not easily quantifiable, dimensions of welfare and environmental protection, McKinsey recommended a comprehensive reform (deregulation) of land use regulations (McKinsey Global Institute, 1998).

The problem is not that the narrow, cost-based McKinsey view is clearly refutable (see ODPM, 2003) but that it echoes and reinforces the normative position of influential interests within the government and provides a simplistic narrative of an overbearing state smothering entrepreneurialism and 'locking jobs in filing cabinets'. The McKinsey study was not a 'one-off' view: the history of UK planning over the past three decades or so is littered with similarly simplistic analyses that provide succour to those who see the world in terms of supply, demand and price signals. Neither is such a view exclusively held by those on the right of the political spectrum (Allmendinger, 2011). This 'Treasury view' of the role of UK planning continues to underpin and justify arguments to dismantle planning controls and has been in the ascendency since 2008 driven by the 'credit crunch' and recession, initially under the tail end of the Labour government but then gaining greater sway under the coalition between 2010 and 2015. Encouraged by think tanks such as the Policy Exchange (2007, 2012) and the Adam Smith Institute (2012) as well as industry groups such as the British Property Federation (BPF, 2008) and the Confederation of British Industry (CBI, 2011) the argument can be summed up as that planning controls thwart com-petitiveness and growth. For the most part this is not an argument for not having any kind of regulation but a specific, industry-supportive form of planning that can include direct intervention and public subsidy where appropriate. The more shrill, libertarian and minimalist perspectives on the need to abolish planning largely from the 1970s and 1980s have given way to arguments for a market-supportive planning based on minimal discretion and greater certainty even if such agendas were often couched in terms of 'cutting red tape'.

However, if the Treasury's simplistic and narrow perspective of planning provides us with too stark a picture then at the other end of the spectrum the more holistic perspectives are too comprehensive and intangible in their evaluations to be meaningful at anything but an abstract level. A focus on planning outcomes such as 'well-being' or sustainable development fits in with a generally supportive view of the role of planning and highlights a range of vague and difficult to measure though positive-sounding impacts of planning (see, for example, Vivid Economics, 2012). That we continue to be faced with such binary analyses of the purpose and impact of planning that pander to normative interests and positions is partly because that which we might term 'modern planning' in the UK was never given an explicit purpose and promised to achieve the resolution of competing issues around land and property in a rational and progressive way.

The state we're in

One outcome of this constant turf war over the objectives and nature of planning is that it constantly finds itself in a transient space at the point of reform, being reformed or implementing reform. In recent years it has become, in Haughton's view, a 'political football':

> In Britain planning is almost a paradigmatic example of a sector used as a 'political football', one that every incoming administration likes to use to explain the failings of the previous administration and demonstrate its own radical credentials. This makes for a bruised sector, used to multiple reforms intended to 'cure' a problem that has been ill-diagnosed.
>
> (2012: 122)

Two broad views currently dominate the debate on the future of planning. The first school of thought privileges the local and argues for much greater weight to be placed upon local considerations in plan making and decision taking. The argument goes that planning is a local issue within a loosely defined and permissive national regime. The second view is that 'less is more' and that planning needs to be greatly reduced and more focused. What planning there is should be nationally consistent and seek to regulate and facilitate development and growth.

More (local) is more

There is a broad current argument that we need more planning that accords with the recent general desire for greater decentralization of policy and decision making. These arguments arise, respectively, from a growing environmental awareness and activism around a more socially just and inclusive planning system on the one hand and a distrust of national politics and policies on the other. Given the focus upon the local it is significant and ironic that the champions of a decentralized planning as a means of resisting new development are national bodies and interest groups such as Greenpeace, Friends of the Earth, the National Trust and the Royal Society for the Protection of Birds. These national bodies have combined with local activism to advance an environmental and social agenda through high-profile protests and challenges to national policies and projects including proposals for a third runway at Heathrow airport, the expansion of nuclear energy and wind power as well as the development of 'fracking', and transport projects such as the proposed High Speed Rail link to Birmingham.

Part of the move by these institutions towards a more localist agenda has been driven by a lack of effective mechanisms to influence and oppose development nationally. The broad thinking is that a more locally led planning will be able to challenge homogenous, national discourses about growth, and instead provide socially inclusive and sustainable futures (e.g. TCPA, 2015). The lack of opportunities for input into planning objectives and outcomes has led to a search for alternatives. Judicial review has provided the main route to challenging planning orthodoxy, although it is limited to contesting the process rather than the substance of planning-related decisions. As a result there have been repeated and increasing calls for the introduction of a third party right of appeal (TRPA) as a method of directly challenging the substance of a decision. At present an applicant can appeal against the decision of the local planning authority (or in the cases of non-determination, against a local planning authority not making a decision). However, this right of appeal does not extend to third parties such as residents and other interest groups. Both the Conservatives and Liberal Democrats included a commitment to introduce a TPRA in their 2010 election manifestos but decided against introducing it when in power from 2010 to 2015. Developers and landowners have been consistently against such a move (e.g. BPF, 2011) while environmental groups have been equally insistent that a TPRA is necessary (e.g. CPRE *et al.*, 2002, 2013). Part of the justification for the introduction of a TPRA was the growth in and expense of judicial and statutory reviews of planning decisions, an avenue that, on the surface at least, is about process rather than the actual decisions. The motivation of the campaigners for the introduction of a TPRA and being able expressly to challenge the substance rather than the process of local decisions was based upon a growing feeling of impotence and the feeling that participation was being used to legitimize rather than inform, or even transform, decisions. Two environmental lawyers were prompted to call for a Tea Party movement for planning with the slogan 'no taxation without representation' (Le-Las and Shirley, 2012).

The coalition government of 2010–15 argued that its new approach of 'planning localism' addressed the concerns that had led to demands for a TPRA, i.e. a locally led, 'bottom-up' system that would give local residents and communities a much greater say in planning decisions. The chief executive of the BPF commented at the time of the general election in 2010 that 'third party right of appeals would be a recipe for chaos. It would clog up the system and undermine everything the Tories have said about being pro-development' (Pearce, 2010: 1).

Naturally, the decision to drop the TPRA and instead adopt localism had nothing to do with the opposition from the development industry and housebuilders, particularly during a recession when the government was keen to promote more not less development. Yet despite genuine concerns about local participation and involvement in planning it is difficult to tease out demands for involvement from local resistance to development.

There is a loose alliance of interests that subscribe to this form of localism, including environmentalists who consider local decision making more likely to be able to stand up to developers, liberals committed to greater decentralization, and idealistic professional bodies and groups that pursue the idea that, if approached in the right way, local planning can transcend conflict. The most vocal advocates, however, are national politicians who regard localism as a popular and low-risk and low-cost strategy countered, if not neutered, by a parallel strategy of pro-growth and development, in other words less is more. Since the general election in 2015 localism has been given a further boost through the commitment to roll out more neighbourhood planning, the commitment to a greater number of elected mayors and City Deals, all of which have been accompanied, confusingly, with proposals that run counter to such devolution and advance a market-supportive and deregulatory agenda.

Less is more

The other current dominant view on planning can be summed up as less is more. This is a common and consistent narrative throughout the recent history of planning that plays to business and development audiences. At various times deregulation has been emphasized by the national government as a strategy for growth and economic success though at certain points there is a heightened focus on shrinking planning control and speeding up the planning process. The last major anti-planning campaign emerged as part of the ideological struggle concerning the allocation of blame for the post-2008 credit crunch and recession. Planning, both generally and in the more specific land use sense, was portrayed as part of the problem – too much regulation as opposed to too little had thwarted economic growth and development.

With a general election scheduled for 2010 and a likely change of government to follow as well as a recession, many lobbyists and sectoral interests took the opportunity to propose planning reform. There was a remarkable degree of consistency in the agendas for reform, including the following:

- abolition of green belts, the introduction of incentives to persuade communities to accept more development and the establishment of simplified planning regimes to promote growth (Policy Exchange, 2007);

- reintroduction of enterprise zones, the extension of permitted development rights, reduction in planning obligation costs and a significant decrease in national planning guidance (British Chambers of Commerce, 2009);
- reduction of supporting information requirements for applications, reducing the time for consultations, outsourcing of plan-making functions and the refocus of local planning away from detailed matters (BPF, 2008);
- relaxation of constraints on development in greenbelts and financial incentives to persuade communities to accept more development (Centre for Cities, 2010);
- reintroduction of enterprise zones, the abolition of regional planning and a reduction in national planning policy (Bow Group, 2009); and
- release of more land for housing and encouragement of local authorities to prepare up-to-date plans (HBF, 2010).

The decrease in development activity was blamed squarely upon the supply side (planning) rather than on the drastic reduction in demand owing to the restriction of credit. The economic crisis had originated in lenders being too ready to provide mortgages that, in many cases, would not be repaid. The 'planning as a supply-side constraint' argument was pushing at an open door – the Conservatives in opposition were keen to win over businesses and the less is more view of planning was to be a key theme once they were in power. According to the Prime Minister planners were the 'enemies of enterprise': 'The town hall officials who take forever with those planning decisions that can be make or break for a business – and the investment and jobs that go with it' (David Cameron, quoted in the *Guardian*, 6 March 2011).

The rollback planning agenda had been gathering pace for some time, however. Concerns about the growth of planning post-2004 under Labour had led to a number of reviews, including the Killian Pretty Review (2008) and shifts in national planning policy towards a much greater emphasis on economic growth and the afterglow of the second Barker report (Barker, 2006; see Allmendinger, 2011). Such concerns were largely overlooked by the significant upwards increase in development activity and demand. When this activity was halted and then reversed from 2008 the less is more planning proponents seized the opportunity.

As well as achieving a level of consistency with respect to reform there was also a degree of potential overlap between the emerging ethos of localism (more local is more) and market-driven (less is more) planning in the move away from a 'one size fits all' system to allow communities to experiment with approaches and develop innovative solutions:

[T]he process of determining the means of planning development is itself a discovery process. It is only by allowing local (including sub-authority) level control over planning that experimentation can take place and the optimal mechanism for planning in each locality can be identified.

(Adam Smith Institute, 2012: para. 9)

This overlap continued with some of the proposals pointing to a more local, market-driven planning through incentives to accept more development (e.g. Policy Exchange, 2007; BPF, 2008a; Centre for Cities, 2010). The underlying logic was that communities would accept more development only if they were allowed to make decisions for themselves and see the benefits. However, this push for localism is not unqualified: nationally important infrastructure projects would continue to be approved by Parliament (Policy Exchange, 2007).

A new framework for the future of planning therefore emerged – less planning and a more market-led, local planning for what remained. This approach influenced policy following the general election in 2010 as, yet again, the purpose, tools and processes of planning shifted. This was not the first time and undoubtedly will not be the last time that planning was subject to fundamental reform and reorientation. Such changes were the latest in a succession of market-related reforms to planning that go back to the early 1980s.

Reconciling 'less and more' planning

These two dominant schools of thought – reducing planning controls while simultaneously expanding and (selectively) localizing them – are not only in tension with one another but provide confusing signals on the purpose of planning for those involved in the system. Some will claim that the objectives for planning and the role of planners in the UK have always been unclear and this is quite deliberate and necessary – creating a consensus across a wide range of interests concerning intervention in land and property markets necessitates a lack of clarity. However, the situation over the past three decades or so has been characterized by an almost frenzied escalation in the number of reforms and changes that have seen planning shift and turn, from crude attempts at simple deregulation to more multifaceted reforms that seek to create a market-supportive, deregulated planning while not alienating growing concerns about environmental protection and urban regeneration. There has also been a recognition that the simplistic less is more understanding of the role of planning does not meet the needs of growth. The provision of housing, particularly affordable housing, schools, public services, and the protection of green spaces, are all important elements of a successful economy. Governments have therefore had to appease multiple audiences and needs, reconciling the irreconcilable in changes to planning.

There are two main consequences of this situation. First, while the fact that planning has been subject to so much reform and reorientation can be linked to the tensions between these two competing views of planning, it also arises as a result of the lack of a coherent view of what planning is for and the resultant vacuum into which a range of ideas fight for dominance. This ideational arena is unusual in the perspectives that planners themselves bring to the debate. Planning and planners have become 'part of the problem' in the sense of withdrawing into a managerialist worldview: planning has become about the management of growth and is no longer concerned with the distributional, ethical or political questions that underpin debates about the objectives and future of planning. In this sense planning is part of the new consensus politics, in that it has become depoliticized and deploys empty phrases such as 'urban renaissance', 'spatial planning' and 'sustainable growth' in order to appeal to a wide range of interests.

The second main dimension is that planners are themselves more directly complicit in these shifts and changes through their role in reconciling the irreconcilable, or 'making reforms work'. Planners manage to achieve the seemingly impossible through a range of techniques and fudges, working to reconcile the inconsistencies and bridging any gaps. In some ways this is a worthy, creative role for planners, and highlights a range of skills and knowledge. However, it misses the wider point that planners have become, in the phrase of Sager, handmaidens of neoliberalism (Sager 2013: xxiii). Yet there is still a denial that the role of planning and planners has shifted to this new, growth-supportive model. According to Sager, it is still not too late:

> Even more than before, public planners must expect opposition from strong market actors who challenge any notion of public interest by pursuing private goals using power strategies that disrupt open and fair deliberation.
>
> (Ibid.: xxi)

While the hope that planners can still seek to act in progressive ways and towards enlightened ends may still linger in the UK, that optimism is forlorn. Planning has retained the outward appearance of acting in the public interest while it has slowly but surely changed and evolved through successive reforms into a system that supports growth. The legitimacy of planning's progressive shell is necessary to continue to deliver its growth-led, market-supportive ends. This shift from a role that sought to reconcile competing interests and demands through open deliberation to a market-supportive role is one thing. That this has been achieved while maintaining the pretence of acting in the public interest is another. Planners and planning in the UK continue to make plans and to determine decisions on the future use of land and property but do so in ways that seek to reconcile the tensions created by the government needing to retain legitimacy and popular acceptance. While businesses and economic interests push for speed and certainty environmental groups and local interests seek greater coordination. The ways in which planners reconcile these competing demands and the incessant reforms of planning is through a range of new techniques and tools. The changing ethos of planning, its contemporary and fluid spaces, scales and politics are the focus of the second half of this book. However, before we reach that I first explore the drivers and influences of such change.

How we got to now

'Planning in England is subject to periodic upheavals … planning reform is now with us on a near permanent basis' (Allmendinger and Haughton, 2015: 29).

How did we get into this situation? It is common if not de rigueur to claim that planning has been reformed repeatedly in the context of neoliberalism. Various changes and outcomes are seen as part of the neoliberalization of planning, a process that started in the late 1970s and early 1980s and has continued ever since. Yet during the decades since this neoliberalization of planning allegedly began there have been distinct and rather different emphases. While the 1980s witnessed attempts to roll back and deregulate planning, the early 1990s were characterized by a strengthening and centralization of planning. Then, the period from 1997–2002 was marked by more deregulation rhetoric while the era between 2002 and 2008 witnessed a 'renaissance of planning'. If planning has been neoliberalized then it is not entirely clear what that means or what has been achieved.

The notion of neoliberalism is a variable one and is subject to sectoral and national variegation. It is also becoming clear that neoliberalism is not coherent, but instead is inchoate and experimental. The overall direction is towards the creation of a market state though, at times and in different ways, skirmishes and temporary reversals might be suffered and accepted, particularly during periods of economic crisis. One important dimension of contemporary neoliberalism is the need to maintain legitimacy as a governing ideology in order to survive challenges and attempts to reverse it. This issue of legitimacy has led to the emergence of a range of tactics, the two most significant of which as far as planning is concerned, are the deployment of post-political nomenclature in order to continue to present a planning system that acts for the wider public good, and the displacement and deferral of political questions and issues through a range of mechanisms. Neoliberal planning is not simply about a crude removal of regulation but a sophisticated capture and roll-out of spatial governance.

The argument of this book is that the planning introduced in 1947 as part of the post-Second World War welfare state has ceased to exist. In its place we now have neoliberal spatial governance. Critical to the continued successful evolution of neoliberal spatial governance has been a range of discourses and tactics appropriated from those seemingly opposed to the creation of market governance. Second modernity arguments about the end of conflict and the emergence and encouragement of consensus-based politics have provided planners with highly influential approaches such as collaborative planning and spatial planning. These tropes of the left have played into the hands of the neoliberals by providing legitimacy to the proposition that the 'big questions' have been determined and that the rest can largely be managed through inclusive, consensual processes backed up by technical studies. There is, of course, an irony in that those who are supposedly most concerned with building a new, democratic future for planning are the pallbearers of its demise. It is this combination of neoliberalization and the need for continued legitimacy that is behind many of the issues that planning and communities are currently facing including disenchantment with planning by politicians and local people. Such disenchantment from a wide range of interest groups further feeds the endless search for new approaches and solutions, thus creating yet more dissatisfaction as planning is reformed and plans are disrupted in the shift to new processes and objectives.

Yet while planners have become depoliticized in order to help to reconcile competing interests and demand, antagonism itself has not disappeared. During the summer of 2011 an extraordinary reaction against the then coalition government's proposed reforms of planning was front-page news on an almost daily basis. The draft National Planning Policy Framework (NPPF) was published in July 2011 without much hype or fanfare. The Conservatives' *Open Source Planning Green Paper* (Conservative Party, 2010b) had outlined proposed reforms of planning while the party was in opposition and included a commitment to reduce the extent of national planning guidance from over 1,000 pages to 50 pages as well as to reintroduce a presumption in favour of sustainable development. The draft NPPF implemented both proposals while simultaneously talking of a commitment to protect green belts and the environment. This balancing act was always going to be tricky to sustain and so it transpired (see Chapter 9). The overall balance was clear – the coalition had listened to development interests and shifted the balance of future planning towards growth without, in the eyes of many, the necessary safeguards and legitimacy. The outcome was familiar to those who remembered the reaction to the attempt by the then Secretary of State for Environment, Nicholas Ridley, to do something similar back in the late 1980s.

What was notable about the furore surrounding the draft NPPF was not so much the reaction itself but who was reacting. Three highly conservative organizations, the National Trust, the Campaign to Protect Rural England (CPRE) and the *Daily Telegraph*, led the charge against the NPPF. Visions of a 'planning free for all' were conjured up and an exegesis of the draft NPPF provided a daily 'horror story' of the likely possibilities of development sprawl. The threat to greenfield sites comfortably elided into an attack on green belts. What was at stake was less a battle over England's green and pleasant land and as much a fight over the heart of the Conservative Party. The outcome was a hastily revised NPPF that provided the language and reassurances that the triad of organizations sought.

But the 'who' of the debate provides a significant insight into the nature of contemporary planning. Neoliberal planning seeks to promote growth and maintain legitimacy through displacing antagonism and conflict (the political). Yet such a displacement is inevitably only partial and temporary as Rancière (1999, 2006) points out. While it is largely assumed and experience tends to point to the re-emergence of the political through street protests and reactions against development from local communities the draft NPPF highlights how powerful conservative interests are also capable of breaking out and challenging attempts artificially to create a consensus. It also helps to explain why reform and counter-reform characterize the era of neoliberal planning.

The challenge to planning

That planning has been hijacked in order to help to pursue growth and to do so in ways that displace and defer open debate arises, in part, from the active and passive complicity of planners themselves. Friedmann (1987) traces the evolution of social and planning theory from the late eighteenth century as different epistemologies and philosophies vied with and influenced each other. Enlightenment cornerstones of scientific method and instrumental rationality combined with ideals of social reform and progress to inform the purpose and ideals of planning. While this fusion of method and idealistic ends waxed and waned, often under the influence of new ideas and approaches as well as in response to seismic events such as wars and depressions, the progressive core of planning purpose through social reform and market intervention by the state and a cadre of professional planners remained. Another common dimension of theory and practice was the nature of conflict. Planning and planners would collate and assemble often opposing and irreconcilable views into decisions and programmes for the general public good. While planners themselves were rightly criticized for substituting their views for those of the wider public (Rydin, 1993) planning itself was an arena in which different views could come together. This placed planning in a transparent, dialectical role between opposing views in a search through reasoned and rational debate for a resolution. The problem, as become clear in the 1960s, was that the opposing views did not ordinarily include those who were on the receiving end of planning. Communities and individuals were left out and subject to outcomes that reflected the 'top-down', 'blueprint' style of government characteristic of post-war social democracy. Growing dissatisfaction with style rather than values was not confined to planning as the 1960s became a decade of protest and questioning of the approach to government and the state.

Glass (1959) and Foley (1960) were among the first to begin to question the vacuum of objectives and theory at the heart of UK planning. McAuslan (1981) and Reade (1987) followed in this vein either bemoaning the lack of a theoretical underpinning or, in the case of McAuslan, competing and irreconcilable theories or ideologies as he termed them:

> Lawyers, planners, politicians and laymen tend to stress a different ideology and argue for changes or reforms in the law or new laws in terms of the ideology they espouse and the resultant cacophony, first translated into law and then continued in its administration and interpretation, leads to confusion and then disarray.
>
> (1981: 2)

This lack of a grounding of planning in a single or clear purpose was exacerbated by a number of challenges that began to emerge in the late 1960s. Such challenges took a range of visible forms and were emerging across the globe, although the events in Paris in May 1968 are held up as emblematic of the resistance to an overly centralized and inaccessible state (see Chapter 3). The oil crisis in the early 1970s also provided a stimulus to new thinking on the left and the right of politics providing challenges to both the assumptions behind and outcomes of land use planning.

The outcome was a challenge to the post-war social democratic consensus and taken for granted thinking about progress and the role of bureaucrats in propping up capitalism. If the 1950s and 1960s had been characterized by economic and social stability underpinned by rational central planning then the 1970s were dominated by social unrest and economic frailty and a growing wariness, if not outright rejection, of the state and its bureaucrats, including planners. On the political right this challenge opened up the opportunity for alternative thinking that rejected the Keynesian orthodoxy and the active state in guiding the economy. A nascent, inchoate and experimental movement that derived its inspiration from the likes of Friedrich Hayek and Milton Friedman emerged (Gough, 2002). The main concern of this drive was to promote monetarism as an alternative to Keynesianism, an alternative that shifted the political focus of attention from labour to capital and included a much reduced role for the state. What would later be labelled neoliberalism began to gain influence and confidence with politicians on the right, largely through the growing influence of a variety of think tanks and the support of some in the print media.

On the left there was a very different reaction that was broadly characterized by two main responses. On the one hand there emerged a reinvigorated and reformulated radical political economy based around critical reflection on the role of the state and planning in sustaining capitalism. Marxist-inspired analyses offered powerful understandings and developed into new more sophisticated approaches to 'new times' through post-Fordism, regulation and regime theory (see Chapter 3). Such views perceived planning as part of the problem rather than the solution, linking planning and planners to the repressive apparatus of the state (Scott and Roweiss, 1977; Harvey, 1978). On the other hand a range of theories emerged that emphasized the reality of social fragmentation and rejected grand totalizing narratives and theories, particularly those belonging to mainstream structuralist Marxism. In place of the unifying structuralism of Marxism, postmodernism and the variety of associated 'posts' such as post-structuralism focused upon complexity, indeterminacy, the social construction of taken for granted 'truths' and the role of power relations in the creation of ideas and beliefs (Dear, 2000). Reacting very differently, the range of postmodern analyses shared the view of 'Marxism for new times' advocates that planners and planning were part of the problem, smothering over diversity and imposing uniformity:

> When Marxism blasted onto the scene (or returned from exile) in the late 1960s, both in Europe and the United States ... certain areas of geography, sociology and city planning became radicalized and intellectualized dramatically, wafting fresh air into erstwhile positivistic subjects, making them interesting and socially relevant in ways they never were.
>
> (Merrifield, 2002: 5)

Both movements influenced planning theory directly and indirectly, although by far the most significant impact was what Moore-Milroy (1991) termed the 'paradigm breakdown' or what Faludi (1973) called the fracturing of theories 'of' and theories 'in' planning (see Allmendinger, 2009). There was no longer a unified and agreed understanding of the role of planning and alternatives to capitalism on the left. While planning theory took up the challenge of the pluralization of theory and was enhanced through the engagement with such ideas, planning practice found itself in a vacuum, criticized for its role in sustaining the status quo and bereft of progressive ideas and thoughts. Increasingly, this void was to be filled by the emerging, more unified ideas of the political right. Although embryonic the evolving thinking concerning the creation of a minimalist, market-supportive state was given time to develop and to become embedded owing to the lack of a unified alternative. At various times, such as the early 1980s, the strategy of 'free market, strong state' (Gamble, 1988) as a distinct era of neoliberalism led to a loss of legitimacy and a political backlash, even from those on the right. Yet, as the then Conservative Prime Minister was renowned for saying at the time, 'there is no alternative'. Such a view works on two levels, highlighting a commitment to the programme but also an accurate assessment of the lack of agreed, alternative ideas. The problem on the left went even deeper as postmodernists actually eschewed such notions and continued to criticize others on the left for seeking to cling onto foundational truths in a rethought Marxism.

It took the collapse of state socialism in Eastern Europe and the Soviet Union from 1989 onwards to provide a more unified approach on the left. Old oppositions and antagonisms fell away and for a short period there was an opportunity to rethink antagonistic positions in the light of the 'end-point of mankind's ideological evolution and the universalization of Western liberal democracy as the final form of human government' (Fukuyama, 1989: 3–4). This opportunity was grasped by a new synthesis of theories that built upon and sought to eradicate oppositions and understand late modern society. Ulrich Beck, Anthony Giddens and others developed the idea of consensus-based politics as a route map for the left in new times. In *Beyond Left and Right* Giddens (1994) explored the impact of globalization and technological change on politics and came to the conclusion that class-based politics has been replaced by identity politics based around lifestyle choices. Consumerism and the market were embedded and the left had to accept that there was no realistic alternative to neoliberalism. Progressive ideals and objectives, such as social justice, fairness and equality remained the goals, although the means to achieve them had changed. The upshot was his notion of the Third Way, a progressive politics for new times that heavily influenced Labour, or New Labour as the party was rebranded.

Some planning theorists fell upon the work of Giddens and others in their attempt both to make sense of new times and to provide progressive, inclusive ways forward for planning. The aim was to search for a planning that was democratic, socially just and environmentally sustainable (Healey, 1993a: 233). One route that became the focus of much work was to build upon the approach of Habermasian communicative rationality, seeking to rethink planning as a form of inter-subjective communication and emphasizing public participation (Healey, 1996; Innes and Booher, 2010). This approach, broadly labelled collaborative planning, sought to embrace the postmodern concern with difference while retaining the possibility of consensus and collective action. Drawing upon the emerging Third Way language of New Labour some in planning academia and practice persuaded the government that the future of planning lay in a new form of collaboration and consensus, concepts that echoed the 'big tent' tenets of New Labour. The opportunity to pursue and implement such an approach came with the election of New Labour in 1997. A fusion of social democratic and liberal market thinking for planning echoed Labour's Third Way philosophy, promising to reconcile traditional tensions that planning had sought to grapple with – according to its champions this new approach to planning or spatial planning (as it was labelled) would be speedy *and* comprehensive, market-supportive *and* socially driven, growth-enabling *and* sustainable (Allmendinger, 2011).

The outcome was a worthy though misguided attempt to reform planning that was sustained on the back of a long period of economic growth. Spatial planning provided a new lexicon for planners as development control became development management and planners were encouraged to develop new skills and knowledge as well as to change their culture in order to deliver positive-sounding though vague concepts such as sustainable development, urban renaissance and smart growth. In retrospect an inclusive, collaborative, progressive planning would inevitably fail to meet the high expectations placed upon it. When frustration within the government concerning the lack of progress in achieving these aspirations began to grow Watson and Crook (2009) rightly asked 'how could the civil servants have got it so wrong?' Despite considerable additional resources planning practice itself remained stubbornly unreformed:

> There is a major failure to take account of neighbouring communities (administrative boundaries still rule); there is a lack of integration in terms of the link between plans and investment; and there is a long way to go to engage effectively with communities.
>
> (Goodstadt, 2009: 8)

More fundamentally the traditional tensions within planning had not been magically removed through open communicative reasoning and collaboration but had been displaced and deferred through a range of mechanisms and rhetorical tools.

The growing realization that the latest era of planning was faltering coincided with the advent of the credit crunch and recession in 2008. Economic growth and development activity during the earlier part of the decade had masked some of the problems and issues, although when development activity started to falter and then came to an abrupt halt, support for spatial planning began to evaporate. A moment of opportunity arose and advocates for new planning approaches emerged to advance alternatives that given the faltering economic situation were particularly focused yet again upon less is more deregulatory models. The pressure for change also included an analysis of why the previous regime had 'failed'. While planning is familiar with being attacked by the political right the consequences of spatial planning led to criticisms and assaults from the left and from others who felt that planning had betrayed its wider public interest ethos and had acted in a duplicitous way to facilitate growth. The era of spatial planning had damaged the reputation of planning and planners.

While Labour distanced itself from spatial planning and began to emphasize a clear, pro-market, deregulated approach the Conservatives and Liberal Democrats started to assemble their own alternatives that combined the perceived need to distance themselves from Labour's top-down regime while accommodating austerity-led public sector cuts and anti-state ideology (see Chapter 5). Following the general election in 2010 and the formation of a Conservative-Liberal Democrat coalition planning found itself being reformed yet again. Three elements of this reformed planning emerged that helped to sustain each other and appeal to different audiences. Localism sought to reverse the national, target-driven approach of Labour with neighbourhood planning, the 'Big Society' would provide the answer to those who asked what would fill the vacuum of a reduced state, and deregulation would speak to the concerns of industry. As with the previous era of spatial planning the experiences of the coalition's approach were mixed (see Chapters 6–9). A large element in the impact of this era of planning was that it had sought to be all things to all interests, a balancing trick that eventually would be exposed as unsustainable particularly when compared with the actual actions of the coalition.

On 10 July 2015 the new Conservative government published its proposals for the further reform of planning (HMG, 2015). The direction of change was indicated in the title *Fixing the Foundations: Creating a More Prosperous Nation*. Again, planning was portrayed as a supply-side constraint with proposals to speed up the preparation of local plans, threats of intervention by the Secretary of State if the authorities did not meet new targets, new compulsory purchase powers and a system of zoning for brownfield land. There is no mention of the Conservative Party election manifesto commitment to expand neighbourhood planning. The emphasis is very much on deregulation and centralization, an approach that not only echoes the top-down, target-driven approach of New Labour but flies in the face of the party's continued stated commitment to localism.

These different periods are explored in detail in this book but the point I wish to make here is that over a period of approximately fifteen years three major reforms of planning had been introduced. Over the previous twenty years planning had been subjected to at least two more major reforms. For comparison, other than the introduction of public participation in 1968 and the introduction of a two-tier system of development planning, both of which could be regarded as adding to the system, the planning system remained relatively unchanged for over thirty years after its introduction in 1947.

From planning to neoliberal spatial governance

What explains this fissiparous and unstable situation? The argument of this book is that planning as it existed in the post-war era has been replaced by neoliberal spatial governance. Early attempts to reduce and minimize planning largely failed but given the lack of alternatives there was the time and space for it to evolve and adapt. From the late 1980s onwards planning was expanded and enhanced in order to support a neoliberal agenda in ways that were very different to the initial simple deregulatory or rollback model. The creation of various state institutions such as Regional Development Agencies (RDAs), the deployment of funding streams and support as well as positive place-making remits for planning at various times over the past thirty years or so provides evidence that neoliberalism is more than a 'minimalist state'. Yet at other times planning has been attacked and reduced as governments seek to present it as a barrier to business and growth. More recent sophisticated reforms have sought both to roll back *and* roll out planning, thus reversing changes that were introduced and reintroducing reforms that had been attempted in the past.

This situation of regular change that seeks to reverse and reintroduce reforms exhibits an underlying pattern. The 'failures' of the spatial era were not the result of a lack of development activity, nor the inability to coordinate the public and private sectors – development activity and housebuilding in particular were relatively high and increasing (though whether this was due to planning or simply the economic situation is debatable). Dissatisfaction and reform arose in that instance from the inherent tensions within any approach to planning, tensions that cannot be reformed away but temporarily resolved through rebalancing and shifting elements. As such the 'rebalancing' of planning will necessitate and defer further reform. The question of what drives this pattern of change is the focus of this book.

Planning in the sense of a state-led regulatory mechanism operated in the public interest has been replaced by and is the host for what I term neoliberal spatial governance. Planning has been both subjected to neoliberalism in the ways it has been reformed and reorientated while also being used as a tool of neoliberalism, helping to create the conditions for growth. Development needs certainty and an interventionist, active planning and state to coordinate multiple actors and work across different scales and spaces. At the same time the same development also needs a minimalist planning and state, making quick decisions about a minimum number of issues. Finally, development needs public legitimacy, both generally and more locally. Participation and involvement of interests beyond the planning authority and developer are necessary in order to ensure that decisions made on behalf of society reflect the wider public interest. Moreover, such wider involvement can delay schemes and raise expectations about what a community may be able to achieve or gain. This can lead to contestation and friction and the calls for further reforms and change.

Added to the above tensions are the complexities, the multiple interests which often conflict, and the cognitive dissonance discussed at the opening of this chapter. The main difference between the post-war system and that of the past three decades or so is a shift in the way in which these tensions have been resolved and the weight placed on the different interests in the determination process. Planners themselves have been a component, if not the key one, in resolving these needs and their associated tensions through the framework within which they operate – the ethos of planning, its laws, policies, spaces, scales and culture. These elements of planning have shifted and are constantly shifting in the endless search for the perfect fix or settlement that resolves these tensions. The 'one size fits all' approach to reform imposed on the wide variety of needs and circumstances of specific places adds to the complexity. If one particular approach to planning seeks to focus on speed at the expense of public involvement and coordination then it is the planners who ensure that the system 'works'. There is also a pendulum effect with a reaction against one approach leading to criticism and a desire to reform again in order to address the deficiencies. The upshot is regular pressure for change and reform, much of which is experimental: failures and setbacks in approaches are an inherent characteristic of neoliberalism. Experimental approaches and initiatives help neoliberalism to 'fail forward' in the absence of any coherent and realistic alternative. Another characteristic is variegation: neoliberal solutions and approaches vary between places and sectors and through time, creating a 'moving map' of experiences. The underlying point is that the state and planning have always played an active role in constructing and reconstructing neoliberalism. Planning and its focus on land in general and cities and regions in particular is an important if not crucial element in national growth and competitiveness. As the crude, deregulatory approaches of the 1980s demonstrated, markets need planning. Cities – the engines of growth and competitiveness – are too important simply to be left to the whims of capital. However, the point is not that markets and cities need planning but what kinds of planning, where and when? These experiences and evolutions of planning are the focus of this book.

Neoliberalism, like capitalism, is inherently unstable and it must evolve. It seeks to stay one step ahead of calls for reform and change. Yet the change itself is always driven by the need to be market-supportive and -focused – alternatives are scripted out through a variety of tools and mechanisms. While different eras of neoliberal spatial governance involve an assemblage of tools and processes the overall incremental and cumulative impact is a shift from one kind of planning to another, one that is both familiar in the terms and processes yet alien in its purpose and ethos. The term 'planning' has been hollowed out of any meaning linked to its origins: 'We are sleep-walking into the abandonment of effective democratic planning based on the 1947 settlement' (Pain, 2015: 263).

Such an evolution would be less of an issue were it not for two consequences. The first is that this shift has been surreptitious, verging upon deceitful. While the purpose of planning has changed, planners have maintained the outward impression of objectivity, neutrality and operating in the wider public interest. When conflict has arisen the usual recourse is to fall back on the 'public interest' defence of needing to mediate and reconcile a range of issues and interests, all of which are presented as being equal. In reality the system is rigged to promote growth even in those areas where it is unnecessary or inappropriate. The upshot of this approach is a suspicion at best and a general discrediting of planning and planners at worst. The second consequence is that long-term strategic planning has been lost. Planning finds itself in a constant state of reform. New sets of objectives, tools and changes are layered onto ongoing reforms making for a confused and confusing panoply of elements that are focused on the short-term. The site or project-led approach for planning through local plans combined with politicians' desire to make an impact mean that long-term strategic thinking arises not through intention but through the accumulation of short-term actions.

Analysing change

Analysing such a changing and fluid evolution of planning necessitates a framework to help us to understand how and in what ways planning has been reformed into neoliberal spatial governance. I explore this change through three lenses: politics, ethos and space/scale. First, neoliberal spatial planning includes new forms of politics and political actions. The creation of modern planning as part of the post-war settlement reflected the contemporary representative style of democracy and the hierarchical expert-driven government of the time. Planners acted in the 'public interest', taking into account a range of views and objectives and drawing upon their expertise. Wider public involvement was limited, although this was to change as demands for participation grew and statutory public involvement was eventually introduced in 1968. The politics of planning remained decidedly antagonistic and representative. Individuals and communities were consulted on proposals with decisions being made either by planners or elected councillors. As environmental concerns grew demands for more involvement and possible third-party rights of appeal and challenge to decisions emerged too. The threat to development and growth prompted the emergence of new forms of politics that sought to obfuscate, defer and displace conflict. Consensus-based inclusionary politics that hinged on broad, difficult to disagree with objectives became part and parcel of planning under neoliberalism. Whether it was in the guise of objectives such as urban renaissance or initiatives such as localism the political and distributional aspects inherent within planning were displaced by politics. Planning and planners became part of a process that sought to manufacture consent for growth through a variety of mechanisms and tools.

Second, the creative and discretionary role of planners in 'smoothing over' the contradictions and helping to reconcile the tensions within neoliberal spatial governance is assisted, in part, by an ethos of planning that it is a set of beliefs and ideals that help to interpret and implement the broader, often national and non-spatial objectives. If planning is given the role of promoting sustainable economic growth, for example, then planners need to interpret this in the light of local circumstance and broader planning doctrine and norms. Different eras of neoliberal spatial governance have been accompanied by a distinctive ethos of what planning is actually for. Yet there is seldom a clear distinction between such principles and customs meaning that there can be and often are multiple and 'layered' purposes, thus creating further confusion and tensions. A clear example was the shift from land use to spatial planning in the 2000s that involved a change from regulatory 'command and control' style planning to a role that was premised upon more multi-scalar growth facilitation and sectoral coordination – spatial governance. Such a shift in ethos was accompanied by new tools, policy guidance and performance management mechanisms. Planners sought to grapple with this change, but struggled to reconcile the component elements and make sense of what it meant for, say, urban regeneration. According to some, spatial planning was actually a return to planning's roots. To others it was as much about promoting growth and development through a combination of 'culture change' and being everything to everyone.

Finally, the evolutionary, disruptive and experimental nature of neoliberal spatial governance has led to the creation and destruction of scales and spaces of planning in the search for the ideal 'fix'. New territorial spaces for planning have emerged and been abolished while other spaces have been privileged and then downplayed. The region – a regular though intermittent space of planning – highlights the tensions between coordination and integration on the one hand and the project-led, site-specific certainty on the other. More interestingly, a range of informal, temporary, fuzzy and soft spaces have materialized in recent years (Haughton *et al.*, 2010) that provide neoliberal spatial governance with the tools to facilitate growth without impeding the legally required processes of public involvement and accountability. Such temporary spaces may become more permanent if they prove to be beneficial or otherwise can be abolished or allowed to wither. The relationship between territorial and soft spaces is left ambiguous and open to interpretation. In the case of Local Enterprise Partnerships (LEPs), for example, the relationship will vary among areas, with some LEPs taking on a larger planning function than others. This process of disruption and experimentation is a key element of neoliberal spatial governance that allows new fixes and models to emerge and change behaviours and outcomes, or perhaps not, and then become subject to evolution themselves.

Of course these three elements (explored in Chapters 7–9) are related. New spaces and scales have gone hand-in-hand with new politics as they displace and defer the political. A new ethos for planning will implicitly and explicitly involve a steer on the spaces and scales of planning. The result is a combination of interdependence, complexity and fluidity that means that the future for planning cannot easily be imagined except as the interplay between the various drivers or themes that underpin and structure change.

The remainder of this book develops the arguments set out in this introduction and is divided into three parts. The first part (Chapters 1–5) sets out the background to the transformation of planning into neoliberal spatial governance. The second part (Chapters 6–8) looks in detail at the nature of neoliberal spatial governance in practice in the first decade of the twenty-first century. These three chapters are structured around the three main characteristics and manifestations of neoliberal spatial governance, namely ethos, politics, and space and scale. The third part (Chapters 9 and 10) explores the recent incarnation of planning – localism – before turning to some analysis and conclusions on the shape of planning and what can be done to reverse its decline.

2 The rise and fall of the consensus on planning

Introduction

For over thirty years, a period I take to be the era of neoliberalism, English planning has been the subject of change and reform by successive governments of the left and the right. Such change has been regular and predictable, swinging first away from regulation towards a more minimalist approach then back towards a more comprehensive role in the search for a 'perfect fix' to enable and facilitate growth. During this period planning has been in a permanent state of impermanence, criticized for 'locking jobs in filing cabinets' under one administration and then lauded as the mechanism to help to address climate change, enable social inclusion and create sustainable places under another. This confused if not schizophrenic attitude towards planning on the part of successive governments of the left and the right stood in contrast with the relative stability of planning from the end of the Second World War until the mid-1970s. The change from stability to instability came about for three main reasons.

The first reason was a determined ideological attack against the post-war social democratic consensus of which land use planning was seen as a part. From 1975 the Conservatives under Margaret Thatcher developed a dogged though inchoate programme of new right-wing ideas that sought to roll back the frontiers of the state while strengthening the residual functions of government. For planning this involved a strategy of deregulation and centralization wrapped in an aggressive rhetoric that sought to blame Britain's relative post-war decline on supply-side constraints including land use controls. Yet in itself such anti-planning thought and rhetoric was not new and had been a consistent and growing theme of right-wing thinking with regard to planning during the post-war era. What marked the post-1979 period following the election of the Conservatives was a determination to implement radical approaches to planning rather than, as previously, to seek to reform planning from within through consensus and with the support and cooperation of planners themselves. The Conservatives were not alone in this strategy of seeking to force change on planning and planners, however. Radical change to planning was also a feature of the Labour governments from 1997, though such reforms sought to expand planning's functions and objectives rather than to minimize them. Previous reforms in the post-war era had been largely within the scope of a consensus around improving the planning system, usually incrementally and in ways that built upon, rather than dismantled, the spirit and purpose of planning. Changes such as the extension of public involvement, the introduction of a two-tier system of development plans and the widening of the scope of planning to include conservation from the late 1960s onwards were accommodated within a broad consensus. Overall, there had been little concerted or serious challenge to the principle of planning itself.

The second reason for this change concerns the reaction and adaptability of planning during this period of more radical reform. Despite regular changes over the last three decades the planning system introduced in 1947 appears superficially similar to that of the second decade of the twenty-first century. Its main components, including the nationalization of development rights, local development plans, and the separation of such plans from decisions on development rights, all remain. Yet planning practice, its purpose, tools, skills and knowledge (to name but a few elements) are, in many cases, very different. The system is adaptive and resilient and remained so throughout this period, absorbing and deflecting change and sometimes turning it to be used in ways that were the opposite of those intended. Such resilience and adaptability derives from the need for vagueness concerning the purpose and scope of planning in order to garner widespread support and to accommodate different and irreconcilable needs with respect to planning as it emerged in the aftermath of the Second World War. Planning was to be all things to all people. Such vagueness allowed planning to evolve, picking up new objectives and tools while dropping others, giving it a resilience as society and people's needs changed. It was this adaptability that facilitated the implementation of more radical changes to planning over the last three decades without the need for wholesale reform of the system itself and it was this adaptability that allowed planning to continue and absorb change, even that of a more radical nature. The outcome of this ability to accommodate reform led to different strategies and tactics on the part of those wanting to effect change, particularly from 2002 onwards. As far as society is concerned, the importance of this resilience is a high degree of stability, which has constricted more radical change and allowed communities a degree of continuity and certainty in planning their areas. However, it is this resilience and adaptability that has, in part, frustrated governments seeking reform and led to further changes.

The third reason for the shift to an era of instability and change was the free rein given to experimentation with neoliberal ideas and policies in the hope of their becoming established as the new orthodoxy for planning. This freedom was a result of the breakdown of the consensus around planning on both the right and the left and the need for what we might term 'reform from within'. During the post-war era there had been a cross-party consensus on planning. This consensus began to break down in the 1970s, which led to the ideological attack by the New Right during the 1980s. The attack from the right is widely known but it was the lack of opposition and possible alternatives on the left that allowed this anti-planning approach to develop, evolve, become established and flourish. The 1970s and 1980s were characterized by fragmentation and relativism on the left on matters concerning the state that provided little in the way of critique or possibilities to the growing hegemony of the right. By the time a more coherent view emerged Labour had begun to embrace many of the tenets of neoliberalism and globalization in its Third Way ethos. From being the party that helped to establish planning Labour become a major critic thereof and developed some radical approaches of its own, outdoing the right in terms of identifying growth-led reforms to planning.

These three drivers – a concerted ideological attack, a growing frustration at the ability of planning to thwart reform, and the emergence of neoliberalism as a viable alternative to the post-war consensus around planning – form the backdrop for what follows. The rise of the more radical challenge to planning from both left and right is covered in the next two chapters. In this chapter I provide the background to two elements highlighted above, that is, the rise of the consensus around planning and the ability of the system to absorb change largely as a result of flexibility and adaptability necessary to accommodate such a breadth and scope for planning. The system was founded on the ability to reconcile the irreconcilable. This chapter sets out where that adaptability emerged from, how the consensus was achieved and why, ultimately, it broke down.

The new orthodoxy

Prior to 1947 land use planning in the UK had been a piecemeal and largely ineffectual affair. Recognition of the need to improve housing conditions to help to justify the tremendous human sacrifice of the First World War coincided with the growing awareness within the ruling elite following events in Russia in 1917 of what might happen if working class loyalty to the system was lost. Such intentions, however, did not translate well into actions or outcomes. The sheer scale of housing renewal and slum clearance provided a significant hurdle to overcome. Over half a million sub-standard houses were demolished during the inter-war years, although this amounted to less than one-fifth of the three million houses identified as being in need of clearance. Efforts were not just concerned with existing housing, however. Various initiatives and subsidies that sought to encourage landowners to develop new housing at lower densities along the lines of garden suburbs were also introduced and then either repealed or inadequately financed to address the scale of the problem.

In terms of actual controls on new development three Acts of Parliament were passed in 1909, 1919 and 1932, each extending the scope of land use control over new housing. The 1909 Act allowed local authorities to plan urban extensions to existing settlements, although the compensation payable to land-owners for loss of development value resulting from such schemes meant that the take-up was low. Compulsory town extension plans to settlements with more than 20,000 inhabitants were introduced in the Housing, Town Planning,

Etc., Act, 1909 signalling the intention to bring new development within the remit of planning controls. Again, take-up among local authorities was low largely owing to the lack of skills and availability of planners within authorities to prepare such schemes. The final attempt to introduce planning controls through the Town and Country Planning Act 1932 met a similar reception to the previous endeavours. The 1932 Act had sought substantially to extend the scope of planning controls, although this ambition had been watered down following the general election of 1931 and the subsequent changes introduced to the Bill by the Conservative-led coalition government.

One consequence of the lack of impact and take-up of new planning provisions was that the suburban housing boom of the 1930s, when completions topped 250,000 per annum for most of the decade, was largely unplanned and unregulated. The extent of inter-war housing growth was staggering. Around four million new homes were built between 1918 and 1939; 2.5 million private, 0.4 million private with public subsidy and 1.1 million public or 'council' homes. The four million additions meant that by 1939 one-third of England's total housing stock had been built during this period. Spatially, the majority of this growth was in the south of England: the built-up area of London in 1939 was five times that of 1918, a growth that had been accelerated by the increased availability of the car, the expansion of the London Underground and the effects of migration from the depressed areas of England to the relative affluence of the south (Reade, 1987: 43). While various attempts at introducing land use planning had faltered, the outcome of this largely unregulated development was a growing acceptance of and consensus around the need to curtail unplanned development and improve existing housing conditions. Such a consensus was underpinned by three broad justifications. The first was the reaction against unregulated development. In addition to suburbanization there were also concerns about what was termed 'ribbon development' along roads. The Restriction of Ribbon Development Act 1935 had been introduced in an attempt to halt the further incursion of new building along roads leading from existing settlements. The environmental and aesthetic impact of such development echoed the arguments of some for the use of urban containment mechanisms such as green belts to control urban sprawl beyond towns, a development that the nascent planning controls were failing to address. As a reaction against such unplanned development the Council for the Protection of Rural England was established in 1926 and began campaigning for controls over urban sprawl. Controls over this kind of unplanned building were improved under the provisions of the Town and Country Planning Act 1932, which included the requirement that planning permission should be sought for new development if a plan was in place. The preparation of such plans was lengthy and ultimately required the approval of Parliament. Without a plan there was little an authority could do. In any event plans tended simply to codify ongoing and proposed development trends, allocating land that would have been built upon in their absence.

The second major justification was unease regarding regional imbalances and the recognition that the depression of the 1930s was hitting some parts of the country much harder than others. While traditional manufacturing jobs were declining in the north of England, newer consumer-based manufacturing was concentrated in the south of the country. Inter-war regional policy in the form of financial aid that sought to encourage firms to locate or relocate in more depressed areas had been ineffectual. A wider concern, particularly with a second world war looming, was explored by the Barlow Commission and focused on the spatial distribution of industry. Following the effectiveness of aerial bombardment in the Spanish Civil War the Commission was established to explore whether some form of industrial dispersal might be expedient. The Commission's conclusions were unequivocal: 'It is not in the national interest, economically, socially or strategically, that a quarter, or even a larger proportion of the population of Great Britain should be concentrated within 20 to 30 miles or so of Central London' (quoted in Reade, 1987: 46).

The recommendations of the Barlow Commission provided clear support for planning based upon the need to address regional economic imbalances, the social consequences of declining areas as well as a strategic, military justification for dispersing manufacturing production. Industrial relocation policy on such a scale would necessitate coordinated national and local level planning and intervention, a leap that would not finally come about until the outbreak of war.

Finally, while there was a growing recognition that some form of regional and local planning was necessary, the dominant national intellectual and political paradigm remained wedded to laissez-faire. There was a not a clear intellectual tradition that underpinned a shift towards greater state intervention. This was to change with the publication in 1936 of Keynes' *General Theory of Employment, Interest and Money* that provided an intellectual and political justification for demand-side interventions and a far more significant role for the state in the economy. Supporters of demand-side approaches could point to the impact of Roosevelt's New Deal programme in the USA and the role of bodies such as the Tennessee Valley Authority in stimulating growth and reducing unemployment. Keynes' work combined with the experiences in the USA provided the political space for the discussion and development of a greater role for the state that was not the socialist or national socialist alternatives to the free market feared by many in government and industry. Instead, there was a clear justification for intervention to 'save capitalism', particularly given events in Russia and Germany, that appealed to those on the political right who were more traditionally opposed to intervention.

The combination of a growing awareness of the need for land use regulations and planning from these different perspectives came together in the wartime conditions of 1939–45. A consensus emerged that grew into an orthodoxy and allowed accelerated fundamental and far-reaching changes in the relationship between the state, the citizen and the market, not simply in land use planning. The experience of wartime was that a planned economy and hitherto unparalleled interventions in the lives of people 'worked' and helped to secure victory. What tied these three themes together was not simply that they all had a clear spatial dimension, though this was significant in the argument that a national system of land use or physical planning was desirable. What was equally important was the dissatisfaction with the ability of politics and politicians to address the issues facing society. In the view of many at the time it was the politicians and the political process that had failed to address the consequences of the Depression and it was the politicians and the political process that had repeatedly failed to introduce a comprehensive system of planning and housing renewal. Instead, it was the 'man from the ministry' who had successfully planned the war effort and it was the soldiers, sailors and airmen that had fought the war itself. Trust and confidence was placed in 'experts' and bureaucrats who, it was felt, could manage the economy and shape society in ways that politicians had proven themselves incapable of.

The era of 'modern' planning in the sense of a comprehensive system comprised of a variety of Parliamentary Acts, institutional arrangements, objectives and assumptions about the nature of society and the value of intervening in land and property markets began to emerge and take shape during wartime, ultimately coming to fruition under the post-war Labour Government. However, if the 'spatial' and the 'expert' provided the broad push for planning then the differences between the positions, particularly the arguments for a strategic regional policy on the one hand, and the detailed aesthetic form of planning control on the other hand, were never resolved. 'Planning' was the common term for both, even though it masked significant differences in underlying philosophy and purpose.

Such an elision of purpose was not helped by the discussions on the need for planning during wartime. If anything, the scope of planning expanded as the experiences of a centrally planned wartime economy helped to overcome any residual reservations. The famous trio of inquiries facilitated this expansion of purpose. The Uthwatt Commission called for 'coordinated planning as a whole compared with confused development in the past' (1942: 7). The Scott Report (1942), probably the most partisan of the three main founding enquiries, came out strongly in favour of protecting rural areas and agricultural land from development while the Barlow Commission (1940) pushed for a comprehensive system of regional planning and policy that would require new institutional apparatus, a significant jump in the scope of planning thought at the time. In contributing to the purpose of planning the three reports added a heady range of objectives and included local, regional and national planning that covered both economic and environmental matters.

As Foley (1960) and McAuslan (1981) have both pointed out, such a wide scope underpins a range of ideologies of planning (they both identify different, sometimes overlapping and sometimes incongruent, streams of thought) that appeal to different interests. Labour and the left more generally have traditionally been more sympathetic to and supportive of social objectives while the Conservatives and the right have preferred minimalist controls that focus upon environmental protection and market efficiency (Foley, 1960). There was no national reconciliation of these different roles and objectives for planning; experts would undertake any harmonization in the 'public interest' based upon widespread trust in public officials and authority. This reconciliation by professionals was part and parcel of the administrative tradition of the UK, which is typical of common law jurisdictions, and which maximizes the discretion of public officials. It allows them significant latitude to determine proposals 'on their own merits' rather than by legally defined standards that are more familiar to continental European jurisdictions. Expectations were high, to say the least. Planners were imbued with an almost godlike aura of comprehension and comprehensiveness (Glass, 1959). This combination of wide discretion, significant yet undefined scope along with an impression of omnipotence and a consensus around the need for planning was a potent mix. Rolled out with the introduction of the welfare state, and the promise to 'wage war' on physical want and squalor which, as the Beveridge Report (1942) put it, arises mainly from a haphazard distribution of industry and population, planning was primed with potential as well as political and popular support.

As Cherry (1996: 87) argues, the advent of war augmented the role of the government in the country's affairs. Extensive state intervention in markets and in the lives of people was accepted and proven. Planning, in the broadest sense and in the more specific form of land use planning, was pushing at an open door. Helping it through that door was the growing influence of industry lobby groups, such as the Town Planning Institute (TPI) and the Garden Cities and Town Planning Association (which later became the Town and Country Planning Association), both of which were involved in highly political lobbying for what they promoted as an apolitical expert-led future run by planners. These 'experts' were to be part of the emerging 'common ground' that permeated discussions on the kind of society that would be created after the war: party and private interests were to be swept aside in the rebuilding of Britain. The broad spectrum of political support was fragile. The left signed up to the 'common ground' as it saw the opportunity to pursue welfare, education and industrial reform, while the right signed up partly out of fear that not to do so would be electoral suicide given the prevailing public mood but also out of pragmatism and concern that a realignment to the left was a concession that was preferable to a national political rupture and the emergence of a hard left that favoured Soviet-style state socialism.

A new planning system would, naturally, require planners. After the effective lobbying to create the system the TPI (as it then was) turned its attention to producing and controlling the supply of planners. The ambiguity necessary for the successful birth of planning was further enhanced and transformed by the TPI into a virtue. Planning was portrayed as both a science and an art that operated in the public interest. At times it would draw upon expert knowledge derived from economics or statistical analysis while at other times it would involve subjective though expert judgement on aesthetics. Both kinds of knowledge would be deployed in the hazy notion of 'public interest' allowing planners to decide what was and what was not relevant. The upshot was that the 'experts' of planning were given considerable discretion and autonomy.

The TPI evolved from being a radical body arguing for change to one protecting the status quo, content with its role as guardian of the newly fledged planning profession. The evolution from a reforming organization to a regulator of state-employed bureaucrats brought with it further tensions and contradictions as planners were, at one and the same time, employees of the state managing land use conflicts in a capitalist economy while simultaneously seeking to achieve wider ill-defined objectives for reform and progressive change (Evans, 1997: 61). The contradiction was particularly acute when planners sought to facilitate growth through creating the conditions necessary for development or investment while simultaneously seeking to operate in the 'public interest'. As Reade puts it:

> [I]deas deriving from these two main sources (detailed design and regional level economic planning) were linked with other social ideas, and elaborated into a veritable web of interlocking and interdependent analyses and prescriptions. The resulting seamless web of remedies embraced many different concerns, and many different fields of specialist knowledge. But it was so put together that virtually any interest group could see in it whatever it wished to see, or found most agreeable.
>
> (1987: 49)

In large part this 'web' was underpinned by the word 'planning'. The Town and Country Planning Act 1947 is rightly described by Hall and Tewdwr-Jones (2011) as the cornerstone of the whole post-war planning system. However, the Act was supplemented by other 'planning-related' legislation. The Distribution of Industry Act 1945 required control over development in the south of England as well as incentives and grants to persuade industry to move in order to be effective, while the New Towns Act 1946 similarly required containment of existing urban areas, particularly London, as part of a programme of population dispersal and housing renewal. Economic and social planning in this broad sense was conflated by planners with planning in the narrower regulation of land use sense and this provided them with a sliding and ambiguous justification and scope. This elision could be deployed to selectively widen or narrow the ambit of planning functions or to justify actions, providing a significant powerful tool for planners in defining and redefining the scope of their role. It was little wonder, then, that the amorphous and difficult to disagree with range of functions of and scope for planning amounted to a 'consensus'. This common ground was a deliberate and highly political construct that masked a particular world view and approach, one that was to dominate planning thought and practice even when it became clear that the consensus around planning was no such thing.

A common ground

The immediate post-war period represented the high-water mark in modernist planning. Enlightenment principles of reason, progress, universalism, empiricism and science underpinned the values, scope, tools and approaches of planning even if these principles did not provide a clear indication of what planning was *for*. When such scientific 'objective' principles and practices met the messy, negotiated and indeterminate world of politics then the 'science' of planning could shift into its other manifestation as an 'art'. A range of influences guided both approaches and helped to fill the vacuum of a clear purpose. One of the leading inspirations for planning as a progressive movement was Thomas Sharpe's popular book *Town Planning* which was first published in 1940. Selling over 250,000 copies *Town Planning* was considered to be a manual for planners on the nature of the 'good town' and provided a passionate argument for a bold collectivist response to the privations and sacrifices of war. The 'good town' would arise from the imposition of technical standards for new development and redevelopment based on population density, light standards, plot ratios and 'socially balanced', self-contained neighbourhoods of 8,000–10,000 people. As for public involvement, Sharpe's approach echoed the predominant perspective of the time: benevolence, combined with professional autonomy and expertise delivered through a national and comprehensive approach, would not only provide the 'good town' but would also be the 'saviour' of democracy:

> The main modern dictators, whatever foul things they may have done in other directions, have certainly been admirably energetic in this [planning] (and it is largely their work in this sphere that makes them tolerable to their peoples – a forceful lesson this for democratic government). Soviet Russia, in the middle of an industrial revolution far more intense and rapid than that which overwhelmed our own towns last century, has been given hundreds of excellently planned and in some ways splendidly equipped new towns and communal centres.
>
> (Sharpe, [1940] 1945: 114)

There was a vague idea that the principles of central planning, a benign bureaucracy and exclusive professional technical skills and knowledge could exist alongside a market economy. However, for some it was the market element of this managed economy approach that stood out as an anomaly. The technical expertise and skills of planners – the wider public interest or collective good that Sharpe and others championed – were in tension if not in opposition to the individualistic, incremental and narrow concerns of the market. Sharpe and others who wrote about planning at the time were aligned with the broad public mood in their arguments for the primacy of a planned future. The nineteenth-century social reform and welfare origins of planning were being expanded as part of a suite of social democratic initiatives including universal education, health care and social security. While some sectors such as coal and rail had been nationalized it was the development of land, rather than land itself that was brought within the purview of the state to be controlled and planned. This was an interim step. Some sought to nationalize land itself, thus further diminishing what was perceived by others as the market element of the market economy.

Post-war practice echoed this Enlightenment modernism and the view of the free market as an anachronism. Planning, as Sandercock (1998: 27) has argued, was characterized by the rational evaluation of options and alternatives, the hierarchical and functionalist segregation of places and neighbourhoods and a belief in progressive and reformist ends based on a taken for granted public interest. The overall approach, in the view of Alison Ravetz, was one of 'clean sweep planning' (1980: 23). The approach was positivistic and evidence based: places, in the phrase of a leading planner of the time, ought to have 'a clear legible structure' (Keeble, 1969: 10). Such structures drew their inspiration from nature and science as planning turned its back on the market-driven incrementalism of nineteenth-century cities: non-conforming uses would be segregated, housing would be planned around self-contained neighbourhoods, cars and people would be separated and green belts would be used to limit urban sprawl.

Underpinning this suite of planning orthodoxies were a range of assumptions and pre-dispositions (Hall and Tewdwr-Jones, 2011). The first was that development and redevelopment would largely be publicly led and funded. New towns and large-scale regeneration would involve a combination of public regulation and direct state-led development. Little attention was given to positive planning that involved the private sector. Development that was not publicly funded was assumed to be minimal and, as a consequence, planning controls over private development were generally regulatory and reactive. In this model planners would allocate land that subsequently would be developed by the private sector, though ensuring that such development actually occurred was not the role of planners or the planning system. The second assumption was that social, economic and physical planning was both desirable and possible. The war had demonstrated that the state could intervene successfully and plan large aspects of citizens' lives for the wider public good. Individual choice and diversity had been subsumed and controlled and the results had included reduced unemployment and improved living conditions for a large proportion of the population. This assumption had two consequences. The first was hubris on the part of planners in their abilities and scope for intervention. The second consequence was a ready-made explanation for when matters (inevitably) did not turn out as planned. The experiences of wartime had demonstrated that planning 'worked'. If it subsequently turned out that plans fell short of expectations then the issue was not with planning per se, but other factors such as insufficient control. In other words, the solution to any failure of planning was more planning.

The third assumption was that the main administrative unit responsible for planning would be the local authority. Coordination of policy and consistency of approach would be the role of the central government and the minister who would approve plans with or without modification. There had been some debate on the scope of local authorities and their functions with some preferring a central minister who would undertake the full functions of local planning. However, a two-tier hierarchical approach based upon the central and the local authorities was assumed echoing the prevalent 'Westminster' model of government. Finally, there was a group of working assumptions that guided the nature of planning and the future. It was anticipated that there would be a stable and immobile population for the purposes of planning. Population growth was expected to be small and predictable. Although a redistribution away from the larger conurbations was envisaged, people were expected to be largely fixed in location – car ownership was low and commuting outside of the south-east of England was minimal. This assumption removed a good deal of complexity from the nature of inputs into the planning process. If the population was largely 'fixed' then there were fewer uncertainties about individual choice and reaction to planning that would need to be taken into account.

These assumptions underpinned planning thought and practice and allowed planners to assume a stable, linear and predictable future that involved few, if any, messy or complex realities. This 'predict and provide' model endured, despite each of the assumptions upon which it was based being found wanting. The simplification of complex realities further underpinned planning's claim to being a science and the heir to the Enlightenment tradition of rationality and positivism. Such simplification of a multifaceted phenomenon also presented technical solutions to what were largely political issues. If planning could take the politics out of topics such as housing and redevelopment then the consensus around planning would be strengthened. In any case, there was little public demand for an alternative to the 'planner-led' approach. The population, as Cherry (1996) points out, was well disciplined after the experiences of wartime siege economy, strict regulation, rationing and the 'man from the ministry' making decisions for the wider public good. A further fillip was the expanding nature of the *dirigiste* state. Land use planning and the nationalization of development rights were overshadowed by the nationalization of industries such as railways, coal, and steel making, the development of national economic planning through a National Plan published in 1965 and expansions in central and local government activities. Nor was the immediate post-war planning system left as a 'one-off' event. The Planning Advisory Group established by the Government in 1964 to look into delays in plan preparation recommended the further expansion of planning, identifying the need for a two-tier system of strategic and detailed plans (PAG, 1965), while the Skeffington report (1969) made recommendations on greater public involvement and the Civic Amenities Act 1967 provided for the creation of Conservation Areas to address public concern over the lack of protection for heritage assets. While it was not all plain sailing, not least the revocation of the betterment and compensation provisions of the 1947 Act, there was a general expansion of the realm and scope of planning throughout the 1950s and 1960s.

The final part of this expansion was the role played by those most directly involved: the planners themselves. The planning profession had benefited from the conducive environment of the immediate post-war era. There had been a conscious effort to promote the 'art and science of town planning' amounting to what Evans refers to as 'classical town planning' (1997: 4). In 1947 there were only 1,700 members of the TPI compared to 1,400 local planning authorities (Ward, 1994: 102). Membership rose and more planning schools emerged, thus leading to the TPI being granted its Royal Charter in 1970. This expansion of the profession and professional planning education led to the usual panoply of consequences as the profession was consulted on policy and began to influence the direction of thinking on issues.

The breakdown of the common ground

The consensus around planning was helped in a political and practical sense by the austerity conditions in post-war Britain and the consequential lack of significant development activity to actually regulate and plan. Yet this was only a temporary situation and cracks in the common ground emerged from a number of directions. One notable though slow burn influence was the appearance of a counter-narrative to central planning and the expansion of the role of the state. This anti-planning critique emerged from both ends of the political spectrum. On the left the emerging analyses of modernity and mainstream structuralist Marxism emanating most notably from the Frankfurt School led by Horkheimer, Adorno, Marcuse and others remained in the realms of (mainly continental) academia and debate, and failed to resonate with the lives and experiences of the wider population. The Frankfurt School of critical social theory had begun to question the narrowness of mainstream Marxist theory and its limits in accounting for the ability of capitalism to survive crises through the support of the state, a state that was being expanded and given new scope in its management of markets. The expanded state was also the subject of critique by Max Weber who questioned the effectiveness of state institutions, positing the replacement of a market tyranny with a bureaucratic one. Such left-leaning critiques were at the margins and made few inroads into the dominant empirical positivism of Saint-Simon, Comte and latterly Durkheim that underpinned the spirit, purpose and tools of central and land use planning. At a more practical day-to-day level state expansion and the nationalization of large parts of the economy were the main components of Labour's manifesto which was being rolled out with little opposition in the post-war years. It is not surprising, then, that the left provided little challenge to the dominant collectivist orthodoxy during this period. Nevertheless, the critiques of state-supported capitalism and the alienating nature and inefficiencies of bureaucracies were developing and would ultimately become far more significant to the left's agenda, as I discuss in the next chapter.

The left was largely content and could see its agenda progressing despite emerging concerns but it was not alone in having anxieties as the right was also stirring, though also at the margins. The post-war social democratic consensus spanned both left and right, although the latter was not entirely supportive of the policies of collectivism, a mixed economy and a welfare state but had acquiesced largely due to political pragmatism. A significant proportion of the Conservative Party was still either suspicious or hostile towards the collectivist underpinnings of the orthodoxy. The reaction against the roll-out of the state was led by the publication of what would become two classics of liberal thinking. Hayek's *The Road to Serfdom* (1944) and Popper's *The Open Society and its Enemies* (1945) were published as ripostes to the expansion of universal social welfare and state-led planning, attacking both the moral foundations and policy implications of socialism. In *The Road to Serfdom* Hayek linked the growth of the role of the state with the inevitability of tyranny and loss of individual freedom. Echoing Adam Smith, Hayek argued that it was the freedom of the market and its unforeseen results of collective consciousness that ensured individual freedom, not centralized planning. Imposing the will of a small minority upon the wider population undermined democracy.

Such arguments began to influence those on the right of the Conservatives. In the UK the One Nation Group (1950), the Bow Group (1951) and the Institute of Economic Affairs (1955) were established to develop free market ideas often challenging the status quo with provocative and unconventional alternatives. It was only a matter of time before these critiques and alternatives shifted their focus from broad centralized planning to land use planning. One of the most contentious elements of the 1947 legislation concerning compensation and betterment was dropped in the 1950s largely due to opposition from property interests, aided by the election of a Conservative government in 1951. Compensation and betterment had been a key plank of the planning system reflecting the argument of the Uthwatt Commission that values reflected the use to which the land could be put. If such uses were now to be determined by the community through the planning system then those deprived of maximizing value and those whose land increased in value should either be compensated or taxed (betterment). This principle had always been controversial among some Conservatives and once the party was in power it was abolished. As well as the more fundamental concerns there was also a widespread feeling that the approach to compensation and betterment was actually putting off much needed development and redevelopment against a backdrop of post-war reconstruction.

Such changes did not inhibit the continued roll-out of land use planning. Nevertheless, the challenge to the certainty that economic and physical planning was the 'natural' way to manage societies and change emerged from a number of directions, paralleling the wider dissatisfaction with and breakdown of the post-war social democratic consensus. Four broad influences stand out. First, there was a growing reaction against the processes and outcomes of planning. At one level there was an emerging unhappiness with the physical manifestations of planning, particularly the idea of functional segregation. A key orthodoxy of post-war planning, echoing the attempts to create healthier living conditions in Victorian cities, was that of segregating 'incompatible' uses such as factories and housing. In the era of the private car such principles extended to keeping pedestrians and motor traffic apart. Jane Jacobs was one of the first to voice the feeling that strict segregation of uses created more harm than good. In her classic book *The Death and Life of Great American Cities* published in 1961 she argued that cities needed close proximity of supposedly incongruent uses as a basis for innovation, entrepreneurship and rich cultural life. In the UK too there was a growing reaction against the homogeneity and uniformity of planning outcomes based upon the segregation of uses championed by Sharpe and others.

However, there was another distributional dimension that had begun to trouble planners. Peter Hall was part of a group of left-leaning planners who had embraced the idea of planning as a way of changing society for the better. It was becoming clear to Hall that planning controls restricted economic activity in ways that disadvantaged the less well off (Allmendinger, 2013). For Hall there was another troubling dimension to planning controls. The spontaneity and freedom to develop and express oneself was being restricted in ways that were never envisaged as being one of the objectives of planning. This libertarianism echoed some of the concerns of the right, although it was driven more by a concern that planning was inhibiting the ability of communities and individuals to 'help themselves'. Hall's solution was 'non-plan', a deliberately provocative proposal to refocus and reinterpret the 'common ground' as being one that was not involved in stultifying, physical restrictions. For him and others on the left planning should not be a top-down imposition of controls but a framework that permitted experimentation and entrepreneurialism not only in an economic but also in a personal sense. Non-plan was a proposal to shift the focus of land use planning back to this concern. However, Hall understood the dangers of being interpreted as calling for an 'end to planning' and the difference between wanting simply to shift the focus and the growing right-wing agenda of abolishing controls altogether:

> Any advocate of non-plan is sure to be misrepresented; we had better repeat what we mean. Simply to demand an end to planning, all planning, would be sentimentalism; it would deny the very basis of economic life in the second half of the 20th century ... we are arguing that the word planning itself is misused; that it has also been used for the imposition of certain physical arrangements, based on value judgements or prejudices; and that it should be scrapped.
>
> (Banham *et al.*, 1969: 442)

As I discuss below, although Hall's ideas were very influential the subtlety of his argument was lost and it was the right that would champion 'non-plan' as a solution. Yet Hall's critique echoed a widely held feeling that planning simply 'wasn't working' in the physical or economic sense. Post-war redevelopment was leading to unpopular, homogenous and unattractive outcomes characterized by the demolition of what was left of Britain's cities and the development of high-rise buildings and urban motorways. The relocation of industry was also failing to achieve its aims with employers seeking to move to areas where there was a good supply of skilled labour and good transport links despite the limitations imposed upon development in such areas by the need for permits and by planning restrictions.

Yet the experiences of planning and its failure to live up to expectations had not penetrated the professional orthodoxies and doctrines of planning itself. Planners and politicians still felt the need to demonstrate that they 'knew best':

I think it is necessary to lead the citizen – guide him. The citizen does not always know exactly what is best; nevertheless we have got to take into account his wishes and his ideas and give him an opportunity of expressing them and give him an opportunity of understanding what is proposed.

(Lewis Silkin, Minister of Town and Country Planning,
quoted in Ward, 1994: 103)

Studies, such as that by Davies (1972), explored the impact of planning on the Rye Hill area of Newcastle during the post-war era and pointed to a growing gap between planners, who had become 'evangelistic bureaucrats', and the communities they were meant to be serving. Rye Hill was an area of Newcastle designated for 'improvement' (i.e. demolition). When the initial plan for Rye Hill was announced by the Chief Planning Officer in 1963, he commented that the plan was a bold one and 'many would be hurt by it'. As one senior planner in the Newcastle Council Planning Department put it: 'You've got to have a touch of arrogance to be a planner – and the basic confidence to know that you're right even when you're wrong, and the present City Planning Officer is such a man' (ibid.: 119). As Davies rightly responds:

If this type of official legitimates his schemes not by reference to the actual consumer, but either in terms if his own self-proclaimed and self-induced charisma or by reference to the range of putative consumers whose wishes or wants he himself can, in impunity define, then how can we deny or control him? The discourse of democracy is vitiated, and we the citizens are forced to give up more and more of the areas of decision making to a group of powerful, highly trained officials possessing, it would appear, a range of quasi-magical potencies.

(Ibid.: 3)

Not only was planning not working within the 'common ground' of the public interest there was no longer, if there ever had been, a public interest to work towards.

A second theme in the breakdown came with studies that began to question the impact of the progressive and redistributive objectives of planning. A major evaluation of the impacts of planning (Hall *et al.*, 1973) pointed to three main consequences: a containment of urban areas; an increase in suburbanization, often beyond the limits of urban areas; and inflation in land and property prices that arose as a result of restrictions on land supply. The containment of urban growth had been largely achieved through the use of green belts but had led to 'leap-frogging' of new development to locations further afield, thus increasing journey times and commuting. Restrictions on the growth of towns and cities and the supply of new building land had inevitably also led to increases in the value of existing development land within settlements. The consequences of planning had therefore undermined some of its progressive ideals by making land and property more expensive, affecting the poorer in society disproportionately (ibid.). Planning was having some effect, particularly in restricting physical development but there were also unintended and undesirable consequences. The wider impacts of such evaluations were significant in helping to underpin the emerging left-wing critiques of planning, particularly within academia but also in groups of like-minded practitioners. For some, such as Thomas (1982), Paris (1982) and Camhis (1979), too much emphasis had been placed on procedure and not enough on planning's role within its social, political and economic context.

This emerging, more critical view argued that the credibility of planning was based on an illusion of control. On the contrary, as Hall *et al.* demonstrated there were clear outcomes of planning that were not only unexpected but unintended. In order to maintain credibility planning had to accept the blame for such outcomes even though they were beyond its control. With the positive powers of state-led development largely removed what powers planning did have were now predominantly regulatory and controlled the private sector (Pickvance, 1982). Consequently, if planning wished to achieve change this had to be through the market, not against it. As Paris (1982), Thomas (1982) and others pointed out this shift in the approach of planning from the positive to the regulatory undermined the aspirations that had helped to justify its introduction. This illusion of control extended to an artifice of public involvement and the general public interest justification for planning: if planning was not making a significant difference to the built environment then neither was public involvement. Planning and public involvement were merely helping to legitimize market-based decisions. For some, the idea that planning simply helped the market to work more efficiently and legitimately was not a surprise (e.g. Harvey, 1985). For others, the illusion of positive planning and the complicity of planners in ignoring the reality of control made them part of the problem.

A final theme concerned more fundamental criticisms focused on the spirit and purpose of planning as it had emerged in the post-war era. As it became clear that planning was not the panacea that had been presented or understood attention began to turn to why this was the case. One possibility concerned the growing mismatch between the notion of planning as 'control' and the more fragmented, complex social and economic realities of the post-war era. Planning had been instituted in accordance with the concept of command and expertise governing what was envisaged as publicly led development and redevelopment. Where development was not publicly led the private sector would be regulated so as to follow public plans and strategies (Hall and Tewdwr-Jones, 2011). However, the ability of the state to undertake redevelopment began to be undermined by financial constraints. Reliance on the private sector to deliver housing and undertake development was far greater than envisaged, particularly in the 1960s. Between 1947 and 1954 over 80 per cent of new housing was funded by the public sector (Ward, 1994: 101). The sterling crisis of 1961 that arose from a growing negative balance of payments driven by an increase in imported goods typified the problems of a long-term relative decline in economic performance and productivity against the UK major European competitors. The consequence was a mismatch between the needs and aspirations of redevelopment and the economic growth needed to help to pay for it. As discussed above, this diminution in the direct development function of the state left planning with a regulatory role. Yet this reactive and regulatory model of planning sat uncomfortably with the need for greater partnership between the public and private sectors which would be necessary to facilitate rather than simply to regulate private development and coordinate public development. In the view of some, planners were not trained or equipped to deal with this new role: 'planning lacked not merely the powers, but also the expertise and theoretical knowledge necessary to tackle the complex environmental problems facing contemporary society' (Evans, 1997: 4).

Other issues also emerged that began to point to a divergence between the post-1947 system and the needs of society. One issue concerned demographic change. Despite a relative economic decline compared to other industrialized countries the UK economy continued to grow in real terms at about 2.8 per cent per annum between 1951 and 1973. This growth helped to feed expectations of improved lifestyles including accommodation. At the same time the population was growing, partly as a result of declining mortality rates. Both economic and demographic influences fed housing demand and highlighted a continuing need for housing. The outcome of increased demand and improved quality was a significant push from the two main political parties to meet this need by building more for less, a push that led to an emphasis on high-rise developments and prefabricated buildings. Reactive and regulatory planning was out of step with this push.

There were other issues with the shift to more regulatory planning. Land use plans were a key aspect of control though it was becoming clear that the system of single-tier plans was failing as it was unable to bridge the need to accommodate both strategic and detailed planning issues. Strategic issues often had a longer duration and needed less revision than more detailed site-specific issues. Yet strategic thinking and coordination took longer to plan and prepare. The upshot was that plan making was unfolding much more slowly than envisaged: only twenty-two of the 145 planning authorities submitted their development plans within the three years required of the 1947 Act (Ward, 1994: 104). Planning was failing to produce the plans necessary for the regulation of privately led development, nor was it delivering on the public sector-led model envisaged.

Such issues should have led to self-reflection on the part of planners and the profession. In fact, it seemed to result in a lack of critical reflection and of recognition that there was, indeed, any problem. Instead, planning managed and internalized such issues:

> [T]he planning system and the profession are far too sure of themselves: land use planning has become a technical doctrine which does not recognize its ambivalence, nor does it consider its limitations. It is, therefore, expressed in terms of far too meticulous standards (with reference to density, for example) on the one hand, and in terms of rather obscure notions (such as that of 'amenity') on the other.
>
> (Glass, 1959, reproduced in Faludi, 1973: 61)

Conclusions

The slow breakdown in the consensus around planning arose for a range of reasons, but while the anti-planning critique of the new right (see Chapter 4) is widely understood it was the growing disillusionment with planning on the political left and the lack of responsiveness from the profession that created the space for the right to propagate its alternatives. For some in the profession it was a lack of commitment to the ideal of planning that was the problem:

> What ... happened was that, exhausted and exalted by the war, we created the finest planning system ever seen, but then lacked the sustained energy to make it produce results sufficiently impressive for the electorate to insist upon its being kept intact. I believe it is wrong to blame inherent defects in the system as some do. It was rather that obviously beneficial results were too few and too slow for it to be seen that the undoubted disadvantages and delays involved for the many members of the public were nevertheless worthwhile.
>
> (Keeble, 1969: 38)

For others on the left planning had become either a way of supporting developers' profits or a means through which good housing had become even less affordable. There thus emerged a divergence of opinion on the future of planning on the part of both main parties and of the planning profession itself, the latter verging on the delusion that the problems of planning were not the fault of planning. More not less planning was the answer. For Keeble, adding to the existing suite of functions and regulations was the 'sane' way to address the problems (1961: 194). However, others on the left had more significant issues not only with planning but also with the role of the state in advanced capitalist societies more generally.

3 New understandings

A reinvigorated and fragmented left

> Humanity will not be free until the last bureaucrat is strangled with the guts of the last capitalist.
>
> (Slogan of the Paris uprisings, May 1968)

Introduction

The slow breakdown of the common ground around planning discussed in the previous chapter took on a new, more fundamental and critical dynamic from the late 1960s. If towards the end of the 1960s there was still a consensus around the benefits of state planning, however fragile and superficial, this had largely been shattered by the mid-1970s. The old certainties and common ground were disappearing and the search was on for new understandings and approaches. The challenge had been growing for some time, although a lack of alternatives and the continuing accord between the main political parties regarding a mixed economy had stymied progress, despite the growing recognition of a need for change. Ruth Glass argued in the late 1950s that

> it is mainly the remembrance of a period of exceptional unanimity, and also the trust in public authority, which keeps the [planning] system going. There are signs that both the memory and the confidence are wearing thin.
>
> (Glass, 1959, reproduced in Faludi, 1973: 62)

The step change from the late 1960s emerged when the critiques of planning began to coincide and to be reinforced by emerging questions in wider society about the role of the state more generally. The challenges and alternatives for planning were to come from both the right and left of the political spectrum. In this chapter I discuss the left's critiques and alternatives to planning, before moving on to the right's response in the next chapter. The terms 'left' and 'right' are broad labels that mask a range of views and attitudes, although they nevertheless serve as useful heuristics for two broad and distinct attitudes towards the role of the state and planning. The mainstream right has broadly viewed planning as a market-supportive mechanism which addresses the imperfections of land and property markets. Such a view has translated, particularly in the past three decades, into reluctant, provisional and critical support underpinned by a broad suspicion of planners and planning as the 'enemies of enterprise'. The left, on the other hand, has traditionally been a more natural ally having originally been responsible for the introduction of the comprehensive system of land use regulation in 1947 as part of a suite of nationalizations of formerly private realms such as industry, transport and natural resources. However, the broad and somewhat uncritical support for planning that characterized the immediate post-war era subsequently gave way to a more discriminating and suspicious view in the 1970s, morphing into a realization that state intervention in land and property markets was not necessarily a natural ally or tool of socialism. Some began to see planning and planners as part of the mechanism of capitalism, while others on the left understood planning as a legacy of modernity that was out of kilter with a complex, fragmented and postmodern society. Of course, there had always been those on the left who were critical of planning, taking the view that planning – in all senses – was a tool of the ruling elite and used to manage capitalism in the interests of capital. Such criticisms became much more prevalent from the late 1960s onwards, leading to both a fall in support for planning and the rise of a plethora of alternatives including more radical approaches. These alternatives provided little in the way of practical responses to planning but were based, instead, upon a more critical and self-reflective attitude of constant critique at best and a dismissal of any kind of collective action as a totalizing imposition at worst. Yet it was not these alternatives per se that were to become the problem but the vacuum that was created by the break-up of a unified understanding of and approach to planning. The breakdown of the consensus and fragmentation of attitudes provided the space that those with right-leaning responses, based upon a nascent neoliberalism, used to gain a foothold in order that their views might evolve into an orthodoxy. It is this changing attitude towards planning on the left, the rise of a plethora of alternatives and the subsequent impact upon planning that I explore in this chapter, before moving on to the right's response in the next.

The 'betrayal' of the left

While the impact of planning on cities and communities in the UK led some on the left to begin to question the objectives and processes of planning during the 1960s the main source of intellectual challenge and point of rupture came from across the English Channel. The events in France between May and June 1968, when Paris was brought to a standstill by a wave of strikes and riots that looked likely to bring down the government of Charles de Gaulle, were the culmination of dissatisfaction with a wide range of issues. The issues that led to the unrest were echoed elsewhere, including in the UK. The events triggered and inspired a host of new left-wing critiques of Marxist theory and contemporary capitalism that were ultimately to fragment the left's understanding of planning and provide new critical thinking about its role. While the fallout of this rupture and subsequent fragmentation would not be fully felt for some years the implications would ultimately be far-reaching and include the spawning of a range of new 'posts' – postmodernism, post-Fordism, post-industrialism, post-Marxism and post-structuralism in particular – that were to dominate planning thought for the subsequent three decades.

Though far-reaching the origins of these shifts in thinking on the left were inauspicious. A series of student-initiated disputes in the French capital quickly evolved into a general strike and street protests that brought the country to a standstill. Orthodox class-based Marxism pointed to ruptures within capitalist societies as being inevitable and part of a logic and dialectic that would ulti-mately end in socialism. Such predictions seemed to be coming true as President de Gaulle fled France during the uprisings. Yet socialism did not emerge at the height of the protests; instead, various elements of the protests began to fight with each other. The French Communist Party labelled the student element of the protests 'rabble rousers' and backed the government's call for new elections that would allow de Gaulle to return to power and normality to return to French society. The consequence of this 'betrayal' of the left by the left was the spark that led many former Marxist philosophers and theorists to reappraise Marxism and the role that theory played in understanding developed capitalist societies, the role of culture and the self, the alienation of workers and class, and the role of bureaucracy in maintaining capitalism.

Questions about these issues had been around for some time – both Friedrich Nietzsche and Martin Heidegger, for example, had provided critiques of moder-nity that had influenced later postmodern thinking, while during the post-war period Jean-Paul Sartre had challenged the reductionist mechanistic determinism of Stalinist Marxism with his existentialist focus on the individual. Another challenge emerged from the *gauchistes* such as Cornelius Castoriadis who analysed the growth and role of bureaucracies whether under socialism or capitalism. According to mainstream socialist doctrine bureaucracies and bureaucratic growth were necessary for state planning. However, Castoriadis argued that bureaucracies under capitalism or communism preserved exploitation – bureaucrats had become a class of their own and the condition of the workers under socialism was not all that different from that under capitalism. In capi-talist economic systems, he argued, bureaucracies were increasingly intervening through the provision of welfare and corporate and trade union bureaucracy to shore up capitalism. The fundamental divisions within capitalism predicted by Marx were being replaced by a new order of divisions between order givers and order takers.

Such analyses and viewpoints had largely been in the shadow of mainstream Marxist thinking until attention began to turn to them in the light of the events of 1968. It was also clear that there was a deeper, more complex social and economic reality than that accounted for in mainstream class-based Marxist theories. While the strikes in France had initially been welcomed by the unions and the powerful Communist Party it quickly became clear that the protests did not sit easily within mainstream Marxist theory and its understanding of class-based conflict. As Hirsh (1981: 140–41) points out, the differences between mainstream Marxist understandings and the realities of the protests in France were subtle but significant. The protests were more concerned with a rejection of cultural norms than an economic crisis and had been led by students, not the working class. Some of the workers who were involved were motivated by grievances with the unions as well as with their conditions, while other not traditionally radical groups such as teachers also became involved and had their own agendas unaligned with those of the students. One upshot was a realization that society and the protests were more complex and less reducible to class-based conflict than previously understood: 'Not only traditional Marxist dogmas disintegrated in May 1968. The liberal myths of stability, integration, depoliticization and consensus in advanced capitalist society exploded as well' (Hirsch, 1981: 141).

The events of May 1968 represented a rejection of social convention driven by the desire for more relaxed social attitudes and the impulse to break free from bureaucracy and alienation rather than, as predicted, a desire for a new socialist order for society. Mainstream Marxist analysis struggled to grasp, never mind explain, these events.

This mismatch and the subsequent reappraisal of a class-based understanding of society was echoed and fuelled by other events that took place beyond the borders of France. The international economic crisis of the early 1970s that brought an end to the long post-war boom introduced a palpable though vague feeling that 'things were different'. Such differences would be later characterized as including globalization, a growing societal and class fragmentation, an increasing significance of information technology and the increasing phenomenon of consumerism. Such shifts and trends challenged mainstream and traditional thinking on the left which increasingly seemed to be out of step with reality. Another consequence of this was a challenge to the role of the state. The top-down, 'one size fits all' approach to planning and land use regulation began to look and feel inappropriate at best, and a conservative obstacle to change and a part of the *ancien régime* at worst,

The challenge to left-wing thinking was fundamental and comprehensive. Advances in electronics and technology towards the end of the 1960s as well as the rise of systems theory in management and the social sciences represented a new era of positivist methodologies based on quantitative modelling of complex phenomena such as cities. The marriage of electronics and communications with the increasing importance of information led to optimistic though influential claims about the coming of a 'post-industrial society' (Bell, 1973):

My basic premise has been that knowledge and information are becoming the strategic resource and the transforming agent of the post-industrial society ... just as the combination of energy, resources and machine technology were the transforming agencies of industrial society.

(Ibid., 1973: 531)

The implications of this shift, according the information and knowledge society advocates, were profound: industrial society had progressed from being space and time bound and was no longer linked to territorially based political and bureaucratic authorities. Post-industrial societies had broken these links eclipsing distance and compressing time, while technology had expanded space into the global and foreshortened time to an instant (Lash and Urry, 1994; Harvey, 1989). Departing from more traditional political economy understandings about the labour theory of value Bell (1980) advanced what he termed a knowledge theory of value, while Toffler (1981: 2–3) argued that the information society amounted to the rise of a new civilization. More measured and critical analyses pointed out that while there were differences there were also substantial continuities between the 'old' and the 'new' and that society and the economy remained essentially capitalist (e.g. Webster, 2006). Lash and Urry (1987), for example, argued that the growth in the significance of information in the economy amounted to no more than the spread of Taylorist techniques of standardization and automation from the factory floor to the office. With the increased significance of information in the economy others chose to rename the terms used in order to reflect the continuities in society rather than the ruptures, preferring 'digital capitalism' (e.g. Schiller, 2000) or 'informational capitalism' (e.g. Castells, 2000).

Information society analyses tended to portray these changes as a progressive departure from industrial society that focused upon a future of prosperity and freedom. Such positive interpretations fed the dominant urban understandings of the time that saw the city as a place to be measured and quantified, mapped and modelled. In publications such as Brian McLoughlin's *Urban and Regional Planning: A Systems Approach* (1969) and George Chadwick's *A Systems View of Planning: Towards a Theory of the Urban and Regional Planning Process* (1971) the future of planning was to have a positivistic destination with the planner as the expert helmsman. The city was a system of inter-connected parts and planners could understand and control it, minimizing 'bad effects' and maximizing individual utility. The laws that governed cities were universal and immutable. If planning itself was facing problems then it was because its models and forecasts were inadequate – more and better planning was needed.

The final major influence on the left towards the end of the 1960s concerned the growing distrust in the decisions and policies of governments and greater calls for greater public involvement. Reactions against the Vietnam War, the civil rights movement in the USA, opposition to road building and the demolition of valued buildings such as Euston Station in London and the nascent environmental movement globally began to challenge taken for granted views. Growing demands for public involvement and a more open and transparent system of government including planning questioned the system's view of planners as infallible experts.

This heady mix of factors, some of which were irreconcilable, represented a direct challenge to those who regarded the city as a place that sat squarely (as orthodox Marxist analyses would have it) in the dominant mode of production and consumption as well as those who were beginning to feel that cities and places were more than simply 'machines for living' as per Corbusier. The challenge was not just a theoretical one for better understanding; it was a challenge for the future of the urban and the role of planning. Marxists had always been more concerned with changing the world than understanding it and Marxist urban theory, such that it was, needed to be relevant to what many on the left term 'new times'. This reinvention of the left's urban thought was to push planning, urban theory and Marxist theory in inspired and challenging new directions and analyses that were to blow away the smug orthodoxy of the planning in the post-war years. The upshot was a rethinking of the role of planning and the city in three broad directions all of which had profound implications.

Marxist urbanism for new times

Spurred on by the challenges outlined above, Marxist revisionism spilled over into the realm of the urban and the role of the city in a range of radical and brilliant extensions of Marxist thought to space and the role of the city from the late 1960s onwards. Two broad trajectories emerged. The first was the approach typified by Manuel Castells' *The Urban Question* (1972) and inspired by the structuralist Marxism of Louis Althusser. For Castells the city was a site of collective consumption and reproduction necessary for crisis management within capitalism. Castells attempted to rethink the relationship between Marxism and the city from within a mainstream Marxist framework. The second stream of thought was led by Henri Lefebvre, Guy Debord and, subsequently, David Harvey and took a different tack that explored how capitalism produced space, commodified it and made cities and space a key element in the survival of capitalism. Harvey (1973), in particular, explored the holistic nature of the urban as well as development in the capitalist system and how the city, through development, redevelopment and public subsidy for regeneration, had become an important productive space of capitalism and not simply a space for social reproduction as understood in classic Marxist theory.

Henri Lefebvre, a left-leaning philosopher and activist, and sometime communist though a committed socialist, was a major figure in the revision of Marxist thought in the post-war era. Lefebvre's approach to the urban had three main elements. First, his take on Marxist theory was heavily influenced by the 'early' pre-1845 Marx and his humanist interpretation of the nature of struggle, exploitation and alienation. The economic realm and class-based relations were important but should not dominate: for Lefebvre Marxism should not be reduced to economic and class-based determinism. Under late capitalism people were increasingly alienated from a range of human relations and sensual experiences both in the home and at work, and post-industrial capitalist society was characterized by social fragmentation across and between classes. Ownership of 'things' or possessions was only one dimension of the human essence: people had other needs concerning human relations and sensual experiences.

This more subjective focus shifted Marxist analysis away from economic relations to everyday life and opened new avenues of Marxist analysis focusing upon culture and advertising (or the 'poetry of modernity', as Lefebvre termed it). Despite increasing standards of living and the affordability of domestic appliances and holidays dissatisfaction prevailed as new forms of contradictions emerged beyond the economic and class-based divisions envisaged by Marx, including the loneliness of overcrowding and the breakdown of familial and social ties. As technology had more or less 'solved' problems of economic production the focus was now more on human development as a basis for revolution. One consequence was that society and economic relations could not be reduced to simplistic, deterministic and 'scientific' laws. Modern capitalist societies continued to exploit and alienate people but in different ways, and people were increasingly colonized by the 'commodity' which shrouded and distracted from the true nature of alienation.

The second dimension to Lefebvre's rethought Marxism flows directly from his analysis of the commodification and colonization of the everyday. Lefebvre reconstructed Marxism from the bottom up, focusing on the complexity of everyday experiences and the sensual. This reversal of the dominant (later structuralist) Marx provided new opportunities for resistance and change, stemming from the bottom up rather than top-down. Part of this rethinking specifically included planning and urbanization. Modernist planning had sought to create 'better' environments through the segregation of non-conforming uses and compartmentalization (e.g. urban and rural, residential and industrial), imposing functional spaces and suppressing the spontaneous and chaotic in human existence. Echoing his concerns with everyday existence Lefebvre argued that planning had separated, controlled and 'planned out' the human exchanges that would help to fulfil the sensual experience and interpersonal interactions. Planning, like capitalism, had helped to alienate people. However, the difference was that this was not necessarily part of the logic of capitalist relations: modernist planning was characteristic of socialist societies too. Spontaneity, vitality and creativity – essential elements of individual need and therefore the true objectives of socialism – had been lost. To reclaim these elements required the facilitation of collective and individual resistance. It was this reclamation of the spontaneity, vitality and creativity that constituted Lefebvre's call for a 'right to the city'. Thus Lefebvre's dialectic took on a new form: class antagonisms central to Marxist thinking were being managed through planning and development. The urban was a site of managed conflict as areas were gentrified through a process of *embourgeoisement*. Gentrification involved the managed movement of workers to new, sterile and controlled outer urban areas. In their place the bourgeoisie colonized the inner districts, carefully managing them and increasingly becoming part of the capitalist production process. Capitalism and planning regarded spontaneity as the enemy.

Although formulated prior to the events of May 1968 Lefebvre's analysis took on a new, increasingly focused form in the aftermath of the protests once it became clear that there was a more complex set of relations concerning the capitalist mode of production. Lefebvre turned his attention to space and the urban emphasizing the contestation between managed and spontaneous space. Space had become the suspect in the mystery of how capitalism had built up resilience to its contradictions as the protests and protestors disappeared and life seemed to return to normal. In Lefebvre's most influential work *La production de l'espace* (*The Production of Space*) (1974) he addresses this question head on and argues that space is socially and therefore politically produced. Space and the urban have changed their function under capitalism from being a site of industrialization to a productive force itself, further deepening and displacing the contradictions within capitalism. Space and the urban have became battlegrounds and are subject to contestation as the bourgeoisie seek to control and manage cities. Space has been commodified and colonized as part of the survival of capitalism. Industrialization had merely been a precursor to the urbanization of capital and the city was now the focus of capital-class conflict and contradiction. While Engels had posited urbanization as a function of capital in the nineteenth century cities had now become a force of production themselves with their own inherent contradictions and conflicts. Cities were not simply a stage upon which contradictions played out (*in* space) but were places that had their own inherent contradictions (*of* space).

Urban development and redevelopment now provided an opportunity for capital to create surplus value creating new contestation with labour and also within capital itself (e.g. where to invest, what kind of development, and how to service development). The state – through planning – had a key role to play in the production of space; coordinating and investing, regulating and designing. The representation of space, involving ideology, power and expert knowledge becomes another dimension in understanding the production of space: zoning, segregation of 'conflicting' uses, urban regeneration, and functional areas are all representations of space and reflected inherent class control and biases. Representations of space could be contrasted with representational space, the space of spontaneity and 'the heart' or 'lived space'. Representations and representational space exist side by side and are linked through everyday spatial practices. Representational space is suppressed and excluded as a threat to capital accumulation through its particularity and the 'right to the city'.

This neo-Marxist analysis of space ran contrary to the contemporary orthodoxy of Marxist theory, particularly in the Soviet Union. It also ran into another obstacle in the form of critiques from more mainstream, structuralist urban Marxist analyses that were also rethinking the role of the urban and planning post-1968. Manuel Castells, a one-time assistant of Lefebvre, presented his own take on Marxist urbanism post-1968 in *The Urban Question. A Marxist Approach* (originally published in French in 1972, with the English edition appearing in 1978). Castells acknowledged the brilliance of Lefebvre's reworked insights but felt the need to provide a more mainstream, structuralist take on the resilience of capital and the role of the urban drawing upon the more scientific Marxism of Louis Althusser. Structuralist Marxists preferred a more analytical and predictable approach that focused on objective structures of capitalism and components of Marxist understanding such as class and contradiction. Structuralism rejected the more subjective, 'lived' experiences of humanist Marxism dismissing them as being 'ideological', i.e. a surface appearance of reality that missed deeper understandings and causalities.

Castells took Althusser's views on ideology and argued that characteristics of society such as crime or homelessness, regarded by some as being reflections of urban living, were in fact the result of capitalist society. According to Castells, Lefebvre's take on the urban had similarly confused cause and effect by arguing that capitalist relations had been replaced by urban relations making industrialization subordinate to urbanization. Alienation and the experiences of everyday urban life theorized by Lefebvre conflated and confused distinct analytical dimensions of Marxism based upon economic relations. Such superficial consequences missed the deeper dependence of the city upon capitalism and class antagonisms. The forms, contradictions and experiences of urban life were not independent of economic practice, the structure in dominance, as Althusser termed it. Individual social practices and experiences are reflective of and conditioned by the economic and form an ideology that helps to mask deeper economic relations and practices.

Castells followed Althusser in arguing that the economic was the dominant influence in any social formation but worked through and interacted with other secondary formations such as the political and cultural. This interrelated complexity points to a unique configuration of social formation dependent upon the situation and context. The urban was a place of production and reproduction, the reproduction of productive forces (e.g. raw materials or labour processes) and the social relations of production (e.g. the skills, availability or health) of labour. Workers must not only be able to work but must also 'know their place' and accept class relations and their place in them. The urban was, for Castells, a part of this reproductive process and a key part of capitalism as well as being a site of collective consumption to facilitate the reproduction of housing, schools and mass transit. These were key to the profitability and survival of capitalism but did not, in themselves, produce a profit. The state in general and the planning system in particular helped to provide and coordinate such collective consumption through social housing, zoning, public spaces and clean air, for example. Such provision helps to offset crises in capitalism even though it initiates new conflicts and contradictions. The dominant class provided the ideology of such urban planning, that is, what is required and where. The upshot was 'planning capture' and politicization: space and place became an extension of capitalist relations with planners acting as the handmaidens. This is not to say that capitalists had it all their own way: structuralists posited a certain degree of independence of the state from the capitalist class and argued that the state works in the longer term interests of capital rather than the shorter term interests of capitalists. The role of the urban as a site of collective consumption was not its own crises and contradictions since new forms of struggle and opposition emerged as a result: urban regeneration and the location of new social housing became politicized and contested. There were also crises relating to state funding of such collective consumption: when state funding started to become problematic the 'blame' could be placed on the state rather than the consequences of capitalist relations. Similarly, the rise of the new petit bourgeoisie of planners and housing professionals also provided a new dimension and intermediaries, distracting from the true nature of urban collective consumption to capitalism.

While Lefebvre had adapted Marxism for the new urban condition Castells had sought to apply Marxism to the urban. However, this was an approach that Castells departed from in his second major work, *City, Class and Power* (1978). This later attempt at a rethought approach was, in Castells' words, a Marxism more concerned with historical relevance than with formal coherence, taking into consideration the rise of new players and agents in the urban including bureaucrats such as planners, and also the way in which there were struggles and conflicts *within* the state. Yet even this concession was not, ultimately, enough and later works such as *The City and the Grassroots* (1983) further developed an agency-focused, non-class-based subjective view of urban change.

The third major exploration of the political economy of planning as a result of the resilience and even the continued expansion of capitalism in the wake of the uprisings and crises of the late 1960s was to come from David Harvey. Like Lefebvre and Castells, Harvey's focus was on the role of the urban in late capitalism. *Social Justice and the City* (1973) was published in the same year as Castells' *The Urban Question,* although it had a different take on the role of planning and the city that, while closer to Lefebvre, was still distinct. For Harvey development and redevelopment of urban space had become more important than and separate from the production of goods as a form of capital accumulation. Cities did not only reproduce labour and the conditions for capital accumulation through collective consumption but were sites of accumulation and class conflict and struggle in their own right. This raises a range of new dimensions including conflicts within different elements of capital – industrial, commercial and housing – over land and space as well as the constant dynamic to produce new, more efficient urban forms. Class struggle is an added dimension to the conflicts and tensions involving the accumulation and the production of space within capital itself. Harvey's approach was developed and refined in *The Limits to Capital* (1982). Here Marxist concerns with overproduction and crises are extended to finance and space as speculation and overproduction and investment in development leads to congealed forms of debt as prices fall amounting to identifiable 'cycles' of growth and stagnation. Planners were a form of urban manager, facilitating this process and 'softening' the consequences for certain groups.

Lefebvre, Castells and Harvey all went on to develop their ideas further (as we shall see in relation to Castells and Harvey below), often in response to criticisms from similar left-wing analyses and reformulations. However, these three totemic and important Marxist interventions and analyses at a time of reflection and questioning of planning in the late 1960s and early 1970s were critical to opening up a space for debate on the left about the role and future of planning. These new interpretations on the urban and planning were significant in the sense of exposing the role of the planner in capitalism and the urban as well as the role of planning itself.

One outcome was a rich seam of new thinking that inspired planners to explore their roles and contributions to space and cities. However, another outcome of the fragmentation of Marxist thought in relation to planning and the urban was to turn the attention of the left generally 'inwards' as the different factions criticized each other as well as the nature of capitalism. A further outcome was the emergence of a debate within planning theory led by the new school of Marxist-inspired planners who attacked planning in general and dominant schools of planning theory and thought in particular. One focus was the continued insistence of planners that they were somehow 'apolitical' and that there was such a thing as a neutral, objective set of theories that justified planning and helped to shape planning action. These new critical perspectives argued that planning theory was 'contentless', was subject to the needs of capital and had emerged through the same social tensions that impact upon the urban. Planning practice was also deemed to be similarly historically situated and determined:

> [Planning is] an ever-changing historical process that is continually shaped and reshaped by broad systems of urban tensions. Thus urban planners in Europe and North America have not turned their attention now to zoning procedures, now to urban renewal, now to expressway construction, simply as a result of the appearance of 'new ideas' within an abstract and self-propelling planning theory. It is only when urban development begins to produce real problems and predicaments that planners attempt to counteract them.
>
> (Dear and Scott, 1981: 13)

While mainstream planning theory was presented by planners as technical 'expert' knowledge, pursued in the 'public interest' planners actually worked to produce and reproduce the conditions necessary for capital accumulation (Harvey, 1985). From being largely ambivalent towards land use planning the left had now been given sufficient reasons to be suspicious at best and hostile at worst.

Postmodernism or the cultural logic of late capitalism

On the left, one reaction to the ability of capitalism to withstand crises and contradictions in the late 1960s and early 1970s was to go back and rethink Marxism, but another was to abandon it altogether. While it would be misleading to identify May 1968 as the sole point of departure for much postmodern thinking it was undoubtedly a spur:

> The May 1968 upheaval contributed in significant ways to later developments of postmodern theory. The student revolts politicized the nature of education in the university system and criticized the production of knowledge as a

means of power and domination ... the students also analyzed the university as a microcosm of a repressive capitalist society and turned their attention to the full range of hidden mechanisms through which a society conveys its knowledge and ensures its survival under the mask of knowledge: newspapers, television, technical schools and the *lycée*.

(Best and Kellner, 1991: 23)

Like the rethought variants of Marxism, postmodern thinking went beyond the immediate crisis to attempt better to understand the transformations in culture and society brought about by rapid industrialization during the post-war era. A particular focus was the increasing significance of consumerism and its effect on society. One target of the rethinking was structuralism and the structuralist core of mainstream Marxism with its emphasis on objectivity, rigour and truth, an emphasis that looked increasingly untenable in the face of a growing complexity and heterogeneity in society. Instead, postmodern thinkers began to argue for a more relativistic, open, subjective and infinite relationship between signified and signifier, and truth and reality that sought to understand the significance of changed conditions in society (the postmodern as new times) and the scope and relevance of social theory (the postmodern as social theory) (Allmendinger, 2000).

An early venture into the postmodern oeuvre, and one of the more well-known, came from Jean François-Lyotard. Like many writers on the postmodern, Lyotard had a long history of engagement with ideas from a variety of sources. He recanted his earlier Marxist orientation in the late 1970s and his contribution to the postmodern debate can be distilled down to two books, *The Postmodern Condition* (1984) and *The Differend* (1988) (first published in 1979 and 1983, respectively). Lyotard's postmodernism concerns a rejection of the grand narratives about Marxism (1984) and '*an incredulity towards meta-narratives*' (though this sounds suspiciously like a grand and totalizing narrative itself). In place of meta-narratives Lyotard instead emphasizes the need for understandings that assume plurality and difference. Drawing on the work of Alan Touraine and Daniel Bell, Lyotard argues in *The Postmodern Condition* that postmodernity has emerged through the conditions of advanced capitalism. Knowledge has been transformed into a commodity in the post-industrial landscape where its nature and use will 'change', though Lyotard does not make it clear how. Following Nietzsche, Lyotard claims that this commodification of knowledge has led science to abandon its search for 'truth' and replace it with a search for 'power'. In addition (and this time drawing on Weber and latterly Habermas) science has come to see instrumental rationality as the only form of legitimate reason. Lyotard's point of departure concerns the role of narratives and the ways in which science claims its legitimacy and has attempted to suppress and ridicule other forms of reason. Lyotard claims that traditional narratives (i.e. spoken) rules and rituals are bound up in self-legitimacy – they need no exterior justification, they just 'are' and no argument or proof is required. However, although science considers such forms of reason 'barbaric' and bases itself on its own transcendental status science cannot ultimately justify itself without recourse to such narratives.

These themes are developed by another major contributor to the postmodern, Michel Foucault. Like Lyotard, Fouault also attacked and distrusted universal truths and universalizing theory but did not reject them outright, seeking instead to problematize and historicize them. Rather than meta-narratives Foucault focused on power and the subject:

> Foucault and others rejected the 'hegemony of Marxism' as rooted in totalizing and essentializing logic that subsumed all forms of oppression and resistance to the fulcrum of labour and exploitation. It become widely understood that power had numerous other sources and strategies, working not only in factories but in schools, hospitals, prisons and throughout culture and everyday life.
>
> (Best and Kellner [1991] 1997: 10)

Foucault's rejection of uni-directional or class-orientated power struggles led him to explore more subtle exercises of power as flows with no locus or 'closure'. Foucault also rejected the Enlightenment view of the subject as sovereign, rational and reflective preferring instead the individual as created through dominant discourses and subject to normalizing power regimes. Foucault's early work on madness draws upon both themes as he undertakes a historic decon-struction of the ways in which madness has been constructed through reason and discourses based on what is regarded as 'normal' and what is 'different'. Those regarded as 'mad' were treated in different ways depending upon the dominant view of the time including, at certain times, exclusion. However, exclusion did not always involve a physical separation but also forms of self-control through routinized and systematized 'codes of conduct' (Rabinow, 1984).

Foucault's is a more disruptive method to understanding and history and seeks to challenge what Lyotard would term meta-narratives of history. His is

> a comparative, historical approach [which] highlights both that madness has no pre-social essence and also that there is nothing natural or inevitable about strategies through which, in modern society, the mad are confined and socially excluded.
>
> (McNay, 1994: 17)

In his subsequent works these themes of a more socially constructed and discursive subject are developed, though he also focuses on the reasons for which one dominant mode of thinking is chosen over another. Foucault's position differs slightly from Lyotard's, however, and allows for agreement or consensus to emerge that amounts to a totalizing history or position rather than the relativist insistence upon the existence of a range of incommensurable discourses.

While Foucault's position and approach to disassembling the universal truths of history was evolving he maintained the need to uncover local lost voices and the potential for infinite productions of meaning. This genealogical method was accompanied by and influenced his take on power. Reductionist views of power, such as the Marxists' insistence on class-based understandings, are replaced:

> Power must be analysed as something which circulates, or rather as something which only functions in the form of a chain. It is never localized here or there, never in anybody's hands, never appropriated as a commodity or piece of wealth. Power is employed and exercised through a net-like organisation. And not only do individuals circulate between its threads; they are always in the position of simultaneously undergoing and exercising this power.
>
> (Ibid., Foucault 1980: 48)

Power is no longer seen as emanating from economic or juridical sources. Instead, power has become an ordering force rather than a restricting or impeding force. In terms of modern society the use of timetables, surveillance, examinations and performance targets seek to 'normalize' the subject, by which Foucault (1976) means the elimination of all 'social and psychological irregularities'. One consequence of this analysis is that as power is decentralized and pluralized then political resistance should be too. The outcome is a politics of resistance:

> It seems to me that the real political task in a society such as ours is to criticise the workings of institutions which appear to be both neutral and independent; to criticize them in such a manner that the political violence which has always exercised itself obscurely through them will be unmasked, so that one can fight them.
>
> (Quoted in Best and Kellner, 1991: 57)

Such an approach has been widely criticized for ignoring the concentrations of power found in, for example, economic institutions or the state and the danger of replacing any claim to truth with simply relativism (Habermas, 1987).

Other former Marxist thinkers such as Jean Baudrillard were to add to the postmodern oeuvre with analyses of the significance of culture and the role of capitalism in the 'death of authenticity' through a procession of simulacra that bear no relation to reality. The resultant 'hyperreal' is a state whereby all referentiality, critical distance and meaning are lost, and whereby people can no longer decide what is real or unreal, right or wrong. This argument, like other responses to new times by former Marxists, is founded on the rethinking of class-based restructuring under Marxism. In the case of Baudrillard (1970, 1972), this is the overlooked significance of consumption in capitalist society whereby consumption of use values based on human needs has been replaced by the consumption of signs or brands. Needs, in Baudrillard's world, are both socially created and socially met, an argument that undermines Marx's inevitability of capitalism's demise and closes off radical alternatives. As with Lyotard and Foucault there is a resistance to meta-narratives and a form of micro-political resistance in Baudrillard's earlier work, though his later work moves him in a more nihilistic direction where there is no truth but a multitude of truths that cannot amount to radical alternatives. Even Foucault's dispersed understanding of power is rejected by Baudrillard (1987) as power is now so fragmented and found in signs, simulations and the media that it is lost and hidden: we cannot trace it. Postmodern society is devoid of meaning and theories. Critics of Baudrillard have focused on his own grand theorizing to the point of abstraction and caricature and parody, seeing what he wants to see and ignoring obvious sources of concentrations of power (Best and Kellner, 1991).

The postmodern and post-structuralist take on the world has not gone without reaction and criticism, particularly from those who reject the idea that Marxism cannot account for new times. In terms of planning two notable reactions stand out. The first is from David Harvey (1989) who sought to integrate the postmodern challenge within his rethought Marxism. The second reaction was more accommodating and sought to embrace the postmodern and explore its meaning and implications for planning.

Harvey had previously sought to deepen and develop the notion of conflict for contemporary cities and include an urban analysis as part of a rethought Marxism. Yet the direction and significance of the postmodern challenge questioned and rejected the deterministic and overarching nature of Marxist thought. It was becoming clear that the postmodern as new times and social theory was gaining a wide following and impact, more so than the attempts to rethink Marxism. Try as he might Harvey argued that the postmodern challenge could no longer be ignored, and he sought to repeat his analysis of contemporary urban conditions within a developed Marxist analysis by painting the postmodern as a consequence of capitalism. Mirroring Fredric Jameson (1991) Harvey argued that what had been termed the postmodern was, in fact, better understood as late modern or the cultural logic of late capitalism. In other words the postmodern is not a break from but an evolution or different form of modernity. In a series of questions that go to the heart of the postmodern challenge Harvey asks:

> Does postmodernism, for example, represent a radical break with modernism, or is it simply a revolt within modernism against a certain form of high modernism ... Is postmodernism a style ... or should we view it strictly as a periodizing concept ... Does it have a revolutionary potential by virtue of its opposition to all forms of meta-narratives ... or is it simply a commercialization and domestication of modernism?
>
> (1989: 42)

Yet Harvey's attempt to portray the postmodern as a component of contemporary capitalism was a sideshow. The challenge to planning thought and practice was leading to fundamental questions about the nature of society and the state, questions that were aided by the challenges of postmodern attitudes:

> It [the postmodern] is *deconstructive* in the sense of questioning and establishing a sceptical distance from conventional beliefs and, more

actively, trying both to ascertain who derives value from upholding their authority and to displace them; *antifoundationalist* in the sense of dispensing with universals as bases of truth; *nondualistic* in the sense of refusing the separation between subjectivity and objectivity along with the array of dualisms it engenders including the splits between truth and opinion, fact and value; and encouraging of *plurality and difference.*

(Moore-Milroy, 1991: 187, emphasis in the original)

The more revolutionary thought of the postmodern appealed more than the evolutionary approach of the late modern revisions of Marx. The themes of the postmodern including the breakdown of transcendental meaning or foundational thought, the discursively created subject, the increasingly fragmented and dispersed nature of the world including a breakdown of political alignments and a more diverse, dispersed and disciplining understanding of power, echoed the uncertainties about planning itself. Yet the postmodern, by its nature, asked far more questions than it answered, particularly for an action-focused field such as planning.

Both the late and postmodern provided new and influential sources of inspiration at a time when planning was searching for answers about its existence and role. One outcome was the emergence of a range of 'locality studies' that sought to explore changing social and spatial relations during an era of economic restructuring. Locality studies rejected structuralist top-down determinism and instead searched for new, more bottom-up influences through the unique configurations of different localities (social, political, economic and cultural) that mediated more global drivers of change: the impact upon local configurations of production and consumption of processes operating at national and global scales could not be simply 'read off' (Duncan and Savage, 1991).

In a subsequent and related shift the growing influence of globalization and the collapse of state socialism in Eastern Europe turned attention onto the region as a new space of economic governance in the 1990s (Storper, 1997), and this was linked to the collapse of Fordist modes of mass production and consumption and the 'hollowing out' of the nation state. Another consequence was a renewed critical geography and planning. The Fordist to post-Fordist debates about new, more flexible forms of capitalism provided a series of challenges to the nature of regulation and government as well as the need to rethink all forms of planning in an era in which 'command and control' was no longer an appropriate or successful strategy (Dear and Scott, 1981; Jessop, 1990).

A third broad reaction was to be found in the emergence of postmodern geography and planning thought led by Ed Soja and former Marxists such as Michael Dear. Dear saw the purpose of the postmodern as being an opportunity to revisit the past with irony and self-consciousness, and not with innocence. In his words he 'passes planning through the postmodern matrix' (1986: 370). Yet Dear was loath to leave behind his critical Marxist past and claimed that the postmodern challenge has been largely intellectual and divorced from the realities of practice which still legitimize the actions of the state and capital (ibid.: 379).

In Dear's view planning's new role under postmodern conditions was to facilitate and support capital in new postmodern urban forms that were evolving as time and space were stretched and globalized. Yet how such a planning would operate or even look was unclear.

Others were more concerned with using the postmodern as a critique of modernist planning. Allmendinger (1998), for example, was not alone in linking planning with modernity and the antithesis of everything that postmodernity emphasizes. Town planners, he argued, tend to look for mastery of the metropolis as a totality by deliberately designing a closed form, whereas postmodernists tend to view the urban process as uncontrollable and chaotic. According to Beauregard (1989), planning was between modernity and postmodernity, with modernist planning seemingly under attack from contemporary social conditions and intellectual challenge. Sandercock (1998) likewise saw the postmodern as a reflection of the diversity and complexity of modern cities and a challenge to modernist conceptions of planning. Yet planning needed to reflect such concerns, not be replaced by them. As she puts it, 'I am a postmodern modernist' (ibid.: 4). For Sandercock, postmodern planning was not derived directly from the tenets of postmodern thinking but was inspired by its themes of non-positivist, hermeneutic, phenomenological understandings and diverse multiverses of ideas and knowledge forms.

Those who explored the relationship between postmodern thought and planning, particularly those who had moved from the comfort of the structuralist meta-narratives of Marxism, were, on the whole, reticent and cautious in their advancement of new forms of planning. The issue was, according to Dear, that so much effort had been put into unpacking planning that we were in danger of creating disarray, literary showmanship and academic intrigue (1986: 372).

A final reaction concerned the consequences and implications from post-structuralist interpretations and understandings derived from, among others, Lefebvre, Castells, Foucault, Latour, Deleuze and Guattari. Post-structuralist thinking led to what has been termed the relational turn in geography and planning that challenged dominant notions of absolute or territorial space (Massey, 2005; Amin, 2004). Relational geographers rejected the notion of space and scale as 'fixed containers' or 'static' and instead posited topologies of dynamic and varied actor networks and spaces as open and cross-cut by many different kinds of mobilities, from flows of people to commodities and information. Conceptions of space have a long history. Back in 1921 Carnap identified three types of space – formal, intuitive and physical (Dikeç, 2012). This threefold distinction has continued to have an influence. Lefebvre (1974) identified *perceived* spaces of everyday life, *conceived* spaces of actors such as planners, and *lived* spaces of imagination that arise from artists and writers, while Harvey (1973) proposed *absolute* (bounded), *relative* (variable depending upon the phenomenon being observed) and *relational* space (nodes within flows of inter-action and spaces of flows). For relational geographers territories or absolute (Harvey) or conceived (Lefebvre) spaces amount to what Massey (2005) has described as 'temporary permanences'. As opposed to the view of cities and space as systems or organisms with an underlying coherence and drivers, relational perspectives highlight that space is always open and is constituted by everyday practices. Both near and far influences constitute space replacing the view of scale as a nested hierarchy moving from the global to the local with one of connectivity.

Despite some overlaps between postmodern/post-structuralist and more 'modernist' planning, particularly including a critique of positivism the overall impact was of a fragmentation of thought and a multitude of possibilities and futures for planning.

The reaction from planning

The reaction within planning theory and practice to the fragmentation of consensus, the breakdown of structuralism, the challenge of diversity, localism and fragmentation was by no means uniform or positive. Some simply ignored or dismissed the challenge, preferring, instead, to retrench into more familiar materialist analyses. Others celebrated the release and opportunities that came from new insights and avenues. Yet there remained a mismatch and uncertainty between what was a modernist enterprise in rationality and closure in the form of the planning enterprise and the need to embrace what was presented as the challenge of new times including the themes of emphemerality, fragmentation, chaos, openness and discontinuity: planning was an exercise in action and public policy and this sat uneasily with the new focus on deconstruction and fluidity. There was also a growing suspicion, if not accusation, that planning and planners were part of the problem at best, and a barrier to new sensitivities and thinking at worst. These fears and the challenge of the 'new' confirmed the view of some in planning that the high modernist project of planning needed to be overhauled (e.g. Sandercock, 1998), inspiring critiques that highlighted the consequences of power-blind planning practices (e.g. Flyvbjerg, 1998). However, if the search was on for new approaches then it was less than clear what postmodern planning or planning for new times would look or 'feel' like. The default and uncritical position was to paint planning, in Mannheim's (1940) phrase, as the rational mastery of the irrational (e.g. Beauregard, 1989; Sandercock, 1998; Hillier, 2002), although the reality was usually more nuanced (Allmendinger, 1998). It is ironic that those arguing against the dominant and overarching meta-narratives were prepared to paint planning en masse in such dominant and overarching ways. Ultimately, planning was a state-enabled practice drawing its legitimacy and processes from statutes and working within multiple and varied institutional, financial and professional contexts. If planning as a process could adapt to the challenges of diversity and fragmentation, the loss of certainty and the need to be inclusive then what would planning as an output that was achieved through plans, strategies and built development look like?

One significant avenue for planning concerned taking on board the relational perspective on space and attempting to make sense of the social construction of space for a discipline and practice wedded to the notion of territorially based plans and strategies (see, for example, Healey, 1997). Yet like postmodern planning such relational planning was largely half-hearted as it sought to blend the precepts of the relational social construction of space with the more fixed, territorial and legal requirements of planning practice. The tensions were greatest among those who championed 'spaces of flows' and those who worked in policy-related fields concerned with economic geography and strategic planning, both of which were becoming part and parcel of the new economic geography school from the mid-1990s and given further impetus in the growing emphasis on regions and devolution in the UK. The emergence of new regional forms of governance and institutional assemblies within the UK highlighted the way in which regions were politically constructed though were created around and constituted territories (Painter, 2010). Territories, understood as delimited, contiguous and coherent political spaces, still mattered (Cochrane, 2012).

A form of truce emerged when relationists responded to the increasing weight of opinion that, as Jones (2009) put it, they had overstated their case. Cochrane (2012: 95) has summed up the response as an attempt to 'reclaim territory'. It was recognized that space can be conceived in relational ways but exists in what Thrift and Amin conceded are limits: 'cities are not free to roam where they will' (2002: 26). Regulations and practices such as planning and bureaucracy mean that relational space is, in reality, a systemized network. As Massey has recently put it:

> Territories are constituted and are to be conceptualized, relationally. Thus, interdependence and identity, difference and connectedness, uneven development and the character of place, are in each pairing two sides of the same coin. They exist in constant tension with each other, each contributing to the formation, and the explanation, of the other.
>
> (2011: 4)

In Cochrane's analysis of the growth of England's south-east region as the latest in a succession of territories that have been the focus of governance, territory matters, even if we cannot always be sure which territory matters when (2012: 104).

The rethinking of the spaces of planning led to some interesting theoretical debates, but little change. It was the post-structuralist debates and postmodern sentiments around a rejection of meta-narratives and explorations of power that had the biggest impact upon planning academia and theory, though often not directly or consistently. Interpreted through the lens of planning, the outcomes of such postmodern challenges were more often characterized by confusion rather than clarity. Foucault's focus on power was an inspiration for many, particularly Forester's *Planning in the Face of Power* (1989) and Hillier's *Shadows of Power* (2002). Often, a form of holism was attempted, bringing together a range of 'posty' concerns:

> I believe that the power and power-plays which planning practitioners both 'face' and engage in are subtle... planning decisions ... cannot be

understood separately from the socially constructed, subjective, territorial identities, meanings and values of the local people and planners concerned.

(Hillier, 2002: 3–4)

Sandercock's *Towards Cosmopolis* (1998) sought to imagine what she terms her postmodern Utopia grounded in the realities of new times around a diminishing role for the state and planning in directing change. In a classic postmodern hedge Sandercock argues that planning should continue to facilitate global economic integration while at the same time acting to facilitate insurgency that addresses social, cultural and environmental justice (1998: 4). Both are to be achieved through the state but in new people-centred, communicative, hermeneutic and community-empowering ways.

A wide range of other post-structuralist and postmodern takes on planning emerged that focused on two broad aspects. First, there was a school of post-modern critique which argued that domineering, repressive and exclusionary 'high modern' planning practices had crowded out other ways of thinking and acting. Instrumentally rational, technocratic, value-neutral and linear processes of high modern planning were presented in simplistic ways as the villains of the piece by planning theorists. Modernist comprehensive planning was the problem and was politically untenable. A new, still to be determined, form of planning was on its way. Planning was emerging in a new era of opportunity.

Second, beyond critique there also emerged a number of explorations of the themes that such a new postmodern planning would be characterized by. Such a new form of planning needed to recognize and reflect upon issues such as diversity, oppression, gender, disability, diverse cultures, sexuality, race and a range of other categories and identities. Yet such works fell down at the next step, with the result that 'what next?' became the common missing or vague component. This lacuna remains unfilled largely because the very nature of modernist planning critiques precluded potentially new meta-narratives of pre-scription. Advocates of new forms of planning advanced their ideas in terms that were necessarily aspirational and vague in order to avoid the trap of pre-scription and domination favouring emergent approaches, understandings and solutions. The result, according to Beauregard, was

> a peculiar form of non-planning in which planners participate in individual projects, often attempting to temper the most egregious negative externalities, while failing to place these projects into any broader framework of urban development, a basic tenet of modernist planning.
>
> (1989: 387)

This may have been the experience in the USA but in the UK there was a widening gulf between academic understandings and planning practice, and the latter were largely ignoring the musings of the former (Allmendinger and Tewdwr-Jones, 1997b).

The communicative turn

If the landscape of influence, thinking and theory was not already complex, fragmented, confused and inchoate enough in the wake of the postmodern challenge, then it was about to take a turn for the worse. From the early 1990s the backdrop of post-positivist, post-modern and neo-modern thinking was supplemented by the powerful critique of Marxism and modernism following the collapse of state socialism in Eastern Europe. The leading exponent of this approach was Jürgen Habermas and his attempt to reconstitute what he termed the project of modernity from the relativism and defeatism of the postmodern challenge. It was an approach that was to prove extremely influential for theory and practice in planning for the subsequent two decades.

For Habermas, modernity had been deformed and dominated by instrumental rationality. He argued that what was needed was a re-emphasis of and reba-lancing towards other forms of rationality, most particularly communicative rationality (1984, 1987). This was an attempt to rescue rather than to ditch the project of modernity. Through their claim to 'scientific knowledge' bureaucrats, including planners, had crowded out other ways of thinking and knowing and distorted power relations in society. While Habermas accepted the point about the growing complexity and fragmentation of society he turned the post-modernists' argument that we should reject the search for agreement on its head: it is precisely because the world is so fragmented that we need to search for agreement. The way forward, he argued, was through communicative rationality whereby speaker and hearer seek common understanding and con-sensus through open discussion. Neo-modernists do not seek to replace instru-mental rationality with communicative rationality but subordinate the former to be an instrument of the latter: action flows from deliberation (Dryzek, 1990).

Such deliberation-based rationality was given a fillip by the events of the late 1980s and early 1990s as state socialism across Eastern Europe began to collapse. The overall impact has been summed up by Fukuyama's hubristic phrase as the 'end of history':

> The unabashed victory of economic and political liberalism [over all compe-titors means] not just the end of the Cold War, or the passing of a parti-cular period of history, but the end of history as such: that is, the end-point of mankind's ideological evolution and the universalization of Western liberal democracy as the final form of human government.
>
> (1989: 3–4)

The loss of alternatives to liberal democracy combined with a decade of deregulatory, New Right governments in the UK and the USA characterized by antagonism and social and economic polarization led to a series of reflections on the nature of such new times, globalization and modernity (e.g. Beck, 1995, 1996, 1998a, 1998b). For planning, the work of Anthony Giddens proved to be particularly significant. Giddens rejected the postmodern turn or, more accurately, the extreme postmodern positions regarding relativism and infinite meaning. Not only was it 'unworthy of serious intellectual consideration' (1990: 46) but 'were anyone to hold such a view (and indeed if it is not inchoate in the first place), they could scarcely write a book about it' (ibid.: 47). In place of postmodernism Giddens had already begun to explore and to seek to bridge the growing gap between more structuralist Marxist and more individual post-modern accounts of society and individual action in *The Constitution of Society* (1984) through his concept of 'structuration'. This early attempt at a Third Way between modernity and postmodernity was followed up with *The Consequences of Modernity* (1990) and *Modernity and Self Identity* (1991), both of which were concerned with the impact of globalization, deregulated financial markets and information technology (IT) – new times – upon society and the individual. Unlike postmodern analyses Giddens focused on the individual coping mechanisms and the reflexive nature of social practices taking on board a range of sometimes overwhelming inputs and acting in ways that could reform such practices. Yet it was Giddens' later work and his 'political turn' that were to have a far greater influence on planning thought and practice.

Dismayed by 1980s-style neoliberalism as much as by structuralist, reformist central-state socialist alternatives Giddens instead proposed his now famous Third Way. In *Beyond Left and Right* (1994) he developed his ideas about the impact of globalization on political activity and how global matters become local matters through mass communication and IT. According to Giddens, people will reflect upon these issues and the risks involved, constantly reinventing and reforming political action and the nature of the identity and the self. In turn, this should mean a greater emphasis on challenging traditions and taken for granted understandings and customs. Habermasian interpersonal and discursive forms of politics based around issues mean that old class-based politics of the left and the right are dead. The nation state has become too small to tackle global issues and too large to address local ones. In *The Third Way* (1998) Giddens goes on to develop and popularize such ideas. Any clear alternative to capitalism carries the implication that traditional politics is breaking down and is becoming a series of lifestyle choices. Politics should be about helping people to make the right choices, choices that will have an impact on them, their family and community.

Giddens provided a cogent and attractive way forward for those on the left who were troubled by the postmodern challenge but who did not want to give up on collective action. The messages were simple and appealing: the left should learn to love the market because only through economic success can social investment and justice be delivered, a line that Blair and his Third Way New Labour were to use. The Third Way was the route between those who said that government was the enemy and those that said that it was the solution. Such an approach was taken on board by the European left, though to differing degrees. In the UK it was Labour, or *New* Labour, that became the vehicle for Third Way ideas. The idea was that Labour would remain true to its values of fairness, social justice, liberty and equality, but the means to achieve them were now to be open to change: in the much overused phrase of the time, what counts is what works. Underpinning this pluralist pragmatism was an acceptance that, in Margaret Thatcher's phrase, there was no alternative. In *Runaway World* (1999) Giddens argued that globalization was the phenomenon that had changed the game and with which there was no resistance or alternative. The neoliberalization of the world economy and the impact on national governments, cultures and society had to be acknowledged and accepted by the left.

The thrust of Giddens' agenda was bolstered by others, such as Castells, who had moved from his previous hard left stance of the 1970s. Castells' *The Rise of the Network Society* (2000) sets out a familiar analysis of 'changed times' and the need for a form of Third Way response to the globalizing economy and its inevitable implications. Habermas (1984) also pointed to the need to accept the 'inevitable' implications of globalization on the nation state and the left. Yet if Giddens and others on the centre left provided a broad or grand-scale understanding of society in new times then Habermas provided his own distinctive and influential contribution of micro-practices or how traditional progressive concerns of the left could be pursued. There had always been critics of modernity who did not wish to abandon it altogether but to reform it and reclaim its original Enlightenment principles. The Frankfurt School of neo-Marxists had attempted to rethink structuralist Marxism and its interpretations thereof by drawing upon a range of other inspirations and rejecting the notion of absolute truth. Of particular recent influence for planning has been the work of Habermas (1984) and his theory of communicative action and the argument that deliberative forms of democracy should seek to be open, undistorted, truth-seeking and empathetic (Allmendinger, 2009).

Part of the postmodern and post-structuralist wake was the turn to deconstruct and better understand practice, particularly the role of language and communication rather than technical tools. Combining different strands and combinations of theory while drawing on Habermas in particular, Forester (1989), Healey (1993a, 1993b) and Schön (1983) began to explore action and how planners attempt to influence politicians' thinking. This work, termed the communicative or argumentative turn (Fischer and Forester, 1993), provided new ways of thinking about and deconstructing planning practice. Implicit in this approach was a frustration with abstraction and theory for the sake of it: planning was meant to change the world not simply to understand it, as Marx put it. However, changing the world required a vision and direction. There was also a frustration, expressed by Healey (1993a) though felt by others, which bemoaned the lack of a progressive purpose for planning, lost within the relativism of the postmodern and post-structuralist accounts. As Peter Hall (1988) pointed out, the argumentative turn with its focus on dialogue, mutual learning and ideal communication was really just 'common sense', and a pragmatic common sense made up of incremental steps towards, well, what? Subsequently adding the prefix 'critical' to 'pragmatism' provides a little more theoretical heft but essentially embraced a liberal incrementalism. The challenge, as Healey put it, was to find a planning that was democratic, socially just and environmentally sustainable (1993a: 233).

According to Healey, some believed that communicative rationality, as promoted by Habermas, offered such a progressive way forward for planning (ibid.: 236). There were a variety of flavours for this new, progressive collaborative style of planning some of which drew on different traditions and schools of thought (e.g. Harper and Stein, 1995; Forester, 1989; Sager, 1994). Collaborative planning, a particular UK approach, drew on the wider communicative turn in planning that was ongoing in the work of Friedman (1987) and Forester (1989) and took inspiration from Innes (1995) among others.

Much has been written about collaborative planning including a good deal of criticism and a resultant revisionism from some and a certain amount of distancing by some former advocates. Given the evolution of thinking it is also difficult to pin collaborative planning down and this has led to some misunderstandings on the part of those who wished to engage with it. It is always easier, particularly with hindsight, to criticize the ideas and positions of those who had a genuine commitment to 'rescuing' planning and planning theory from the ambiguity and indeterminacy of the 'post-challenge'. Yet the collaborative approach needs to be critically understood as the mainstream response from the left to the paradigm breakdown and its impact in the light of the subsequent developments in planning theory and practice.

There is not the space here to explore the variety of influences and developments in collaborative planning theory (see Sager, 2013 for a comprehensive discussion). Collaborative planning sat on the fence between modernism and postmodernism, accepting the postmodern challenge but not giving up on consensus or, as it was sometimes put, mutual understanding: 'the progressive challenge is ... to find ways of acknowledging different ways of experiencing and understanding while seeking to "make sense together"' (Healey, 1993a: 236). Using a language that was beginning to take hold in the New Left following the 1989 collapse of socialism in Eastern Europe collaborative advocates argued that the progressive values that underpinned planning were sound but the means of achieving them, particularly instrumental rationality and scientific understanding, did not value diversity and difference. There are a wide variety of communicative and collaborative approaches to and understandings of planning, yet there are some common characteristics or propositions for communicative planning. Under a collaborative understanding planning is characterized by:

- multiple discourses of which instrumental rationality is but one. Other ways of knowing should be brought to the fore, including aesthetic experiences such as poetry and story-telling;
- no common language or understanding among diverse communities exists. Planning should therefore seek what it can in terms of mutual understanding. This is to be achieved through respectful (agonistic) discussion;
- inventiveness in the ways in which such discussions are undertaken (the who, where, what and when) and reflective about the processes. All forms of knowledge should be included in such argumentation: nothing is inadmissible except the claim that something is inadmissible (a claim that is

similar to that of the postmodernist rejection of master narratives being a master narrative itself);

- openness and fluidity. Planning and planners should maintain a critical and reflexive stance, drawing upon Habermasian criteria of comprehensibility, integrity, legitimacy and truth. To ensure that individuals, groups, discourses and knowledge are not excluded planners should also be creative in searching out 'lost' and exposing dominant voices; and

- the goal of mutual agreement based upon interdiscursive understanding against a backdrop of constant critique in order to ensure continued openness and possible alternatives.

Collaborative approaches are predicated upon the assumption that fixed preferences may be altered once they have been confronted by other views and understandings, a process of mutual learning rather than a negotiation around fixed and predetermined interests: 'Through such processes of argumentation we may come to agree, or accept a process of agreeing, on what should be done, without necessarily arriving at a unified view of our respective lifeworlds' (Healey, 1993a: 244).

Collaborative advocates rejected the two main claims against communicative planning, namely that it ignored powerful structuring forces such as global capital and dominant local interests and that it was a form of pragmatic, mutual adjustment rather than a new progressive approach to planning. This pragmatic mutual adjustment meant that rather than being a progressive approach for new times collaborative planning was accused of being the handmaiden of neoliberalism (see Bengs, 2005; Purcell, 2009). The response to such criticisms can be summarized as 'what's the alternative?' and 'this is what planners do in any case' (for a more contemporary development of collaborative planning theory see Sager, 2013). Other criticisms, particularly following empirical studies of communicative and collaborative planning in practice were less easily dismissed (see, for example, Ploger, 2004; Hillier, 2002; Flyvbjerg, 1998; Allmendinger and Tewdwr-Jones, 1998; McGuirk, 2005). Equally, there are studies that seek to claim that collaborative consensus building 'works' (e.g. Innes and Booher, 2010), though one wonders about the degree of confirmation bias in such evaluations.

It may be, as Hillier and Healey (2008: 6) claim, that collaborative planning has been misrecognized and misrepresented but the recent recasting as an attempt to 'improve strategic spatial planning by paying attention to procedural issues such as institutional design of arenas, routines and styles of discussion to provide better solutions to problems of collective concern' is itself a misrepresentation (ibid.: 7). The advocates of collaborative planning protest too much. There is no doubt that collaborative planning was an understanding of an agenda for consensus building in modern complex societies focusing upon the micro-practices of local planning. It remains so (see Innes and Booher, 2010). However, the point here is not to evaluate collaborative planning and rationality but to highlight the extent of its impact on planning, whether or not the 'metaphor', as Hillier and Healey (2008: 6) put it, was misused.

While advocates acknowledge that 'complete consensus may not be achieved' (Innes and Booher, 2010: 6), it is the search and prospect, if not the promise of consensus, that constitutes the attractive 'metaphor' of collaborative planning, both on the political left and right. Although some advocates complain that collaborative processes for planning were misunderstood as a collaborative planning *tout court* it is hardly surprising that such a 'misunderstanding' took place, if it did, when advocates proclaim that 'for the many wicked problems we face, collaborative planning is more likely to generate feasible and legitimate decisions than traditional decision making' (ibid.: 7). The nuance is lost in the advocacy particularly in an era in which the 'big questions' have been 'answered' and we are now concerned with simply managing micro-level change.

Collaborative planning was not the only route taken by planning theory during the 1990s and beyond but it was, without doubt, the most significant and influential, particularly in the UK. The themes of consensus, participation, progressive ends and a new ethical purpose provided a cogent and well-meaning focus for planning and the left. Yet collaborative planning provided many challenges for those actually charged with translating it into practice. One outcome was a displacement of activity and thought. Academics and practitioners grappled with the varied, complex, abstract and inchoate range of ideas and theories with the latter largely abandoning them as unworkable and impractical. Sager (2013: ch. 8) contends that planning theorists have a responsibility to the end use of theory yet it was by no means clear what those ends would look like. Further, the very nature of collaborative planning precluded prescription on what it might look like; to do so would be prescriptive.

A second consequence was very practical. At the time that collaborative planning was in the ascendency on the left planning practice in the UK was under sustained attack and critique from the right. What Dear has termed a pastiche of practices (1986: 227) was no match for the ideological attack of the New Right and the day-to-day realities of budget cuts, privatization and institutional reorganization in local government. The lack of a coherent alternative to the neoliberal dominance, particularly during the 1980s, was aided by the eschewal of the master-narrative of progressive politics. Such dreaded master-narratives were replaced with new, empty narratives about social justice, diversity and difference, though the focus of such worthy aims was to be on the delivery of a micro-politics of practice. This led some to accuse collaborative planning of being, in Sager's phrase, 'politically naïve and acting as if spellbound by their own good intentions' (2013: xix).

Conclusions

For a variety of reasons the left accepted the challenge of new times and rethought planning by engaging with postmodern and post-structuralist ideas. Postmodern, neo-modern, relational and critical pragmatism approaches emerged underpinned by a bewildering array of philosophies, social and political theories and practices. What connected this disparate range of approaches and subjects was an emphasis upon the self, an exploration of the role of difference, a rejection of positivism and structuralism and of overarching, reductionist class-based and conflict-driven theories of societal evolution.

Moore-Milroy (1991) has termed this Cambrian-like explosion in planning theory a paradigm breakdown. From the late 1980s planning theory became a pick and mix of theories and thinking – a dash of Foucault, a smidgen of Lefebvre, a hint of Latour and a pinch of Habermas – to end up in an ever increasing hotchpotch of confused, confusing and largely incommensurable narratives.

However, such a breakdown was characteristic of the left, not of the right, as I explore in the next chapter. In one sense then there was a postmodernization of planning, awash in a sea of incommensurable thinking and practices. As Healey put it 'we cannot know where this [collaborative planning] can take us. But we can act with hope and ambition to achieve future possibilities' (1993a: 244).

It would be wrong to understand such a search as a neutral and inevitable consequence of the postmodern challenge. The postmodern, post-structuralist and neo-modern turns were not simply reactions to the breakdown of modernism and structuralism but a political project with an agenda, however muddled and inchoate. The agenda was a loose one and coalesced around what Hillier and Healey (2008: 205) describe as diversities of identity, culture, multiple knowledges and modes of expression. Social theory is never neutral. Collaborative planning theory was not merely devised but was packaged for a wider audience of academics, practitioners, communities and politicians and deployed language and images that would help to 'sell' it more successfully than its rivals. Collaborative planning sought to balance diversity and consensus in a search for the Holy Grail of the new wave of planning theory – a progressive framework that was sensitive to difference and particularity. Such a search rightly sought to politicize those aspects of the social that had hitherto been ignored or overlooked – issues concerning diversity, difference, the personal and the individual – and in doing so eclipse or decentre the economic. This was a clear normative agenda for those committed, in Healey's words, 'to planning as a democratic enterprise aimed at promoting social justice and environmental sustainability' (1993a: 233).

The claim that such thinking had little direct impact upon planning (Davoudi and Strange, 2009) misses important points about the fragmentation of the left, the diversion of attention within planning academia, the gap between theory and practice and, most significantly, the creation of politically neutral language and a resistance to imposition (grand narratives) that made it difficult to project what planning was seeking to achieve beyond the most abstract and general of intentions. This postmodern sensibility permeated planning academia along with other influences around spatial relativity and notions of consensus and partnership-based governance to provide a very loose agenda and one that offered an opportunity for others to co-opt. If modernist planning was structuralist, domineering and arrogant then postmodern planning, in all its guises and manifestations, was supine, vacuous and empty.

The left and planning fragmented into a variety of identity-based politics losing the coherence of universalism (which had lost its legitimacy) and replacing it, instead, with a set of new and vague master-narratives based on difference, diversity and social justice. Yet explaining what such grand aims would mean for planning was both difficult and also anathema – being explicit about ends and means would violate difference and diversity while also closing down alternative options. One upshot was a growing irritation. Another was more significant. Without a coherent and progressive alternative narrative planning was subject to the onslaught from the New Right during the 1980s.

If, as Lenin claimed, democracy was the perfect shell for capitalism then collaborative planning was the perfect shell for the neoliberalization of planning. However, this was not quite as straightforward as some have claimed. The neoliberal challenge was itself by no means secured at the time. The 1980s constituted a particular deregulatory form of neoliberalism that by 1990 was judged to have failed. Yet without a clear alternative the project of neoliberalism was given time to reassemble and reconstitute itself into new, more complex and variable forms that deployed the language of the left in order to neutralize it.

4 New understandings
A reinvigorated and unified right

Introduction

The events that led to the student protests in Paris and the slow breakdown of the post-war social democratic settlement in the UK were not exclusively the concern of the left. The breakdown of the consensus around state-led planning from the early 1970s also led to the search for new ideas and approaches from the right in the UK. While the left's point of departure had been the attempt to understand the role of cities and planning in the continued existence of capitalism, those on the right focused more on what they perceived as the role of the state and planning in slowly throttling economic growth and personal freedom: the left blamed planning for propping up capitalism while the right blamed planning for curtailing it. For some it was time to explore new approaches and roll back the state:

> The 1950s and 1960s marked a period of economic and social stability which nurtured a belief in the efficacy of science, technology and rational planning. The massive uncertainties faced by Western economies during the 1970s have heralded a retreat from social experimentation and a restatement of libertarian principles.
>
> (Sorensen and Day, 1981: 390)

The shared political space around planning that had existed from the mid-1940s bifurcated from the early 1970s with the right developing an approach that looked to nineteenth-century liberalism updated to meet the context of radically altered political and economic dimensions and new times. This updating of classic liberalism for new times has subsequently evolved into what has been widely labelled neoliberalism.

Neoliberalism is now generally perceived to be a resilient and variegated form of governance that has underpinned many of the changes to planning in the UK, particularly from the 1980s onwards (Allmendinger and Haughton, 2013). However, during the 1970s neoliberals sought a new understanding of the state, the economy and society, including planning, within an ideological framework of traditional liberal tenets based around a tightly delimited political sphere which does not encroach upon the essentially private realms of economic and social exchange. This nascent, inchoate and experimental alternative to the post-war consensus was by no means a natural or even obvious successor to the status quo. Neoliberalism had to be nurtured and imposed in a contested landscape of alternatives (Peck, 2010) including the emerging response of the left. Current forms of neoliberal governance are more nuanced, complex and variable, and in some cases as interventionist as the state-heavy, top-down form of government that was eventually perceived to be damaging and threatening by its original advocates. Yet the attitude towards the role of the state is not the only distinguishing feature between the attitudes of the left and the right to new times. Part of the imposition and nurturing of neoliberal forms of governance, including planning, involved portraying democracy itself as part of the problem. Neoliberalism and neoliberals share

> a profoundly suspicious, skeptical and anti-political culture; the globalization thesis suggests the increasingly anachronistic nature of political intervention in an era of external economic constraint, inviting a fundamental reappraisal of the previously unquestioned capacity of political processes to shape societal trajectories. Both conspire to discredit the 'political' in contemporary societies, raising a series of questions about the nature of politics, the space for political deliberation in an era of globalization, and the role of political analysis in holding power to account.
>
> (Hay, 2007: 5)

Neoliberal is the label placed upon a variety of responses from the right towards what was perceived and portrayed as the crisis of liberal democracies. The early responses and alternatives involved, broadly, deregulation, state restructuring and the ascendency of private interests. This rather crude rollback form of neoliberalism has given way to a pervasive and almost imperceptible background framework for planning that is (deliberately) difficult to grasp. Part of this difficulty in pointing to neoliberal forms of planning is the problem of identifying a moving and evolving phenomenon as well as capturing and engaging with the huge literature on the topic and national and sub-national variegation in what amounts to a variety of neoliberalisms. While it is still possible to characterize neoliberalism as a 'reassertion of a classical liberal economic argument: society functions better under a market logic than any other logic, especially a state-directed one' (Purcell, 2009: 141) the actual practices of neoliberalism involve a far more complex fusion of state-market relations to the point where it becomes difficult to disentangle the parts from their sum. Rollback deregulatory forms have evolved into what some have termed rolled-out neoliberalism or even, during the turmoil of the economic crisis and recession, 'roiling' neoliberalism (Peck, 2010). Simple state deregulation creates crises within markets and capitalism exacerbating those inherent within capitalism itself. Such crises typically involve an oversupply of goods and services, and a lack of coordination of markets and investment leads to crises in capitalism (Hay, 1996) as well as providing opportunities to challenge and replace neoliberalism as a governing ideology. As such the state, including planning, is needed to help to deliver more efficient markets, smoothing out supply in ways that provide opportunities for sustainable growth while ensuring public interest and legitimacy. What is clear is that current, dominant neoliberalism sees the state, including planning, as essential to current forms of economic growth: neoliberalism is more concerned with state capture and the reorientation of state interests than in state abolition. Yet state appropriation is not an outcome but a process as neoliberalism is a fluid, dynamic, unstable and creative phenomenon made anew through time and space in response to changing and variable challenges and circumstances (Peck and Tickell, 2002; Peck, 2010).

This central role for planning was not obvious in the 1970s when the alternative to the state and planning appeared to be no planning. The failure of the crude, deregulatory agenda which formed part of the Thatcher government's approach during the 1980s pointed to the need to reform planning, not to abolish it. It also highlighted the need to play a sophisticated game and one that would ultimately involve the appropriation of many of the left's narratives and nomenclature in order to provide a legitimacy and wider appeal to the market state.

This chapter provides a background to the right's alternative to social democracy and state-led planning that can be seen as a parallel to the previous chapter. In doing so I seek to emphasize three dimensions:

- Neoliberalism does not amount to a reduced state but the capture and reorientation of the state towards the creation of what Harvey (2006) terms the 'market state'. The market state involves a reorientation of state activities in order to avoid crises and challenges to market-based government. In terms of changes to planning such an appreciation helps us better to understand what appears to be the paradox of neoliberal planning; that is, the seeming extension and creation of new pro-planning governmentalities throughout the 1990s and 2000s.
- Experimentation and contestation are inherent features of neoliberalism as it is mediated through social, economic and political contexts at different times. Its inherent instability – largely derived from tensions within neoliberalism itself – combined with its mediation or contestation require neoliberalism to be adaptable and dynamic and place a particular emphasis upon the role of state actors, including planners, in managing the contradictions and manifestations.
- There is a need to maintain the legitimacy of neoliberalism in order for its survival as a governing ideology. This highlights neoliberalism as an ideological project as it seeks to normalize the notion and tenets of free markets as being 'obvious' or in the general interests of society. This legitimacy is achieved through a variety of means and governmentalities, most particularly in the planning field concerning discourses and mechanisms that present inclusive notions of partnership and consensus.

It is this last point that highlights the link between the two trajectories of planning on the left and the right: neoliberalism needs planning to help to maintain markets and neoliberal forms of planning need legitimacy and accountability. Neoliberals of different shades and varieties needed to appeal to a wide constituency in order to maintain the appeal of market-led government and its position as a governing ideology. To help to achieve this some of the language and ideas of the left including notions of inclusion, coordination and integration were and are deployed as well as positive-sounding, non-partisan phrases and polices concerning sustainable development, smart growth and urban renaissance (Allmendinger, 2011).

This chapter has three parts. First, I provide a brief overview of the emergence and characteristics of neoliberalism as the right's response to the 'crisis' of social democracy. I emphasize that neoliberalism is a process and an outcome and that it is contested and experimental in nature, and always exists in hybrid form. Second, following Gamble (2009), I emphasize the different strands of neoliberalism and how these have provided tensions for the neoliberalization of planning and the use of planning as a tool of neoliberalism. Finally, I explore the contradictions and limits of neoliberalism as a project for planning and how, in order to retain legitimacy and momentum, a ruling ideology and a range of governmentalities have emerged drawing upon the ideas and discourses of the left to provide a veneer of collectivism and state-led planning in the wider public interest while maintaining the core of market-supportive minimal planning.

The rise and rise of neoliberalism

Despite disciplinary and personal emphases there is a common narrative that relates the emergence and evolution of neoliberalism as a distinctive political-economic philosophy to the breakdown of Keynesian orthodoxy in the late 1960s and early 1970s as governments around the globe struggled to control rising inflation and unemployment. Where applied, Keynesianism had successfully managed to stabilize economic cycles and output particularly in the post-war era. Keynesian-managed economies were characterized by low, stable unemployment and low inflation. This situation began to break down in the late 1960s and with the oil crisis of 1973 economies began to experience both persistently high unemployment and high inflation. As tax revenues fell and welfare payments soared alternatives to Keynesianism as a system of government had their moment of opportunity. Two critiques and alternatives to the Keynesian orthodoxy stood out. First, monetarism spearheaded the attack on Keynesianism by offering an alternative to fiscal demand management. According to monetarists inflation was related to money supply rather than being a consequence of aggregate demand. The monetarist critique and alternative was as much ideological as economic and implied a much reduced role for the state in economic management. This more ideological dimension constituted the second main critique of Keynesianism and was founded on a traditional liberal riposte to state involvement and mechanisms including wage and price controls. This

'Austrian School' retort led by, among others, Friedrich Hayek, emphasized the need to reintroduce 'sound money': Keynesianism had distorted market signals, risk and the 'discipline' of bankruptcy. Dismantling and replacing Keynesianism was not simply a matter of changing macroeconomic policy as a range of powerful vested interests had emerged that benefited from the increased role of the state in a managed, social democratic economy. Such interests included those who benefited from the welfare state as well as those that had increased importance in a planned economy such as the trade unions.

As Gamble (2009: 79) points out the real significance of the monetarist riposte was political not economic. Monetarism represented a shift in the balance of power from labour to capital. Consequently, replacing Keynesianism included the need to confront a variety of state apparatuses and interests. Monetarism was not enough and needed a complimentary approach to the role of the state. This fusion of monetarism with an anti-planning and anti-state ideology combined with a penchant for individual freedom was and remains the foundation of neoliberalism. Such a symbiosis is not unproblematic and without tensions, however, particularly regarding the role of the state.

The traditional nineteenth-century laissez-faire view of the state had been overtaken by events and even the most ardent of liberals conceded that in advanced economies the state was needed not only to police the market but also to protect markets from social democratic 'counter-attacks' and the short-termism of politicians. Capitalism itself had also evolved from that which concerned nineteenth-century liberals and was now more corporate leading to concerns about the power of big business in rigging 'free markets' and creating monopolies. Thus, neoliberalism's predilection is for a small, residual state, although there is also a need for the market to be policed and regulated by a strong, active state and one that is able to resist the temptation for politicians and interests to lobby for market intervention. As Peck (2010) argues, neoliberalism has always been about 'state capture' and reorientation as much as state dismantling. However, a small, active and centralized state also needs to address issues of support and legitimacy: the Keynesian state and its welfare dimensions enjoyed widespread popular support (Purcell, 2009) and the long-term legitimacy and popularity of the neoliberal alternative. At the same time, as Offe (1984) argues, the state must also appear to be a neutral arbiter of interests to preserve its legitimacy. There was a danger that simply 'rolling back' the state would undermine support for neoliberal modes of economic governance. As a consequence the neoliberal desire to replace Keynesianism and take on the interests that supported and benefited from it required a pragmatic approach not only to maintain legitimacy but also to mediate and construct neoliberal modes of governance in the light of existing economic, social and institutional landscapes. This eye on electoral populism and the need periodically to devise neoliberalism anew in order to address the consequences of previous approaches and experiments has led to a faltering, though resilient, ontogeny. The attack on Keynesianism and the welfare state in developed countries has been approached at times in a piecemeal fashion and at other times in a punctuated way. The election of Margaret Thatcher in the UK and Ronald Reagan in the USA represented a more punctuated phase of domestic neoliberalism, while the embedding of neoliberal thinking as policy orthodoxy in the 1990s in organizations such as the World Bank and the International Monetary Fund, via the 'Washington consensus' characterized a different and more international phase.

While questions about the nature and scope of the state and the need to maintain the legitimacy of neoliberalism blunted the shifts from Keynesianism there was a third problem that, in terms of changes to planning, overshadows both. Neoliberalism has always been a loose amalgam of ideas but there are two dominant though antonymous strands within it (Gamble, 2009). On the one hand there is a laissez-faire strand that is based on the idea that there should be as few impediments as possible to markets. On the other hand there is also a social market strand that has a more interventionist role for the state interposing in markets to ensure that they maximize possibilities and minimize the emergence of monopolies. While both strands privilege markets and are underpinned by an active state the former assigns to the state the role of removing obstacles to markets while the latter gives the state a role in creating the necessary conditions for market operations such as institutional and legal frameworks, investment in social capital, the provision of welfare safety nets and environmental protection. There is a potentially large cleft between laissez-faire and social market liberalism in practice, and the experiences of the past four decades both in the UK and elsewhere highlight the extent of such a gap in relation to models of neoliberal governance, the role of the state and the nature of planning. What bridges the two is the common acceptance of the primacy of markets in social relations and the need for a strong state to resist counter-attacks and either to remove obstacles to markets or create the necessary conditions for them to operate most effectively and efficiently – a relationship explored by Polanyi (1944) among others. Nevertheless, given the variety of ideas and tensions it is not surprising that, as Harvey points out, some of the strands of neoliberal thinking are not entirely coherent (2006: 21). Nor, it should be emphasized, are neoliberal policies and outcomes.

If matters were not already complex enough neoliberalism in the UK context has also been adopted by different political parties and interpreted and mediated through ideological and historical lenses that make the evolution and roll-out of neoliberalism even more Gordian. As Jessop and Peck (1998) argue, the pressure of electoral cycles and day-to-day politics can act as a significant driver of influence on policy that is separate from the needs of the market. Elements of the Conservative Party in the UK turned towards laissez-faire neoliberalism in the mid-1970s though this was always mediated with more traditional Conservative concerns with environmental protection particularly in rural areas, traditional 'family values', a distaste for immigration and the European Community (EC)/ European Union even though the latter two have strong laissez-faire credentials with respect to the free movement of goods, services and labour. There were also overlaps such as the common predisposition to concepts such as the rule of law which neoliberals and Conservatives championed over the more discretionary, bureaucratic nature of administration and policy implementation in the UK. While there were some symbiotic policies there were also numerous examples of initiatives that undermined one another or were vague purely to avoid contradiction, thus leaving agents such as planners charged with their implementation but confused as to the purpose of such policies (Allmendinger, 1998).

The New Right Conservatives in the UK were not alone in struggling to mediate neoliberal thinking with practical politics. According to some, New Labour's Third Way was merely a form of neoliberalism seen through the lens of Labour's more traditional concerns with social justice (Callinicos, 2002). The pragmatism over 'means' towards what Labour argued were traditional 'ends' allowed for an eclectic mix of market-based solutions and policies combined with some more traditional statist approaches. In planning there was a clear strategy of supporting economic development and growth particularly through significant levels of increased house building. This growth-driven strategy was to be delivered through a range of more traditional top-down statist mechanisms including binding targets, deregulation and incentives to local authorities in order to facilitate growth and the imposition of arm's length agencies. At the same time other currents of New Labour policy that derived from concerns about climate change and environmental protection cut across and leavened growth strategies emphasizing increased building standards and the cost of mitigation measures (Allmendinger, 2011). These and other multiple streams of policy and delivery mechanisms amounted to a 'congested state' often 'getting in the way' of implementation (NAO, 2007, 2008; HoC ODPM, 2003).

However, one major difference between 'new' and 'old' Labour concerned the degree of experimentation in delivery and tools. At one level experimentation under neoliberalism is an inherent characteristic, a consequence of the diversity of streams of thought within neoliberalism combined with the mediation of such notions through existing social, economic, political and institutional contexts and the need to account for party political traditions and negotiation. New Labour made a virtue out of vice with respect to this and relabelled experimentation with the slogan 'what counts is what works'. Peck and Tickell (2002) encourage us to think of neoliberal contestation and experimentation as being closely related. As a socially produced, historically and geographically specific phenomenon the outcomes and practices of neoliberalism should be perceived as a restructuring strategy that defies a simple neoliberal norm. All neoliberalisms are contested or mediated and neoliberalism only ever exists in hybrid or 'messy' forms (ibid.: 35). According to this view, experimentation is a result of the search for what works best in the existing circumstances. However, at another level there is a more deliberate strategy of experimentation in the constant search for successful institutional and scalar 'fixes', challenging the acceptable and the norm in the hunt for new and better neoliberal forms. In some cases this will involve deliberate challenges and confrontational stances, an approach summed up by Margaret Thatcher's phrase 'there is no alternative' during the early 1980s. During this era there were clear examples of little comprise or mediation of neoliberal principles with existing social, economic and political conditions. The forced sale of council houses, for example, was successfully undertaken by the government which took little account of the objections and resistance from local authorities.

It will be clear from the above that the notion of neoliberalism is used in a number of senses. Neoliberalism can be summed up as:

- an understanding of the changing nature of policies, regulations and institutions that can be regarded through a neo- or post-Marxist lens as the restoration of power of the capitalist class in advanced capitalism (Harvey, 2006). Neoliberalism as a form of analysis takes some tenets of Marxism and adapts and evolves them for contemporary capitalism allowing for a more diverse understanding of the interests and identities of class, a more balanced approach to the role of agency and a less functionalist view of the local state;
- a set of ideas or theories to restore the conditions for capital accumulation drawing upon a range of sources and inspiration. This includes a number of influential economists, historians and philosophers such as Friedrich Hayek and Milton Friedman. According to Gough (2002), neoliberalism seeks to free markets and private property from 'socialization', that is, state interference and infringement by 'others'; and
- an uneven and contested form of economic governance built around creating a market state (Robison, 2006: xii). It is important to understand neoliberalism as an output *and* a process. Neoliberalism is in creative tension with and is mediated through existing institutional, social and political arrangements at the national and sub-national level.

These last two points provide neoliberalism with what we might term 'external' tensions, e.g. in mediating neoliberalism through existing forms and institutions of governance and 'internal' tensions, such as distinct emphases on the understanding of a particular issue and the approach that should be taken to address it between different tenets of neoliberal theory. As a consequence of these external and internal tensions neoliberalism is characterized by variability and fluidity in terms of its policy and institutional outputs or solutions.

The right's critique of planning

One thing that should have become clear from the preceding discussion is the dynamic, multifaceted and evolutionary nature of neoliberalism. One is tempted to ask that if neoliberalism is everything then perhaps it is nothing? If we can consider both Thatcher and Blair as neoliberals, albeit in very different ways, then perhaps the term itself is lacking precision or usefulness. As Brenner *et al.* (2010) conclude, the widespread use of the notions of neoliberalism and neoliberalization has been accompanied by considerable imprecision, confusion and controversy. As far as planning is concerned how useful is the notion of neoliberalism in understanding change?

As with the exploration of alternatives in the light of the breakdown of the post-war social democratic consensus from the left (see Chapter 3), early incarnations of neoliberal thought were inchoate though less diffuse than their counterparts on the left. There had always been a minority view that planning controls in the UK were too detailed and prescriptive. The events of the late 1960s and 1970s provided a fillip to such views, even though such a stimulus was more economic than social. One influential critique was provided by Jane Jacobs in her book *The Death and Life of Great American Cities: The Failure of Town Planning* (1961). Another early provocation and call for reform in the UK came not from the free market ideologues of the right but from a member of the Labour Party and highly respected planning academic Peter Hall. Hall co-authored an article in *New Society* in 1969 called '*Non-Plan: An Experiment in Freedom*' (Banham *et al.*, 1969) which argued that during the post-war era planning had not only failed to make life better but had actually made matters worse. Such critiques expressed a general dissatisfaction with planning for both left and right (as discussed in Chapter 2) and fed the general mood that planning had somehow 'got it wrong'.

Distinct though related critiques of and alternatives for planning emerged from the right. One influential early strand proposed a return to laissez-faire liberalism updated to the conditions of advanced societies and cities. This strand did not involve the removal of planning but a form of *de minimus* planning, a residualized core that would be concerned with the specific issues that arise in the unique circumstances of urban life. The liberal critique of planning is also an attitude or stance on the role and significance of planners. According to this view planners are part of a self-interested and powerful class of state officials who seek to maximize their own position at the expense of others. An inspiration for much of the liberal turn in planning as in liberalism in general was the work of Hayek (1944, 1960) and Friedman (1962). For liberals, freedom encourages greater creativity which leads to more interesting and varied lifestyles. Drawing on Hayek, Sorenson and Day set out in their argument for the liberalization of planning that 'social formations which emphasise individual liberty are generally more creative, productive, dynamic, responsive to human needs and flexible than those which do not' (1981: 391).

Yet freedom is not absolute and there are circumstances in which superior authority will be necessary to address a range of negative externalities that arise in urban living. Hayek was clear that cities and people were complex and often did not mix in ways that meant that individual freedom was absolute:

> In many respects, the close contiguity of city life invalidates the assumptions underlying any simple division of property rights. In such conditions it is true only to a limited extent that whatever an owner does with his property will affect only him and nobody else. What economists call the 'neighbor-hood effects,' i.e. the effects of what one does to one's property on that of others, assume major importance. The usefulness of almost any piece of property in a city will in fact depend in part on what one's immediate

neighbors do and in part on the communal services without which effective use of the land by separate owners would be nearly impossible.

(1960: 341)

Under liberal thinking the curtailment of individual freedom and intervention in markets by the state should be focused on such 'neighbourhood effects', particularly those arising from conflicting land uses and the physical quality of structures. Where such issues do not arise, or where they are trivial then they are best left to individuals to resolve. In such circumstances there is no role for planning in intervening in the freedom of owners to develop and use their property as they see fit. At another level planning can also be justified under liberal thinking through its role in coordinating the provision of essential public goods such as communications and infrastructure as well as the preservation of historic places and environmentally and ecologically sensitive areas. However, the tools of such intervention should themselves be market based, e.g. tax incentives or, where absolutely necessary, rule based. Markets work most efficiently through certainty and consistency in public decisions and this points to a 'rule of law' based planning whereby policies should be clear and decisions should be taken in accordance with such rules. Liberal analyses argue that discretionary approaches to planning such as that of the UK create market uncertainty. The certainty of the zoning-based systems that are more common in North America and other parts of Europe are preferable.

As well as the critique of the planning system and approach to decision making a further critique focused upon planners themselves. In the view of liberals planners regard themselves as the fount of all wisdom regarding land use and development (Sorensen and Day, 1981). Those who worked for the state in the pursuit of the public good were regarded by Hayek as *'the greatest danger to liberty today'* (1960: 262, emphasis added). Such a critique echoed and drew succour from the Public Choice School of analysis which emphasized a 'new class' of bureaucrats who made decisions and allocated resources in ways that benefited them rather than the broader public good that they aspired to serve. According to Public Choice Theory, increased intervention by the state in the economy and civil society leads to the politicization of all areas of life, increased expectations of what could be achieved by the state and demands for increases in intervention when such expectations were inevitably dashed (Hay, 1996: 98). This 'governmental overload' analysis argues that the state has raised expectations and resource commitments beyond what is sustainable or achievable. In terms of planning the public choice and government overload perspectives on the economic and political crises of the 1970s highlighted the role of planners and other public sector professionals in perpetuating a system that was clearly inappropriate and in need of reform because it served the interests of planners themselves, not society (Pennington, 2000). Interestingly, the focus upon planners and other public sector officials from the right mirrored the left's analysis in some ways: Habermas and Offe had highlighted the role of public officials in sustaining capitalism by adopting new governing mechanisms in the face of crises, whereas the right argued that the same officials had led to the state becoming ungovernable by expanding their roles and making decisions that favour their own interests, and then justifying them by reference to the amorphous and vague notion of the 'public interest'.

It is important to stress that liberalism is not homogeneous and that there are distinct emphases within a broad liberal school. One distinction is between libertarians who stress personal freedom and those who stress market freedom. In libertarian thinking the economic is subsumed within the freedom of the individual as a parallel and symbiotic stream of thinking helping to guide the approach to intervention and planning where it can be justified. Individual freedom, within limits and with exceptions, is the objective and markets, market mechanisms and price signals are the means through which this is best achieved. There are overlaps, although these two strands can point in different directions when applied to concrete policy areas such as planning. Such differences become more acute and important when political dimensions are taken into account, most notably the adoption by the New Right, a point that is covered further on in this chapter.

The liberal riposte began to involve a number of critiques and analyses from within planning both consciously and unconsciously. Early works included Jacobs' *Death and Life of Great American Cities,* (1961), Banham *et al.*'s *Non-Plan: An Experiment in Freedom* (1969), Douglas Lee's *Requiem for Large Scale Planning Models* (1973), Banfield's *Unheavenly Cities Revisited* (1974), Peter Hall's Freeports idea and, critically, Bernard Siegan's work on 'unplanned' Houston, *Land Use Without Zoning* (1972). Jacobs provided a critical take on post-war planning in the US context but in terms that translated into UK experience. Her argument, prefiguring Hall's analysis of the role of planning in UK inner city decline during the mid-1970s, was that planning had failed to halt the decline in US cities and had even contributed to their continued stagnation. The reason was that planners had failed to understand the complexity of cities and societies and had sought to impose simplified models and understandings taken from such luminaries as Ebenezer Howard and le Corbusier. Jacobs argued that there was a mismatch between the day-to-day complexity of everyday life and the theories and models that constitute the toolbox and mindset of planners. Rather than imposing theories and ideas upon cities, planners should instead seek a better understanding of how cities really work and what constitutes a successful city. The segregation of what planners consider to be non-conforming uses, e.g. businesses and homes, is actually what makes places diverse, creative and attractive. Where negative externalities and conflicting uses, such as noise and pollution, do arise then they are best dealt with through specific legal measures rather than as part and parcel of land use control. Planning should seek to create the conditions for diversity, allowing space for 'ideas and opportunities to flourish' (Jacobs, 1961: 255). Planning should intervene to seek to create diversity through restricting the emergence of mono-uses and protecting uses that struggle to compete economically with those that can outbid them for land and property.

Banfield's *Unheavenly City* ([1970] 1974) explored the urban unrest and riots in US cities in the late 1960s. Like Jacobs, he argues that the problems of inner cities cannot be addressed through rational public intervention in the form of planning. Planning seeks to address problems and issues concerning amenity, convenience and business advantages that would otherwise take care of themselves or are unimportant; the way that a city appears (i.e. its urban form) may be ugly but this is not important compared to its function. 'Ugly' areas can be useful if not essential in allowing low rent uses to locate and develop. There are some issues that public policy, including planning, should address such as health, although these are both specific and limited. Though US in origin the broad arguments of Jacobs and Banfield were echoed in the UK critiques and approaches of Banham *et al.* (1969), Hall (1977a, 1977b), Bracewell-Milnes (1974) and Jones (1982) among others. Of these the most significant influence on the development of alternatives for the right came from Hall both as joint author of *Non-Plan: An Experiment in Freedom* (Banham *et al.*, 1969) as well as his development of the ideas of non-plan into what he termed Freeports (Hall, 1977a, 1977b), a much wider and more controversial proposal to remove planning and other controls from selected areas of inner cities.

Hall and his non-plan collaborators were firmly located on the left of British politics but like others on the left they had begun to come to the view that land use planning was not the panacea to urban problems that many had thought. Rather than establishing a comprehensive connection between national economic and local physical planning the focus for planning had become an aesthetic choice. A panoply of regulations and processes had crowded out difference and individual expression. Non-plan involved the experimental removal of planning regulations across wide areas to see what would happen without such detailed controls:

> Between us, Peter Hall and I floated this maverick thought: could things be any worse if there was no planning at all? They might even be somewhat better. We were especially concerned at the attempt to impose aesthetic choices on people who might have very different choices of their own. Why not, we wondered, suggest an experiment in getting along without planning and seeing what emerged? We called it 'Non-Plan'.
>
> (Barker, 2000: 4)

If the intention was to provoke a debate on the nature and future of planning then the outcome was not entirely as envisaged, particularly as non-plan began to influence thinking on the right (Allmendinger, 2013).

Hall further developed his analysis of the negative outcomes of planning in two of his more well-known works, *The Containment of Urban England* (1973) and *Great Planning Disasters* (1980). *The Containment of Urban England* explored the implications of restricting urban growth around towns and cities through green belts and highlighted three main implications. First, the study argued that the planning system had failed to provide sufficient housing or employment opportunities for poorer, unskilled workers and their families in urban areas. Second, planning had led to significant inflation in land and property prices by constraining the expansion of towns and cities, encouraging an increase in the density of new development within cities. The combination of implications of the first two findings led to the third consequence of the planning system, namely the rise in commuting as housing and employment land was increasingly separated by the use of containment policies such as green belts. The economic and social consequences of 'successful' containment, particularly the impact on land prices and subsequent housing affordability have remained a theme of laissez-faire critics of planning ever since (e.g. Evans, 1991; Evans and Hartwich, 2006; Pennington, 2000).

The liberal critique of and alternatives to planning were promoted, in part, through the use of examples of privately planned developments such as Georgian Bath, the 'attractive chaos' of medieval street patterns such as York and Siegan's work on the experiences of non-plan in Houston, USA. Echoing libertarian concerns Siegan argued that markets should be allowed to operate efficiently, that public planning is a form of market interference that leads to more problems than it solves and that planners and planning are open to political interference and have too much discretion. The proof Siegan offers is found in Houston, where private controls over land and development have led to rational market-efficient outcomes that do not amount to chaos. Such private controls come in the form of covenants that run with the land and require changes to be approved by those in the covenanted area. Such approaches are more common in North America and often involve far more restrictions and are more pre-scriptive than public planning controls. Nevertheless, such an approach appeals to libertarians because such controls are private and (mostly) monitored and enforced by local communities.

Despite criticisms concerning a lack of strategic coordination of such site-based controls private sector alternatives and the examples of places such as Houston were influential upon libertarian critiques of planning in the UK. Drawing directly upon Siegan's work Robert Jones argued that:

> Defenders of planning are apt to conjure up visions of the hideous and garish free for all which would result if it were removed. It is quite possible, though, that the resultant order might be more to popular tastes and con-venience than is the environment imposed by the planning class. If we examine what might occur in the absence of local authority planning controls, the result is by no means the tasteless and shoddy chaos which that class suggests.
>
> (1982: 21–22)

It is worth highlighting a couple of points from the above in passing. First, Jones (who was a Conservative Member of Parliament and involved in the legislative attempts to deregulate planning in the 1980s) points to '*local authority* planning controls' rather than other forms of control and regulation.

One form of control he mentions further on in the text quoted above is economic forces that 'act to locate residential, commercial and industrial properties in their most appropriate areas' (ibid.: 22). Other forms of non-local authority control include the wider use of restrictive covenants. The second point concerns the phrase 'class' to describe planners and defenders of planning, comprehending the right's understanding of the nature of planners and planning as being a self-interested community that pushes for increases in regulation in order to justify its position and perpetuate intervention in the market.

The attacks on planning from the right and left were pushing at an open door: it was broadly agreed that 'something' needed to be done. However, rolling back planning controls to some ill-defined, halcyon era of private property rights and restrictive covenants was never a realistic possibility. Even Hall's deliberately provocative take on the need for change in planning had admitted as much:

> Any advocate of non-plan is sure to be misrepresented; we had better repeat what we mean. Simply to demand an end to planning, all planning, would be sentimentalism; it would deny the very basis of economic life in the second half of the 20th century ... we are arguing the word planning itself is misused; that it has also been used for the imposition of certain physical arrangements, based upon value judgements or prejudices; and that it should be scrapped.
>
> (Banham *et al.*, 1969: 442)

Howling at the moon was never going to get the libertarians very far. They needed a realistic and politically acceptable range of alternatives as well as a host to carry their hopes for a smaller market-focused state and planning. Selective deregulation was a possibility and successive governments from left and right had periodically tried this to electively deregulate, only to undermine such changes later with expansions of planning controls into new areas and policy objectives. Some form of planning, even for the emerging New Right, was a given. In their paean to libertarianism and planning Sorenson and Day call for selective rather than wholesale deregulation: 'Those who value freedom rightly question the goals, methods, institutions and impact of bureaucratic activities such as urban planning with a view to eradicating *those aspects which are unnecessary or ineffective*' (1981: 390–391, emphasis added).

Politically, the removal of planning controls was very sensitive. Accompanying the free market libertarians was a strong, conservative element within the right that remained suspicious of ideology and the market as well as being wedded to controls and regulations that provided some limits to development, particularly in rural areas. Such controls were also popular with rural inhabitants and voters who wished to maintain their little bit of England as 'green and pleasant'. This core of more traditional (what Thatcher would later term 'wet' Conservatives) may have disliked the idea of planning but accepted the outcomes and the cost as the price that needed to be paid to protect the countryside from development. Planning deregulation was clearly on the agenda, although the extent of reform remained open to question.

Attacks on planning and other forms of 'socialism' were more general in nature, although the alternatives were treated with more circumspection. Libertarians needed to proceed carefully, selectively and even experimentally. One such experiment provided a key direction for planning. The idea of non-plan in the late 1960s had been an attempt to begin a debate on the nature of planning from a liberal perspective. Hall's next major intervention was to develop the notion into a more concrete and politically sensitive form. From an almost light-hearted, anarchistic proposal to free up individuals to express themselves as an experiment in non-plan, Hall was to move on to the realities of Britain's inner cities and the successive failure to tackle industrial decline, population loss and social unrest. As part of a package of more orthodox proposals to tackle and reverse inner city decline Hall also proposed a more radical, last-ditch solution that he termed Freeports:

> It would result in a final possible answer, which I would call the Freeport solution. This is essentially an essay in non-plan. Small, selected areas of inner cities would be simply thrown open to all kinds of initiative, with minimal control. In other words, we would try and recreate the Hong Kong of the 1950s and 1960s inside inner Liverpool or Glasgow.
>
> (1977b: 5)

Freeports went further than non-plan and were not simply about planning: exchange controls, customs duties and taxes would be removed and there would be a free movement of labour and capital. The areas would be outside the scope of social services, industrial and other regulations:

> Residence in the area would be based on choice. Since the special taxation and customs arrangements would render the area ineligible for Common Market membership, it would be most appropriately administered as a British Crown Colony or protectorate; the Isle of Man provides one model. Existing residents – and there would not be many – would be free to stay or leave, since they would hold UK passports. However, if they stayed they would have to do so on new terms, under the laws and regulations of the Crown Colony. Their tax levels would be much reduced, but so would their benefits. And if they tried to enter the United Kingdom they might not be allowed to do so until their social security payments were made up.
>
> (Ibid.)

Deregulation of planning per se would have a range of advantages but selective deregulation could be used to create a form of comparative advantage, providing some areas with benefits over others and possibly reversing inner city decline. Selective deregulation would also help to 'win the argument' that there was little to fear from rolling back the planned state and plenty to gain.

From critique to practice: the rise of the New Right and the neoliberalization of planning

The general background of critiques and alternatives from the right provided a rich, broad and largely consistent agenda. Such an agenda was to help to inform the changes to and the direction of UK planning throughout the 1980s under what is now widely regarded as a neoliberal agenda. Neoliberalism is a catch-all phrase that covers a wide range of positions and governmentalities and came into more widespread and mainstream use during the 1990s. While it is often retrospectively applied to the emerging ideas of the New Right during the 1970s and their implementation during the 1980s the New Right is used here as a particular phase of neoliberal thinking. The natural host for the ideas of the right's critique of planning in the UK was the Conservative Party, though other parties shared some of their concerns, particularly about the role of planning in restricting growth and personal freedom. For some on the left in the 1970s, including Peter Hall, planning had shifted from being part of the suite of radical market interventions in the mid- to late 1940s concerned with helping to create a mixed economy, and had instead become a middle-class-dominated mechanism for protecting areas from new development including economic development (McCormick, 1991). The economic and social crises of the 1970s had political consequences for left and right with the former seeking to govern as a minority party supported by the Liberals from 1974–79 against a backdrop of rising inflation and unemployment. During this period the left entered one of its characteristic periods of intense internal rivalry within the Labour movement that was to continue well into the 1980s. The Conservative Party, on the other hand, had a similar though less fractious internal realignment and under its new leader Margaret Thatcher, elected in 1975, shifted to the right. This shift took on board new thinking and critiques of state–market relations within the context of the Conservatism, pragmatic politics and an electoral strategy. This amounted to a *New* Right (Gamble, 1988), one that melded a range of influences and ideas to come to a specifically UK flavour of neoliberal thinking. While the New Right does not come close to mapping on to the Conservative Party there are complementarities between the more traditional, one-nation Conservatism with its penchant for authoritarianism and the more liberally minded free marketeers. The main overlap concerns electoral success: if the New Right within the Conservative leadership and wider party could achieve electoral success then the tensions between the two could be overlooked. However, there were also more fundamental, ideological overlaps. As one of the leading lights of the New Right, Keith Joseph, put it, monetarism is not enough: 'monetary contraction in a mixed economy strangles the private sector unless the state sector contracts with it and reduces its take from the national income' (1976: 52).

A reduced state should not be a weak state, however. The market needs policing to help to ensure that the consequences of the free market do not lead to the emergence of monopolies and political instability. In place of the one-nation approach of welfare and the redistribution of wealth a strong, authoritarian state is necessary. A liberal state needs a strong state. Yet this is not the only connection between the liberal and authoritarian strands of the New Right; there was also a joint distrust of the public sector, a common view that public bureaucrats constitute a new self-interested class and a joint distrust of socialism.

The fusion of liberalism and authoritarianism under a New Right agenda provided little in the way of concrete policy direction for planning in the 1970s and the early 1980s. Policy development was being exogenously led by think tanks, individuals such as Hall or initiatives and ideas from other jurisdictions such as North America. The then Shadow Chancellor, Geoffrey Howe, had picked up on Peter Hall's Freeports and met him to discuss the translation of the idea into practical policy (Allmendinger, 2013). While the left had been deeply critical of Hall's Freeports, seeing them as a reversal of the post-war welfare state, Howe picked up on the notion and language of 'areas of fairly shameless free enterprise' (Hall, 1977b: 5). Using the cover of Hall's left-wing credentials to demonstrate the non-partisan nature of deregulation Howe announced the Conservatives' proposal for a series of Freeports renamed Enterprise Zones (EZs) at a speech in June 1978. Such zones would be areas where detailed planning regulations would cease to apply and only basic controls over health and safety and pay issues would exist.

Other initiatives and policies also tended to involve deregulation, centralization or a combination of the two (Allmendinger and Thomas, 1998). In 1980 the Conservative government issued new guidance on material considerations (the issues that local planning authorities could take into account in determining planning proposals). The introduction of Urban Development Corporations (UDCs) (based on the model found in some US cities) in 1980 involved significant state intervention in the form of financial incentives, infrastructure provision, compulsory purchase of land and simplified planning regimes. UDCs involved a massive shift in redevelopment responsibility to the centre through the appointment of the boards of the corporations, financing and policy direction. Whether through deregulation, centralization or both, the local interests were the main losers.

This pragmatic coalition of free market liberals pushing for deregulation and authoritarians with a distrust of local decision making and planners was fused with a political practicality and realism that included more traditional tools of land assembly and incentives to help to create demand. It would be wrong to present these strands of thinking as being held by distinct groups or tribes within the New Right. They often constituted a form of cognitive dissonance as individuals sought to reconcile an instinct to deregulate and reorientate the state through the recognition that markets needed to be created and stimulated in some situations. The state, including planning, was a necessary evil though its form and approach could be better aligned to those of a market state including a centralization of controls and minimization of local discretion.

Needless to say the implementation and policy development of this hybrid agenda from 1979 exposed some of these tensions, particularly with regards to planning. There was also a hard-headed political dimension that influenced the roll-out of the New Right's agenda. The rhetoric of radical change and deregulation summed up by Thatcher's infamous phrases 'there is no alternative' and 'the lady's not for turning' energized supporters but worried those who feared the deregulation of planning would lead to sprawl and the 'concreting' of the countryside. One outcome was a strange double talk from the government: while advancing a rhetoric of radicalism through enterprise-supportive deregulation ministers were simultaneously reassuring those concerned that the agenda would not be too radical. The first Secretary of State under Thatcher, Michael Heseltine, comforted concerned constituents and shire-based MPs that '*I have no intention of wrecking the planning system developed in the last forty years or so*' (quoted in Thornley, 1991: 122, emphasis added), while another planning minister was more explicit:

> There will be those that say we are intent on weakening the planning system. Nothing could be further from the truth. A strong and effective planning system is the best way to encourage sensible development and to protect the countryside where it is necessary.
>
> (Nicholas Ridley, quoted in Thornley, 1991: 123)

The provisional nature of this support, i.e. 'deregulation where necessary', provided enough scope for change to be introduced. One upshot was that policy was sometimes 'confused' and lacking clarity of objectives. Another was that policy was presented to multiple audiences in different ways. UDCs, for example, often accompanied EZs as in the case of the London Docklands. The deregulatory characteristics of both were played up to certain audiences and the argument that removing planning controls would, to paraphrase one Secretary of State, unlock jobs from filing cabinets. Yet another dimension, perhaps more important in the success of such areas, was the *dirigiste* role of the state in compulsorily purchasing land, decontaminating it, putting in the necessary infrastructure and offering significant fiscal benefits to developers and occupiers. This more traditional, highly centralized role for the state was downplayed in order to focus attention upon the impact of removing planning controls. For planners and local communities this mixed message proved problematic: planning was simultaneously being deregulated and rolled out in forms that resembled the functions of new town development corporations. Non-plan had, in fact, turned out not to be quite as expected.

This policy confusion was supplemented at times with what we might term policy dilution through a 'watering down' or downplaying of the radical nature of policy following pressure within the government and the Conservative Party itself. While the liberal inclination was to deregulate or reorientate planning towards market principles there was still a significant proportion of traditional and natural Conservative voters who felt that planning regulations were there to protect England's 'green and pleasant land', particularly the bit that they inhabited. This NIMBY attitude started to focus policy change upon 'other' areas, particularly urban locations. The permitted development rights regime was liberalized in order to allow businesses and householders to undertake development without the need to obtain planning permission from local authorities though such changes did not apply to Areas of Outstanding Natural Beauty, National Parks or Conservation Areas. This deregulation was also accompanied and equalled with increased centralization of control and minimization of local discretion. The procedures for local plan adoption were simplified while the increased use of government circulars sought to dictate the matters that local authorities could consider when dealing with proposals for development.

The third main adulteration of liberal thinking for planning arose from the application of free market principles onto complex and by now embedded regulatory frameworks that, while by no means perfect, enjoyed support from a wide spectrum of actors involved in development. The New Right's focus was upon creating flexibility, although markets also liked certainty and consistency even if they did not actually need it, and it was this element for which non-plan had failed to take account. Industry, including housebuilders and developers, complained of the burdensome nature of regulations and the time taken to achieve planning permission. Government talk of 'a bonfire of controls' was largely a reaction to bodies such as the CBI that was calling for deregulation. Yet industry was wary of the unknown and the implications of deregulation. Those who financed development were also cautious if not suspicious of what could amount to a supply-side shock as the flow of land and property on the market became a torrent. The logic was that lifting supply-side constraints would increase supply, although how much and where was largely unknown. All things being equal an increase in supply would lead to a decrease in prices, yet loans and mortgages of existing properties and schemes had been secured against a backdrop of a steady and reliable supply. The free market liberals' proposals were starting to worry the market that they sought to privilege. This backdrop goes some way to explaining how a radical New Right that implemented far-reaching changes in other areas such as the sale of council houses, privatization of nationalized industries and deregulation of the financial services had a much more modest record of change in planning.

It was not a lack of ideas or policies that led to a demure approach to planning; after all, the Centre for Policy Studies, the Institute of Economic Affairs and the Adam Smith Institute had all propagated ideas and alternatives. Nor was there a lack of will, despite the protestations of ministers, to dismantle planning controls. The Local Government Planning and Land Act 1980 and Circular 22/80 were both early indications of radical intent regarding planning. What undermined the changes to planning and the New Right's agenda was the conservatism within parts of the party, its supporters and the market itself.

As an era of rolled-back neoliberalism the New Right's approach was, at best, mixed. The libertarian instincts and rhetoric came up against problems in their translation into policy and in their effectiveness. This opened up the New Right to criticisms of being obsessed with deregulation when, in fact, their approach drew more upon the rhetoric of 'rolling back the frontiers of the state' while approaching planning policy in a more mixed and eclectic way.

The lessons from the 1980s were important in the evolution of liberal to neoliberal thinking. If market government was to prosper it needed to be more subtle and nuanced, presentationally more astute and ready to introduce diversions with an eye on the long term. It was these tensions that were to help the evolution of neoliberal thinking and help to explain the significant changes in approach to planning under the Conservatives from 1991.

Conclusions

The thinking about the role of planning during the 1970s and 1980s had broadly mirrored the emerging New Right attitude towards the role of the state, the removal of supply-side constraints and the need for a liberalized economy. Yet while the intellectual foundations of planning reform came from the work of Hayek among others, the propagation and translation of ideas – 'winning the argument' – was achieved in part through the active role of think tanks such as the Institute of Economic Affairs (established in 1955), the Centre for Policy Studies (established in 1974) and the Adam Smith Institute (established in 1977) as well as industry mouthpieces such as the *Estates Gazette*. The outcome was a growing body of thought, publications and attitudes that decried planning and argued that national economic growth and personal liberty would benefit from a rollback of regulation. This more rhetorical and attitudinal impact was far more significant than the actual measures introduced during the 1980s, particularly given the sensitivity regarding deregulation exhibited by many in the Conservative Party.

Beyond the rhetorical success the actual impact of the changes to planning during the 1980s was minimal. Despite some radical intent there was a watering down of ideas and approaches as Freeports evolved into EZs and thereafter into Simplified Planning Zones (SPZs). Such dilution came about because of the practical implications of deregulation as much as a suspicion of free market policies within the Conservative Party itself. However, the broader reason was that crude deregulation was not in itself market supportive. While property interests could rally to the call for less regulation and state intervention the certainty provided by planning at a more site-specific level was critical to investment and profit. Rather than crude deregulation property interests actually wanted a market-supportive planning, a system that shifted its balance back towards enabling and facilitating rather than regulating and controlling. Developers, landowners and investors needed certainty and consistency as well as flexibility. At the same time the process needed to be quick whilst retaining legitimacy.

The growing popularity and success of the Green Party in the late 1980s as the environment began to emerge on the political agenda led to a shift in attitude and rhetoric from the main parties. The unsubtle and one-sided model of planning as a burden on business needed more nuancing and balance. Besides, planning could be the way in which the government could persuade the electorate that it was sensitive to environmental needs. Whether this shift is defined as an evolution or a U-turn the change was facilitated by the replacement of Margaret Thatcher with John Major as party leader and prime minister in 1990 and a major amendment to planning in 1991.

From 1991 planning would be reformed again by the introduction of a 'plan-led' approach (Allmendinger and Thomas, 1998). Rather than continuing a market-led, case-by-case approach the government, underpinned by a presumption in favour of development, began to issue national planning policy and amended legislation that required decisions to be made in accordance with the local development plan – a presumption in favour of the development plan. This shift towards centralization and hierarchy both countered the ability of local authorities to interpret planning guidance in ways that were contrary to government intentions while instilling a more consistent market-led ethos. The lessons from the 1980s had been learned – planning would be reformed and reorientated to support the market.

The alternatives to this approach and a possible counter-narrative were unforthcoming: the left were lost in a morass of contemplation and reflection. If, as claimed by Moore-Milroy, there was a paradigm breakdown in planning, then it was on the left not the right. The right was clear and purposeful in its approach, pragmatically adopting and adapting a range of ideas drawn from different sources in order to create and then maintain a new governing ideology. Building upon the lessons from the 1980s the way was now open for the further round of experimentation and evolution.

5 From New Right to neoliberal spatial governance

Introduction

If, as argued in the previous chapter, the right's changes to planning during the 1980s were largely a practical failure, how can it be claimed that planning, in the UK and beyond, is still the focus of ongoing neoliberalization? (see, for example, Purcell, 2009; Gunder, 2010; Andersen and Pløger, 2007; McGuirk, 2005). If the aim of neoliberalism over the past three decades or so, including the 1980s, has simply been to deregulate planning, minimizing it to a regulatory rump, it would be judged a failure particularly given planning's current scale and scope which (broadly) is little different to that which existed in the early 1970s. The New Right's initial attempts to reduce the size and influence of the state and planning during the 1980s can be summed up as a crude, deregulatory and centralizing approach melded with and tempered by political and practical concerns. As I argued in the previous chapter neoliberalism is more than a rolled-back, minimal state. The role of the state, including planning, under neoliberalism is 'to create and preserve an institutional framework appropriate to (market) practices' (Harvey 2006: 145). As Gamble (2009: 63) puts it, the neoliberal state is a regulatory state, not a laissez-faire state. The survival of neoliberalism as a governing ideology in the 1990s required a more flexible, variable and experimental approach that shifted and took opportunities to shape the role of the state, but not necessarily to reduce it. Neoliberal planning did not amount to Hall's non-plan but was a fusion of a market-based, growth-focused planning, and a planning that was implemented with sufficient public interest legitimacy to be seen to be acting in the wider needs of society.

This position, which has been termed neoliberal spatial governance (Allmendinger, 2011; Allmendinger and Haughton, 2012), has not emerged through a conscious strategy of a 'guiding hand' but through a series of experiments and trials, some of which have succeeded and some not. This evolutionary roll-out of neoliberalism has been essential to ensure that the moving target of neoliberal spatial governance adapts to opportunities, setbacks and successes. Since the early 1990s, in the aftermath of the New Right's approach during the 1980s, planning was expanded and enhanced in order to support a neoliberal agenda in ways that were very different to the simple deregulatory or rollback model. The creation of RDAs, regional Government Offices and the panoply of policy guidance, funding streams and supporting institutional arrangements from the late 1990s to 2010 for example, highlight that neoliberal planning can have more than a 'nightwatchman' role and be concerned with growth management and support. Yet while some claim that neoliberalism offers 'a simple and straight-forward criterion for the direction of policy' (Gamble, 2009: 27) this does not really tell us about actual practices in areas such as planning under the influence of neoliberalism: there is no neoliberal 'toolkit' in complex and developed economies but rather a set of broad predispositions that are mediated and arbitrated through existing though evolving institutional and policy landscapes.

This is not to say that neoliberalism is uncontested, either by alternative governing ideologies or internally through tensions over the speed or scope of change; sometimes a series of neoliberalisms or possibilities are best understood as being in tension. Such an array of sometimes contradictory neoliberalisms and the mediation of neoliberal tenets through unique circumstances of places and sectors such as health and education has relevance for planning and particularly planning as practiced in countries with a common law tradition and high levels of administrative discretion. As I discussed in Chapter 1, the day-to-day practices of sectors such as planning work within overlapping and multi-scalar legal, policy, professional and institutional frameworks. Such assemblages are evolving and are driven by a wide range of factors leaving significant discretion and choice to professionals and localities to interpret instruments and policies in the light of specific, local circumstances. This allows for a wide though circumscribed variegation in neoliberal roll-out. While the 'fundamental mission of the neo-liberal state is to create a "good business climate" and therefore to optimize conditions for capital accumulation no matter what the consequences for employment and social well-being' (Harvey, 2006: 25) this leaves open a wide spectrum of possibilities and subtleties.

> There is no inexorable logic of state or scalar restructuring waiting to be uncovered, even if from time to time particular tendencies can be identified. On the contrary, it is always necessary to explore with care what is actu-ally happening – to identify the interests in play and the ways in which economic and political processes come together and (sometimes) break apart as governmental territories are put together and, equally often, taken apart. What is apparent is that the existence and nature – the borders – of territorial politics cannot simply be taken for granted. But that does not mean that these issues are irrelevant or can be dismissed as somehow old fashioned. On the contrary territory continues to be a focus around which politics is actively conducted and pursued, and a great deal of activity continues to be orientated towards the reimagination and sometimes invention of particular territories within which and around which political initiatives and political programmes may be developed and implemented.
>
> (Cochrane, 2012: 105)

The capture and reorientation of planning has been achieved not through a full-frontal attack on deregulation and minimization but through a reorientation of the practices and objectives of planning towards market governance and also, crucially, the deployment of nomenclature and language to distract attention and reassure wider society that planning still operates in the public interest. This legitimacy was the missing element from the deregulatory approach of the New Right. Ironically, it has been provided not by the right but by the left, particularly following the emergence of New Labour in the mid-1990s and its attempts to find a 'third way' between the free market and the post-war social democracy. It was Labour that helped to develop the language for planning around socially aware progress and growth.

Despite their very different backgrounds, implications and trajectories both the left and the right have influenced current planning and its transformation into neoliberal spatial governance. This transformation of planning has been variable and multifaceted. However, there are three main elements that are part of any understanding of change. The first is that planning has been both subjected to neoliberalism in the sense of being reorientated and altered as well as being a tool of neoliberalism, i.e. as a mechanism to help to create more productive, competitive places. The second element concerns the tensions within neoliberalism between rollback deregulation on the one hand, and rolled-out, market-supportive and -facilitating forms of planning on the other. Such tensions play out differently in space and time, but crucially both manifestations, e.g. policies, can undermine each other. Third, and following on from the first two elements, it is important to understand how neoliberal spatial governance has actually manifested itself through time and how tensions and the notion of planning as a subject and object of neoliberalism have played out and evolved. This chapter develops these three elements.

Planning as a subject and object of neoliberalism

Superficially, there appears to be, at best, a tension and, at worst, confusion at the heart of planning reform over the past three decades or so. Despite the differences in approach planning has been simultaneously rolled out into new market-supportive roles as well as minimized and rolled back. The paradox of planning reform has been that change has involved both 'less' and 'more'. One way out of this paradox is to introduce the idea that planning is both an *object* and a *subject* of neoliberalization. By subject I mean subjected to neoliberalism. By object I mean the way in which planning has been used as a tool of neoliberalism. As a subject of neoliberalism planning's scope, scales, tools and objectives are periodically challenged and altered in a restless and fruitless search for the 'perfect fix' of regulation and market freedom. Such changes are driven by both laissez-faire and social market strands of neoliberalism. In other words planning has been subject to both attempts to reduce its role and minimize its regulatory 'burden' as well as to moves to develop a more proactive and market-facilitative approach that emphasizes partnerships, skills and knowledge. 'State capture', as

Peck (2010) puts it, has sought to embed neoliberalism within sectors such as planning through changing the culture, objectives and values of planning in subtle, and not so subtle, ways. Deregulation during the 1980s was an early crude and largely ineffectual approach to subject planning to neoliberalism. More sophisticated subsequent strategies sought to reorientate planning practices through the deployment of New Public Management (NPM) techniques such as targets and incentives, the greater use of IT and more codified and less discretionary tools such as Local Development Orders.

As an object of neoliberalism planning has also been tasked with a range of objectives including the necessity to facilitate what Marxists would term economic and social reproduction or, more prosaically, economically vibrant and resilient places. For neoliberals the city is the intersection of such state-market relations. As Jessop points out, neoliberalism needs cities to manage the

> interface between the local economy and global flows, between the potentially conflicting demands of local sustainability and local well-being and those of international competitiveness, and between the challenges of social exclusion and global polarization and the continuing demands for liberalization, deregulation, privatization and so on.
>
> (2002: 466)

Cities and their hinterlands – functional economic areas – are too important to the success of neoliberalism to be left to the whim and caprice of the free market (Gough, 2002). There is an important if not critical role for planning in the management of cities to both promote and facilitate economic activity and oversee the consequences of activity such as inequality (Imrie and Raco, 2003; Columb, 2007). The actual strategies through which planning facilitates and manages the consequences of neoliberalism are evolving and reflect the more general tensions within neoliberalism around the desire to minimize market imperfections and the recognition that such interventions are also needed.

Table 5.1 sets out a range of different initiatives following the distinction between planning as a *subject* and *object* of neoliberalism and the two main neoliberal attitudes towards the role of the state, what I would term laissez-faire and managing markets. The list of initiatives within each category is by no means exhaustive. It is also necessary to emphasize that these approaches are not necessarily in tension with one another. For example, privatization of planning (planning as a subject of neoliberalization) has continued throughout the 1980s, 1990s and 2000s to the point where there are some local planning authorities that contract out their plan-making functions. Yet subjecting planning to privatization has not stopped state expansion under more social market 'urban entrepreneurialism', particularly during the 2000s, and actually complements a more flexible or zoning-based approach to planning – setting out clear criteria 'up front', while reducing the discretion of decision makers implies fewer planners.

Notwithstanding these issues, the general point of Table 5.1 is that one of the reasons why planning has changed with regularity over the past few decades is

Table 5.1 Tensions in neoliberal changes to planning

	Planning as subjected to neoliberalism	Planning as an object or tool of neoliberalism
Laissez-faire	'Privatization' of planning functions and policy: contracting out of planning functions such as plan making and supporting information requirements (Higgins and Allmendinger, 1999).	Flexible or deregulated planning: creating zoning-based approaches within the UK discretionary system, e.g. EZs and SPZs (Allmendinger, 1997, 2006) Allmendinger and Thomas, 1998).
	NPM techniques: targets and incentives to make certain kinds of decisions quicker, focus on quantity over quality in decision making (Massey and Pyper, 2005).	Quangos: Use of arm's length bodies to bypass local authorities, e.g. UDCs (Imrie and Thomas, 1999; Wilks-Heeg, 1996).
	Deregulation: removal of planning regulations and reorientation of planning guidance (Allmendinger, 2011; Allmendinger and Thomas, 1998).	Competitive Bidding: new funding mechanisms to instil entrepreneurial culture across the public and private sectors and departmental silos, e.g. Single Regeneration Budget (Rhodes *et al.*, 2002).
	Abolition of bodies and scales of planning: removal of tiers of planning bodies and simplification of planning hierarchy, e.g. abolition of metropolitan county councils in 1986, RSSs and Government Offices in 2011 (Allmendinger, 2011).	'Project-led' planning: downplaying of plan making and plan significance (Allmendinger and Tewdwr-Jones, 1997b).
		New private finance measures: shifting responsibility for funding improvement and development to the private sector, e.g. Business Improvement Districts (Lloyd *et al.*, 2003).
		Infrastructure funding: simplifying planning obligations to reduce costs and increase consistency, e.g. Community Infrastructure Levy (Allmendinger, 2011).
Managing markets	'Culture change': training and guidance to promote a more positive, 'delivery-focused' attitude, e.g. development management (Morphet, 2011).	'Urban entrepreneurialism': creating attractive conditions for mobile capital and 'business-friendly' planning contexts (Newman and Thornley, 1997).
	Re-regulation: shifting the focus of planners' work through guidance and advice from external advisory bodies such as the Commission on Architecture and the Built Environment (CABE), the Planning Advisory Service and the publication of good practice guidance, e.g. Planning Policy Statement companions.	Public-private partnerships: creation of new delivery and coordination bodies, e.g. Homes and Community Agency, RDAs (Geddes, 2006).
	Processes and products: new planning mechanisms such as Local Development Frameworks (LDFs), new scales and processes of planning in order to address, for example, climate change, increased demands for involvement and social inclusion (Allmendinger, 2011).	Urban renaissance agenda: creating 'successful places' through mixed-use development and gentrification (Imrie *et al.*, 2009).
		Consistency and certainty: creating 'level playing field' for investors across country through significant expansion of national planning guidance and introduction of the 'plan-led' approach (Allmendinger, 2006).

because of the tensions and contradictions between the approaches inherent in planning as a subject and object of neoliberalism. There are numerous examples of where they coincided: the creation and management of success-ful places – planning as an object of neoliberalism – requires an active role for planning while planning as a subject is largely concerned with minimiz-ing or limiting intervention. Making quick decisions and having simple coherent strategies provides markets with certainty and reduces risk. At the same time planners are called upon to create and facilitate markets through, for example, regeneration and working with multiple actors across scales and sectors. The search for a 'fix' that gives planners an expansive role in making successful places but in ways that are minimalist has been a source of constant tension, leading to contradictions, lack of clarity and calls for further change.

Table 5.1 provides an indication of how object and subject and laissez-faire and managed market-driven changes existed, often simultaneously, even in eras when, rhetorically at least, the overall theme of government was domi-nated by a particular approach. For example, during the 1980s there was a strong laissez-faire approach from central government that focused upon planning as a subject of neoliberalism (e.g. deregulation, abolition of scales, etc.) and planning as an object of neoliberalism (e.g. flexible zoning-based planning and project-led planning). However, there was also a little acknowledged managed market approach through the use of UDCs and EZs that sought to redevelop areas through investment in land assembly, decon-tamination, infrastructure provision and the provision of fiscal incentives. There was also a rather selective laissez-faire agenda both to planning as a subject and object of neoliberalism. In large parts of mainly Conservative-voting, rural England there was support for planning controls and processes in order to thwart new development. Such tensions and political realities effectively undermined many of the changes (Allmendinger and Thomas, 1998; Allmendinger, 2011).

Other more recent eras of planning also exhibit such issues. From 2004 New Labour, the planning profession and economic interests such as the CBI and the Home Builders Federation (HBF) devised an approach that recognized and tried to reconcile the laissez-faire and managed market dimensions to neoliberalism while also addressing planning as both a subject and object of neoliberalism. This conscious strategy, broadly termed the 'spatial turn', attempted to fuse planning as an object and subject of neoliberalism through a sophisticated growth-based strategy of targets, market-incentivized performance, inclusive discourses, partnership forms of governance, deregulation and increased resources to the sector (Allmendinger and Haughton, 2011a; Haughton and Allmendinger, 2010). This 'win-win' strategy, like others before, ultimately failed to achieve its objectives, thus underscoring Peck's (2010) view that neoliberal experiments 'fail forward'. I discuss spatial planning in greater detail elsewhere in this book. Here I want to make two points in relation to the discussion of neoliberalism. Spatial planning, like other neoliberal planning strategies, was a victim of the tensions (object and subject, laissez-faire and managed market) and resultant consequences of neoliberalism. As planners struggled to come to terms with changes to their roles (e.g. privatization, culture change, reregulation) as well as with new processes and products of planning (e.g. RSSs, LDFs) towards new, managed market objectives (e.g. urban renaissance) there were also more laissez-faire attempts to make planning work faster and meet performance targets. The upshot was frustration and a lack of achievement that ultimately led to the replacement of spatial planning with the next era of change, localism.

The distinction between planning as a subject and object of neoliberalism builds upon the laissez-faire managed market distinction and takes us some way towards making sense of constant change in planning under neoliberalism by emphasizing the dual and sometimes conflicting agendas as well as the incessant need to constantly reform. It also adds to the argument that rejects the view of a linear progression towards an ever more perfect neoliberal state. As Peck (2010) reminds us there are setbacks and periods when neoliberal preferences and tenets are blended with more *dirigiste* state strategies. There was a period after the credit crunch in 2008 when some felt that neoliberalism's time had come. In retrospect we now know that such hopes were to be replaced with despair as neoliberalism demonstrated its embeddedness and a new era or 'fix' emerged, particularly after the general election in May 2010. The wider point about setbacks and reversals holds, however. The localism agenda remains inchoate and incipient as different interests struggle over its properties and implications for planning. Some elements, such as neighbourhood planning have introduced new and potentially threatening strategies for growth that could emerge as new forms of intervention and regulation. Other elements, such as the abolition of Regional Strategies and a more minimalist approach to national planning policy, represent more core neoliberal concerns.

Variegated neoliberalism and planning

Deconstructing neoliberalism and approaching any understanding from the lens of a particular policy area such as planning highlights the tensions, contradictions and synergies of different strands or elements of neoliberalism. The constant search for new policy, scalar and institutional 'fixes' in planning amounts to variegated neoliberalism (Peck and Tickell, 2002; Macartney, 2011): the rise and fall of spatial planning and the emergence of localism or the Big Society from 2010 highlights such variegation and evolution. However, variegation also covers the tensions and variances *within* a particular neoliberal era or settlement. For example, the managed market and laissez-faire strands of planning often lead to different approaches within the same timescale as discussed above. As well as capturing the differences between and within particular eras of neoliberalism there is a third dimension of my use of variegation that concerns the need to understand neoliberalism from the experiences of a particular sector or context. Variegation is to neoliberalism what situated and contextual history is to Marxism. Marx was at pains to point out the importance of understanding the specific differences between capitalist societies: capitalism and the relations between elements of society varied historically between different places. For Marx there are no eternal abstract theories or categories. Instead, we need to look to the specifics of socio-historical relations in a particular society and develop theories from the 'ground up' in order to understand society and thereby be able to change it. Commentators and analysts of neoliberalism similarly emphasize the importance of context and the variability of 'actual neoliberalism' between places and sectors and through time.

Debates within neoliberalism over how to characterize particular conjunctures or crises, especially in the period after 2008, can descend into abstract and fruitless analyses of prefixes and whether we are experiencing 'post-neoliberalism' or 'post-capitalism' (Altvater, 2009) while missing the shifting relations and opportunities to shape outcomes and futures within particular societies (Hart, 2010). Nevertheless, while understanding the variability of neoliberalism is both desirable and necessary, constructing what Harvey (2006: 87) refers to as a *'moving map of neoliberalization'* is problematic not least because most states that have taken a neoliberal turn have done so only partially. The uneven spatial nature is further compounded by the contestation of neoliberalism within states, leading to temporary reversals and setbacks in the process of neoliberalization and the mediation and transformation of neoliberal tenets through national institutions and policy mechanisms and processes.

Neoliberalism varies through time, between sectors and across space and territories. Such variegation is the outcome of a basic, operational logic mediated through the diverse regulatory landscapes and institutional assemblages of different places that are themselves a result of previous rounds of regulatory contestation (Brenner *et al.* 2010). While such variegations are an agreed characteristic of neoliberalism there is an understandable and conscious tendency towards abstraction in periodizations. The conjunctures and ruptures of neoliberalization that amount to a simultaneous destruction and creation, or what Hegel and Marx termed *aufheben*, are experienced differently in different places. Extracting commonalities and themes in the context of such variegation can only be achieved through abstraction.

Focusing on a policy sector and regulatory regime such as planning helps to 'bridge the gap' between more macro-level abstraction and more meso- and micro-level processes, thus highlighting some of the rolling institutional dynamics with their specific trajectories and momentum that cannot be 'read off' from more regimes of 'system-level' accounts (see Hodkinson, 2011, for another account and example of this). The ongoing debate between 'strong' theories of neoliberalism, which emphasize more abstract and global dimensions and 'weak' theories which focus more on hybridity, contingency and contradiction in local manifestations is to a large degree a distraction (see, for example,

Gibson-Graham, 2008 and Hackworth and Moriah, 2006). The two approaches are best seen as complementary, rather than one being conceptually subordinate, or one being closer to political dynamics than the other. They function at different levels of abstraction and with different forms of pertinence. Periodizations of operative processes at meso level can map out differently than those at a more macro level. Moreover, system-level periodizations do not necessarily 'contain' policy field periodizations in a similar manner to a Russian nesting doll, since they operate at different levels of abstraction and reflect on different political dynamics. So we might expect different periodizations of neoliberalism to emerge, reflecting diverse institutional domains and historical experiences. Nonetheless we might also expect something to be holding them together, which is why we find it useful here to frame our discussion in relation to rollback and roll-out accounts of neoliberalization (Peck and Tickell, 2002). By introducing a sectoral perspective our aim is to develop a deeper understanding of the evolutionary and transformative nature of neoliberalization, in the process challenging and adding to our understanding of the ways in which planning itself has been transformed over the past thirty years.

It is a truism to say that there are a variety of neoliberalisms. As Peck and Tickell put it 'although neoliberalism privileges the unitary logic of the market while advocating supposedly universal cures and one-best-way policy strategies, it is inherently much more variegated than such self-representations suggest' (2002: 387). The mediation of neoliberal tenets or strands is particularly important in both the UK and planning. Despite devolution the UK remains a unitary state with a first-past-the-post electoral system and a fuzzy relationship between the legislature and the executive. This tends to produce governments that can pass legislation and impose policies without a great deal of interference at the national level. Nevertheless, while this 'Westminster' model based around distinct central-local relations has been shown to ignore the significance of sub-national bodies in policy implementation (Marsh and Rhodes, 1992) and the role and autonomy of actors including professions such as planning in policy implementation it does highlight the importance of governing ideologies within parties as key to the mediation of neoliberalism. Changes to planning under neoliberalism broadly echo the two main tenets of UK neoliberalism – the managed market and laissez-faire strands – and the tensions between them. But what we can add through a detailed exploration of planning is a richness to such understandings highlighting the policy implications of different neoliberal models, how and in what circumstances one approach is chosen and deployed over another, how different manifestations of neoliberalism exist simultaneously, the agency dimension of 'who chooses?' different neoliberal strategies and how crises emerge and are resolved. In doing so we are drawing upon more macro understandings while also adding to them in order 'to explore the concrete practices of rescaling in a theoretically informed and *informing* fashion' (Peck, 2002: 333, emphasis in the original). I do this below by focusing upon two dimensions of change through time (temporal variegation) and within planning and across space (sectoral and spatial variegation).

Temporal variegation

There was a good deal of discussion, speculation and not a little wishful thinking concerning the implications and significance for neoliberalism of the financial crisis and recession that started in 2008. Despite a mantra about the superiority of markets lasting over four decades neoliberals became very sudden converts to the need for an active role for the state. State 'bailouts', or incidents of the government 'repeatedly saving markets from their own mistakes', as Stiglitz (2010: xx) puts it, did not amount to some kind of Keynesian revival but the rediscovery of a Keynesian truth, that government plays a critical role in free markets. Neoliberalism is a form of market-orientated regulation but, as Karl Polanyi (1944) argued, the road to free markets was opened and kept open by continuous state intervention:

> There was nothing natural about laissez-faire; free markets could never have come into being by merely allowing things to take their course. Just as cotton manufacturers – the leading free trade industry – were created by the help of protective tariffs, export bounties, and indirect wage subsidies, laissez-faire was enforced by the state.
>
> (1944: 139)

The state has always been a key component in constructing and reconstructing neoliberalism and at the same time it has been an object of that same market-orientated regulatory restructuring. Of course, this has not stopped neoliberals from blaming the state and its regulators rather than the market for the recession. The outcome of the 2008 financial crisis was not the return to Keynesianism, but the replacement of one set of neoliberal strategies with another.

The point here is that neoliberalism, in Peck's phrase, 'fails forward' (2010: 5): crises, evolution and adaptability are key characteristics. The ruptures within neoliberalism are inevitable and lead to a struggle over future forms: 'It's [neoliberalism's] success as an ideological project reflects its deeply contra-dictory nature, as a combination of dogmatism and adaptability, strategic intent and opportunistic exploitation, programmatic vision and tactical smarts, principle and hypocrisy' (Peck, 2010: 4). At times of crises and transition 'only the state has the ability to reorganize capitalism and create the conditions for a new period of expansion' (Gamble, 2009: 97).

This discussion draws attention to the temporal variegations and nature of neoliberalism. Peck and Tickell (2002), for example, distinguish between different eras of neoliberalism, with the late 1970s and 1980s characterized by deregulation and a rhetoric of minimal state (or rollback) neoliberalism, while the 1990s and 2000s experiments in neoliberalization were typified by the roll-out of a variety of supportive state forms and modes of governance. More recently a slightly different terminology has posited the 1970s and 1980s as 'disarticulated neoliberalism' leading on to a period from the 1990s of 'deepening neoliberalism' (Brenner, et al. 2010; see also Peck, 2010, ch. 1).

In any characterization of different eras the emphasis is on managing the contradictions of early experiments in de- and re-regulation and continuously reformulating the role of the state in relation to the market and civil society. Different eras have distinctive strategies. As such there is a continuing interplay of aspects of the rollback/roll-out, disarticulated/deepening dimensions of neoliberalization while, sometimes taking two steps forward and one step back, neoliberalism 'feels its way', thus ceding ground to political expediency. This leads Peck (2010: 25) to argue that in the current economic crisis we may be witnessing a 'roiling neoliberalism, as a still dominant but deeply flawed "settlement", increasingly buffeted by crises'. The important point here is that it is possible to discern major shifts in the way in which neoliberal thinking is presented and operationalized, not least as the contradictions of early deregulatory approaches became apparent. However, while such conceptualizations are abstract they serve as a useful heuristic against which we should explore and evaluate different sectors and national responses as the precise manifestations of regulatory experiments at both system and policy field levels will always be temporally and spatially variegated.

In relation to temporal variegation of neoliberalism planning in the UK experienced a broad attempt at rollback deregulation in the 1980s along with other areas of state activity. Nevertheless, deregulation and market orientation led to a series of consequences including the creation of uncertainty as former regulatory regimes were replaced with more market-orientated and supportive decision-making frameworks. Local communities, developers, land and property-owners and businesses welcomed greater freedom for themselves but disliked the same freedom for others. The rollback of planning controls led to a spate of new settlement proposals in the south-east of England which had previously been restricted. As a consequence local, mainly Conservative-voting communities coordinated a campaign of resistance and lobbied MPs to reverse the deregulatory strategy (Ward, 1994). Thus at a more fine-grained level the experiences of planning highlight how an era portrayed as deregulatory was tempered by the need to ensure political and market support.

The rethink and reorientation of rollback neoliberalism in planning was the lack of enthusiasm of the property industry. Initiatives such as SPZs introduced in 1986 allowed landowners to request the adoption of an alternative, simplified system of land use controls, one that was more common to continental European or North American zoning systems. To the surprise of the government and contrary to neoliberal orthodoxy such zoning-based approaches were unpopular. In the conclusion of Allmendinger and Thomas the rollback strategy amounted to a 'spectacular misreading of the market supportive role of planning' (1998: 240): property values depended to a high degree on the restriction of supply and the certainty provided by planning regulations. The result was a rethink and change in strategy. There was no 'crisis' such as a recession but a rationality and legitimization crisis that arose from a lack of support and impact within society and the market and the withdrawal of political support within the government. The consequence was the emergence of a new experiment in neoliberal planning from the late 1980s that built upon the lessons of rollback.

The story of neoliberal planning is more complex and nuanced than a succession of neoliberal 'experiments'. As discussed above the notion of neoliberalism was itself contested and this had material consequences for policy fields such as planning. Neoliberalization of planning ironically placed the planner centre stage as an object of neoliberalism through deregulation but as a subject of neoliberalism in creatively managing the tensions and manifestations. This latter dimension required discretion and autonomy that worked both ways in facilitating and resisting neoliberalization. Neoliberal governmentality, particularly in the early days, had a lot to learn. However, an important dimension in any neoliberal strategy is the rhetorical dimension to the changes and eras or 'winning the argument' about the superiority of a market state to a social democratic state.

Finally, the nature of the state, so critical to neoliberalism, changed. Planning is an arm of the state and we can analyse the evolution of neoliberalism from a state-centred perspective focusing upon the cultures, governance, institutions and mechanisms of planning. While planning was not subject to contracting out or privatization of functions that befell housing it was subject to an attempt at 'culture change' (Allmendinger, 2011). What Gamble (2009) calls the 'depoliticization' of policy was an increasingly key feature of planning through the use of arm's length commissions. However, this went further than simply the privatization of policy and included the depoliticization of planning itself through its governance arrangements and objectives. Part of neoliberal strategy towards planning from 2004 was to seek to 'normalize' market-led solutions by deliberately realigning planning with a growth strategy while presenting an illusion of partnership and participation.

Sectoral and spatial variegation

As well as temporal variegation neoliberalism varies between sectors and across scales and space. A range of distinctive scalar strategies have been employed by the UK government which have reworked the scales of planning as a tool of neoliberal spatial governance. During the 1980s such top-down deregulatory strategies were based upon either a laissez-faire free market tenet or managed market neoliberal tenets. The laissez-faire initiatives were largely national (e.g. the changes to the Use Classes Order) while the managed market dominated initiatives were spatially more targeted or select. However, the distinctions are not entirely clear and in some instances there was an overlap. Initiatives included both laissez-faire and managed market tenets: UDCs and EZs involved deregulation and significant market-shaping intervention (Thornley, 1991). There are two significant conclusions to be drawn from this observation. The first is that spatial variegation operates at both the national and sub-national level. The second concerns the nature and success of spatially variegated neoliberal experiments.

A recent national-scale neoliberal experiment concerns devolution. While there has always been a degree of spatial variegation in policy between England, Scotland, Wales and Northern Ireland this differentiation accelerated from 1998 onwards following New Labour's devolution programme. In planning devolution increased variegation and this has been felt through differentiated policy contexts and frames linked to new planning spaces (Haughton *et al.*, 2010). Devolution has been widely read as being a series of experiments in reworking the scales and sectoral boundaries of the state in the search of new approaches for stimulating economic growth. In more recent times the creation of LEPs and City Deals has also seen the introduction of new state-led experimental spaces of planning.

> [Neoliberalism] is best seen as an evolving and reflexive market-led approach to economic management, where the core concern with re-regulation in favour of market forces is accompanied by considerable diversity between territories in how the resultant processes of experimentation evolve.
>
> (Ibid.: 9)

Nevertheless, such experiments in spatially variegated neoliberalism are riven through with tensions that have been characterized as including centripetal forces 'pushing' for differentiation and experimentation on the one hand and centrifugal forces 'pulling' such variability back to a more common regulatory environment on the other. In the UK such tensions have inevitably favoured consistency and experiments in spatial variegated neoliberalism have been highly circumscribed and centrally controlled. Ultimately, while there has been some experimentation and differentiation such spatial variegation has been marginal (Haughton *et al.*, 2010). Part of the reason for this relates to the influence of UK-wide policy communities and 'learning' that provide a limit on more radical change. Another reason concerns the deliberate attempt to restrict diversity through the use of concordats between, for example, the Scottish Executive and the UK Parliament on the scope of divergence. However, the most significant factor concerns the influence of businesses and economic interests on policy agendas.

There has long been a concern among business and economic interests that devolution would lead to a less sympathetic neoliberal policy and regulatory environment, particularly in Scotland where the scope for difference was felt to be more significant. This 'scare story' has been deployed by business interests in order to resist and thwart planning change, such as the proposed third party right of appeal. However, spatially variegated neoliberalism is not only to be found at the national level flowing from deliberate processes of devolution. A variety of new scales and spaces of planning linked to economic and neoliberal agendas have emerged in recent years. I explore these new 'hard' and 'soft' spaces of planning in Chapter 8.

The temporal, spatial and sectoral variegation of neoliberalism has not been automatic or uncontested. Experience highlights how neoliberal spatial governance has been rolled out in the face of the challenges presented by other competing discourses concerning, for example, climate change and sustainable development. Neoliberalization is creative and flexible in meeting such challenges, unfolding in pragmatic and spatially variable ways as neoliberal principles translate into a range of policy and governance approaches, responding to both existing and emerging institutional arrangements and social, economic and political landscapes (see Brenner and Theodore, 2002). One result is that neoliberalism may be subject to temporary setbacks accepting these as necessary battles lost in the longer war of neoliberalization. As Raco (2005) rightly argues, we should not necessarily assume that in all circumstances the particular strategy of the state will be consistent with broader neoliberal tenets. We can also expect hybrids between neoliberalism and other philosophies to exist (Peck, 2010).

Periodizing the neoliberalization of planning

Having discussed the temporal and spatial variegation of neoliberalism I now wish to turn to how this has manifested itself in planning. However, this is not a straightforward task. Part of the success of the neoliberalization of planning is that superficially planning looks similar, with a consistency in terminology and familiar institutions and concepts. Yet there are important and distinct shifts. Table 5.2 attempts to capture some of these through comparing the changes in specific dimensions of planning.

Table 5.2 serves to highlight the enduring characteristics of planning between its shift from being a regulatory mechanism to a form of neoliberal spatial governance. For example, it is not that neoliberal planning has dispensed with scale and hierarchies, but instead has introduced new forms and understandings of scale and hierarchy that help to deliver growth. The contrast with the crude deregulatory approach of the 1980s could not be starker: non-plan has been replaced by market-supportive plan.

A further dimension that is worth highlighting is the evolution of such changes though subtle and evolutionary shifts. Periodizations of neoliberalism are usually and necessarily painted with a broad brush. The nuances of national and sectoral experiences are largely overlooked. Global abstractions of neoliberalization highlight eras of rollback and roll-out, disarticulated and deepening (see, for example, Peck and Tickell, 2002). Such periodizations are conscious of the temporal, spatial and sectoral variegations of neoliberalism and act as a necessary starting point in the understanding of more nuanced and micro-level understandings. In this section I attempt a more fine-grained, sectoral and spatial periodization of neoliberalism focusing on the changes to planning in England over the past few decades. This approach seeks to fill in some of the detail from more broad brush approaches and understand the dimensions and drivers of

Table 5.2 Selected key characteristics of regulatory and neoliberal spatial governance

Dimension	Regulatory planning	Neoliberal spatial governance	Change
Scale and hierarchy	Planning linked to administrative boundaries of local and regional government. Hierarchical relationship between scales of planning provides consistency and conformity.	Increasing use of soft space forms of strategies and governance at all scales to create functional planning areas and to facilitate development. 'Hard' or statutory spaces remain as residualized regulatory spaces.	Flexible and relational spaces and scales overlaid onto top-down hierarchies of planning and government.
Space	New planning spaces followed administrative or institutional reform.	Linking and coordinating institutions through cost-efficient strategies and visions rather than expensive and time-consuming institutional reorganizations.	Rigid to flexible and temporary.
Inputs	Some tradition of external inputs into strategy making thought process linear and state-led.	Privatization and visioning through international competitions drawing upon comparisons of 'successful' places. Allows difficult issues to be raised and tested with deniability if unpopular.	State-led to privatized.
Purpose	Planning acts in the wider public interest balancing competing demands on land and property though within overall market-supportive framework.	Focus upon economically 'successful places' with emphasis upon 'sustainable growth' and 'win-win' outcomes. Trade-offs and distributional issues and consequences downplayed.	Mediated, public interest to growth focused.

Dimension	Regulatory planning	Neoliberal spatial governance	Change
Mechanisms	Strategies and plans durable with fixed lifespans and timescales.	Strategies and tools of planning created and destroyed easily and cheaply in constant search for successful strategies and fixes. Easy exit if deemed ineffective or inappropriate.	Enduring to ephemeral.
Role of plans	Land use strategies key statutory documents within local government.	Governance and strategies separate or alongside existing planning regulatory structures and processes. Draws upon other regulatory frameworks and traditions.	Single plan to multitude of plans and strategies.
Role of state in development	State-led development more common – rowing not steering.	Execution and implementation dependent upon a wide variety of state and non-state actors.	Direct to indirect.
Ethos	Range of orthodoxies of planning concerning protection of the countryside and separation of uses underpins land use policies.	Radical visions used to unsettle and challenge orthodoxies and path dependencies.	Orthodox to heterodox.
Relationship to market	Planning manages growth mediating between market and other interests.	Planning and strategies orientated towards partnering and facilitating market. Performance and outcomes of strategies and governance judged and rewarded through market incentives.	Market-supportive to market-driven.
Relationship between plans	Strategic planning through national and regional scales balances local with other aspirations.	Competition between places encouraged as part of experimental and market-driven governance strategy.	Balanced growth to competition between places.

Table 5.2 (continued)

Dimension	Regulatory planning	Neoliberal spatial governance	Change
Governance	Clear hierarchy of state actors and responsibilities.	Multiple public and private governance institutions with sometimes overlapping geographical areas and areas of strategic responsibility, engendering both competition and cooperation across governance bodies.	Simplicity to multiplicity.
Accountability	Engagement limited within professionally driven processes and discourses. Consultation of preferred options rather than engagement in determination of options.	Relying for legitimacy on non-representative forms of democracy, or indirect links through nominated 'members' from elected bodies, in favour of participative and direct (e.g. referenda or project-specific public consultation exercises).	Democratically limited to remaking democracy.
Role of professionals	Range of professionally driven orthodoxies and doctrines help to define the objectives and processes of planning.	Actively engaged in strategies for changing public opinion through various tactics of presenting alternative strategies or governance bodies as problematic.	Closed discourses to open and active discourses.

change in planning. From a more sectorally driven understanding a host of issues and questions emerge such as how was neoliberalism governed and managed within a complex landscape of institutions and actor networks? Was there resistance to neoliberalization, what forms did this take and in what circumstances was it successful?

There are two underlying dimensions to my periodization of neoliberal planning. First, the periodization set out in Table 5.3 is based on a tripartite distinction which posits neoliberalism as an overarching *philosophy* within which *paradigms* provide underlying assumptions and organizing principles that allow policy actors to interpret situations within common frames, defining the problems to be solved and the methods to solve them through the third level of *policies* (Allmendinger and Haughton, 2012). Policies are developed by policy actors in response to particular issues and are constructed and debated within the limits established by paradigms and philosophies. This is commonly referred to as a neo-institutionalist understanding (see Schmidt, 2008; Lowndes, 1996, 2005).

The distinction between philosophies, paradigms and policies acknowledges the importance of discursive frames within which options and strategies are understood but it also highlights differences in duration and persistence. Paradigms and policies evolve and change in the medium term through public debate. Paradigms, such as the deregulatory, pro-business approach between 1979 and 1990 (see Table 5.3), constitute distinct eras of neoliberal philosophy. Given the different and sometimes contradictory strands of neoliberal thinking paradigms represent temporary settlements and compromises that characterize a particular approach. As can be seen from Table 5.3 they also have attendant policies that represent the material, day-to-day manifestations of neoliberalism. Policies are mainly facilitative of neoliberalism but can also deflect and resist it. Under this framework philosophies are a relatively enduring collection of underlying assumptions and tenets while paradigms and concomitant policies evolve in response to 'crises' connected with the outcomes or contradictions of neoliberalism.

This threefold distinction between philosophies, paradigms and policies reflects fundamental features of UK planning which, despite the normative and to lesser degrees practical shifts towards more networked forms of governance, remains predominantly embedded within cascading, hierarchical state processes and institutional frameworks. This allows for a 'policy tether' and helps to ensure that national neoliberal paradigms are influential and that local policies are pursuant to wider objectives. Yet the discretionary and semi-autonomous nature of planning allows for the creative interpretation of paradigms, 'making sense' of them to fit local circumstances. The spaces between paradigms and policies become 'creative gaps' in which there is an invitation to interpret and construct approaches to material, specific and local issues within a broader understanding. This provides for policy and institutional experiments, evolution and feedback within paradigms.

Table 5.3 Periodizing English planning as a form of neoliberal spatial governance

Era	Dominant paradigm	Key themes	Dominant scales	Key scalar tensions or scalar fault lines	Key moments and policies	Outcomes
1979–91	Pro-business, deregulatory approach: rollback neoliberalism.	Planning system reactionary and explicitly market focused. Conditional local experimentation (e.g. EZs, UDCs, SPZs). Release enterprise and reduce regulatory burdens. Dismantling apparatus for regional strategy making. Disbelief in ability of planning's ability to be long-term in its strategic gaze.	National through market-driven legislation and policy. Minimization of local discretion through use of zoning mechanisms and appointed boards. Some centrally prescribed local experimentation, notably UDCs and EZs.	National vs regional, as regional institutions dismantled or downgraded some areas created informal regional planning bodies. National vs metropolitan counties (with met counties abolished 1986). National impatience with local government (e.g. in some cases UDCs imposed).	Local Government, Planning and Land Act 1980 introduced EZs and UDCs. Circular 22/80 removing design from planning considerations. Housing and Planning Act 1986 introduced SPZs. 'The Future of Development Plans' Consultation, 1986 removing the need to prepare development plans. 'Lifting the Burden' White Paper, 1985 1987 Use Classes Order introduced B1 Use Class allowing change of use from industry to offices without need to obtain planning permission. Emphasis upon speed of decision making in development control, monitored through targets.	Uncertainty for communities and landowners over future development. Large number of new settlement proposals introduced that threatened government popularity. Local authorities often ignored policy changes undermining them. Evidence that some high-profile initiatives such as SPZs were used for ends other than those envisaged by Government, i.e. increasing regulation. Growing environmental concerns towards the latter part of the era, especially after 1989, helped to force a rethink.

Era	Dominant paradigm	Key themes	Dominant scales	Key scalar tensions or scalar fault lines	Key moments and policies	Outcomes
1991–97	Centralized, hierarchal, policy-led: 'state steering'.	Plan-led, proactive planning. Expansion of central policy guidance, introduction of plan-led approach to ensure consistency and certainty.	National and local. Reintroduction of regional steering through devolution of Government Offices.	Counties and national government (especially Home Counties in relation to housing numbers).	Planning and Compensation Act 1991 introduced 'plan-led' approach representing a U-turn. Planning Policy Guidance (PPG) 1, General Policy and Principles and PPG 12 Development Plans, 1992 both set out new proactive planning framework. Government office of regions role enhanced (c.1994). Kyoto Agreement, 1997 provided further impetus to planning to mitigate impact of climate change.	Rigid, hierarchical control required plans and policies to be up to date and material. This was often not the case and system fell back into project-led approach of previous era. Separation of plan from permission meant that certainty over future development was provisional and dependent upon securing planning permission. System remained slow.
1997–2000	Rolled-out neoliberalism. Pragmatic and fluid: searching for a new scalar fix.	Devolution and economic development through RDAs.	Resurgence in regional and devolved nation planning and economic development. New regional strategies and organizations.	National vs regional and new nations as devolution opened up possibility of divergent strategies.	Modernising Planning Green Paper, 1998. Urban Task Force Urban Renaissance 1998. McKinsey Report, 1998. Scotland Act 1998, Wales Act 1998, Regional Development Agency Act 1998. Regional Assembly model rolled out from 1998.	Devolution and rescaling ignored more fundamental issues with development plans and development control. New fix simply added an additional level of regulation which, combined with emerging new agendas such as urban renaissance, exposed a complex sets of processes and plans.

Table 5.3 (continued)

Era	Dominant paradigm	Key themes	Dominant scales	Key scalar tensions or scalar fault lines	Key moments and policies	Outcomes
2000–02	Speed and certainty: rescaling agendas and debates.	Speed and certainty of planning service through targets and incentives. 'Modernization' and 'culture change' through proposed new system of development plans at regional and local scales.	National and regional. National level to provide themes and objectives, the regional scale to determine outputs from system such as housing targets. The local level would identify sites.	Aim of democratically elected regional assemblies was dropped after north east referendum. Lack of legitimacy stored up problems over housing and growth-led strategies in the future.	Local Government Act, 2000 introduced local Strategic Partnerships and Community Strategies. Urban White Paper, 2000 (as above) CBI Planning Brief, 2001 criticized slowness and uncertainty of planning. Planning Green Paper, 2001 proposed to speed up and create greater certainty through new system of development plans. Business Planning Zones (BPZs). Planning Delivery Grant aimed to speed up development control.	The proposed new system of development plans came under heavy criticism from House of Commons Select Committee and Royal Commission on Environmental Pollution. Complex objectives including sustainable development could not be achieved with a scaled-back system. Change of Secretary of State in 2002 led to U-turn on objectives of new system, but not the new system of development planning.

Era	Dominant paradigm	Key themes	Dominant scales	Key scalar tensions or scalar fault lines	Key moments and policies	Outcomes
2002–06	Spatial planning: housing and development without conflict.	Multi-sectoral and multi-scalar coordination and integration of development. Sustainable development and climate change through development. Move from 'balancing' objectives of each other to win-win approach. Metaregions promoted to pursue growth in Thames Gateway and Northern Way.	Scalar functionality: national scale provided discourses around sustainable growth, regional tier provided targets across local and sub-regional boundaries, local scale implemented and delivered through new, more easily prepared and adopted development plans. Housing market remains dysfunctional, overheated in south while struggling in parts of north. Four national growth areas designated in south, plus nine housing renewal pathfinders in North and Midlands.	Regional tier increasingly seen as imposing growth creating tensions with elected local tier. City regions increasingly identified as being critical to deliver housing growth and economic development. Required complex, multi-agency partnerships. Overlooked aspect of system was development control which became politicized and the focus for contestation.	Planning and Compulsory Purchase Act, 2004 introduced new system of development planning. Sustainable Communities Plan, 2003 emphasized growth strategy. Barker Review, 2004 focused upon housing delivery. Egan Review, 2004 explored the skills needed within the built environment professions to deliver growth agenda. PPS 1 and PPS 12, 2005 introduced notion of spatial planning. Local Area/Multi-Area Agreements (MAAs) introduced to help to promote sub-regional and multi-tier partnerships. Planning Advisory Service and Advisory Team Large Applications to assist Authorities (ATLAS), 2004 among other measures introduced to help to manage and facilitate new growth agenda.	Strategic behaviour on part of local planning authorities meant that targets achieved though speed not improved. Skills deficit and lack of resources within local planning authorities limited roll out of new approach. Mismatch between local government boundaries and functional (e.g. sub-regional) planning areas undermines delivery requiring complex and unwieldy partnership 'glue'. Lack of incentives for communities to accept more development. Multiple objectives caused confusion on the ground – what was sustainable development? Lack of understanding of the point of the new approach: Stafford & Lichfield Core Strategies found unsound, 2006.

Table 5.3 (continued)

Era	Dominant paradigm	Key themes	Dominant scales	Key scalar tensions or scalar fault lines	Key moments and policies	Outcomes
2006–10	Economic-led delivery: scaling back ambitions.	Explicitly economy and competition focused. Delivery and outcomes prioritized Re-parameterizing consensus-based approach, notably Infrastructure Planning Commission.	National and sub-regional. City regions and MAAs as sub-regional forms experimented with.	Regions and national. Devolved nations and national as they struggle to gain new powers and regions as they face possible abolition.	Planning Act 2008 introduced Infrastructure Planning Commission. PPS 4 heralded new competition led policy, particularly on retail. Killian Pretty Review, 2008 led to widespread streamlining of planning processes. Barker Review, 2006 highlighted the importance of economic development in sustainable development. Planning White Paper, 2007 reformed the reformed system. Sub-National Review and Taking Forward Sub-National Review, 2008 highlighted sub-regional planning PPS 12, 2008 streamlined plan-led approach.	Economic downturn has temporarily removed some of the growing conflict around development. However, clear refocus of system, polices and outcomes to more explicit growth agenda. Resistance from some local planning authorities over top-down housing and development targets.

Era	Dominant paradigm	Key themes	Dominant scales	Key scalar tensions or scalar fault lines	Key moments and policies	Outcomes
					Framework for Regeneration, 2008 focused on economic case for regeneration. Development Management Consultation, 2009 further attempt to create a pro-development culture change in planning. Local Democracy, Economic Development and Construction Act 2009 merged regional spatial and economic strategies. Infrastructure Planning Commission established and National Policy Statements on energy published. Community Infrastructure Levy that seeks to minimize local discretion introduced.	

Table 5.3 (continued)

Era	Dominant paradigm	Key themes	Dominant scales	Key scalar tensions or scalar fault lines	Key moments and policies	Outcomes
2010–	Pro-market localism. Deregulation of controls and targets. Loosening of policy cascade and hierarchy.	Localism. Greater control over development if a plan is in place. Termed 'Open Source Planning' by coalition. Allowing variation in approaches and policies within loose national framework.	National through permission attitude towards local variegation. Sub-regional through the 'duty to cooperate' across administrative boundaries. Local. Local planning to reflect local priorities within promarket context. Simplified planning regimes and necessity to have plan in place to be able to resist development pressure.	Local versus local. Resisting development in high demand, mainly southern English localities leads to emergence of NIMLA (Not in My Local Area) attitudes. Wealthy areas choosing to forego financial inducement to bring forward more housing development. The word 'region' becomes almost unmentionable in policy circles.	Coalition government agenda for planning expected in a Localism Bill. National Infrastructure Planning Commission folded into the Planning Inspectorate. White Paper on Local Economic Growth in Nov 2010 emphasizes functional, sub-regional planning for economic growth and prosperity.	Abolition of RSSs and RDAs and creation of 24 LEPs between regional and local levels. Withdrawal of Core Strategies in some areas. Decrease in expected housing delivery regardless of recession. Density targets abolished.

Table 5.3 sets out several distinctive dominant paradigms and links these with a range of strategies and policies. Such an approach enables a better appreciation of the punctuated and natural evolution of planning, the distinctive approaches and eras and the patterns of change, including repetition and experimentation. Thus, for example, UDCs and EZs were policies or strategies within the distinct deregulatory planning paradigm of 1979–91. The periods in Table 5.3 provide a broad starting point though, like all heuristics, the distinctions suggest clear boundaries between the eras, while in reality such clarity is misleading and masks and overlaps contradictions and 'ragged edges'. As well as being a key characteristic of the 1979–91 paradigm UDCs appeared again during 2002–06 though in a modified form more aligned to the then paradigm that emphasized community engagement. Similarly, while EZs were a flagship policy of the 1980s they were being considered by the coalition government in 2011. As I noted earlier, the 1980s planning 'presumption in favour of development' had been dropped by the 1990s, but in 2010 the coalition announced its intention to create a very similar, if subtly nuanced, reversion to a 'presumption in favour of sustainable development' (Conservative Party, 2010a). My framework plays down the idea of a linear account of progress in planning, and instead highlights patterns of regular change shaped by an underlying logic and mediated through institutional economics and social/professional contexts. The patterns of change highlight dead ends, U-turns and the multiplicity of ways in which planning experiments are unleashed or recalled. Evolution is based on changes in professional thinking and discourse, involving episodic and incomplete learning from the past and or present, enmeshed within a fast-moving political context which alters the boundaries of what is feasible.

The second feature of this approach concerns the nature of the periods themselves (Hay and Farrall, 2011) and is based on the identification of distinct eras of coherent, substantive policy content. The fifth column in Table 5.3 sets out such key moments and policies with secondary policy dimensions and implications, in particular scalar dominance (third column) and scalar tensions and fault lines (fourth column) helping to define distinct eras. Based on this methodology Table 5.3 sets out seven distinctive periods of planning from 1979 onwards. Each period has a dominant paradigm and associated dominant scales for policy innovation, signature policy moments, and scalar fault-lines.

What is apparent from Table 5.3 is the unsettled (and unsettling) pursuit of a stable mode of spatial governance and the inevitability of further periods of change as new configurations emerge and replace existing paradigms. What is also evident is that each era is distinguished by different emphases, tools, policies, instruments, discourses and scales. This is not to suggest that each paradigm is a simple reaction against the inevitable failure of planning to address the tensions within neoliberalism. While there is an element of reaction there is also a degree of evolution and learning as subsequent approaches build upon, rearrange and add to the institutional and policy fixes of each previous era. Equally, there is also a degree of comparative learning from within a jurisdiction (e.g. other sectors and regulatory frameworks) and outwith (e.g. approaches used in other countries).

The periodization reveals quite starkly the way in which scalar tensions have been ever present throughout the past thirty years as politicians have sought new scalar fixes that transcend some of the barriers, as they see them, to effective planning. This suggests that these barriers provide greater obstacles than merely having to find the appropriate scales for strategic thinking and delivery. It also suggests the folly of unrealistic expectations about the ability of any newly empowered scale of governance, such as 'regions' or 'city regions', to provide a 'silver bullet' solution to long-standing planning problems. Indeed, Table 5.3 is suggestive of the prosaic realities of the historical as well as contemporary institutional dynamics of planning, which has long seen itself as coordinating others in pursuit of the good society.

Conclusions

There are three main points I wish to emphasize in this chapter. First, the unsettled pursuit of neoliberalism through planning has significant implications for the scales and spaces of planning as highlighted in Table 5.3. Planning reform and change is both restless and regular though this cyclical change provides a challenge to planning itself. For example, long-term strategic planning, particularly at the regional level, requires significant investment of time and resources. Regular reform even over a ten-year cycle does not provide the necessary continuity for strategic planning, particularly around major infrastructure investment for the public sector and land assembly and investment for the private sector. Such disruption means that planners adapt to new approaches, scales and spaces in the knowledge that such an investment will likely be futile in the inevitable event of more reform. So the different eras of neoliberalism are both unstable and deficient, leading to sub-optimal regimes that will inevitably lead to calls for further reform.

Second, while neoliberalism is restless and regular it is important to note its contingent and variable nature in relation to planning. As a set of ideas and theories around freeing markets and private property from 'socialization' (Gough, 2002) neoliberalism lacks purchase and needs a 'host' to act as the focus and mediate the ideational. There is also an important day-to-day role in resolving tensions and contradictions within neoliberalism itself as well as helping to conjure up experiments in neoliberal planning. This day-to-day role places an emphasis upon and is undertaken by planners charged with place making either consciously or unconsciously. There are numerous opportunities for this creative role. Table 5.3, for example, identifies key scalar tensions or fault lines highlighting the contradictions and spaces of opportunity where neoliberalism is actively managed and facilitated. This active and creative role for agency echoes and adds to some of the debates about 'strong' and 'weak' interpretations of neoliberalism (Gibson-Graham, 2008). One further dimension largely overlooked in this debate concerns the 'ruptures' between these different eras and the role of planners in managing transitions between different paradigms and related policy, scalar and governance change. Neoliberalism could not be as resilient or enduring without a willing partner – the term 'collaborative planning' takes on a new and quite different meaning when looked at in this way. I explore this more in the next chapter where we discuss crises and crisis management in relation to planning and planners. Under neoliberalism planners take on the role of 'problem solvers' not just in relation to development but also in resolving tensions in the system within which they work.

Finally, despite the restless, regular and contingent nature of reform the 'big picture' of change is one of planning being appropriated in various ways to act as a form of neoliberal spatial governance. The transformation of planning into neoliberal spatial governance has not been straightforward or unproblematic. While the crude, deregulatory approach of the 1980s was resisted by planners the neoliberalization of planning has been a more subtle affair willingly facilitated by, inter alia, planners and academics, partly to further what was regarded as a progressive agenda and partly to thwart the possibility of a further round of deregulation. While variable in space and time the shifts in planning can be understood to involve three elements or constants. The first concerns the narratives or discourses that help to 'make sense' of reform and change in any particular era as well as distinguishing and justifying change. The ethos of a particular era of neoliberal spatial governance – spatial planning, localism, etc. – gives a direction and purpose as well as helping planners to 'fix' or restore the inherent tensions within any particular regime or era of neoliberalism. The second constant element in reform is the ways in which space and scale are created, abolished and reformed as part of this restless search for a market supportive and facilitative planning. Each era has a variety of new spaces of planning and/or places increased or decreased significance upon existing spaces. Finally, the governance and politics of planning are subject to change and reform. On the one hand a more active, aware and informed public seeks to engage with issues concerning growth and change in the built and natural environment. On the other hand growth strategies require certainty and speed. Planners are therefore drawn into reconciling the need for accountability and transparency for a pro-growth agenda that they need to portray as in the 'public interest'. The upshot has been the emergence of new forms of politics that seek to manage such tensions in planning.

The next chapters are structured around these three elements – ethos, space/scale and politics – and explore how planning has been shaped into neoliberal spatial governance through these lenses.

6 A new ethos

Introduction

Following the collapse of state socialism in Eastern Europe, from the late 1980s the way was open for neoliberalism to spread and evolve unencumbered by ideological alternatives. The left's search for new forms of progressive theory and practice led to fragmentation and multiplicity, leaving the field clear for a more relaxed and experimental neoliberalism with a market-based and -supportive planning. Yet the victory of the market and its subsequent and enhanced dominance as a form of governance was to be found not in the eradication or minimalization of the state and public bodies to a 'nightwatchman' role as attempted during the 1980s, but in a more subtle approach that could now draw upon and employ some of the language and notions of the left relating to social inclusion and progress. This colonization came as much from an acceptance by the left that, in the words of Margaret Thatcher, 'there is no alternative', as it did from the right's concern to legitimize and consolidate market-based government. If the public was increasingly focused upon issues such as the environment, housing affordability, climate change and social inclusion then these issues needed to be addressed in ways that were market orientated. Neoliberalism fuses public legitimacy with a market-supportive and -orientated planning. As the New Right had discovered the crude deregulation of the state and planning characteristic of the 1980s ignored the needs of the market that required a supportive state as well as a legitimate one.

As I argued in Chapter 4 the Conservative governments of the 1980s and 1990s had attempted to reform planning first through deregulation and then centralization. Neither approach was successful in achieving the aims of a minimalist, market-supportive planning. The reasons for this failure came down to the complex and symbiotic relationship between planning and land and property markets. The nationalizing of development rights affected landowners though the planning system itself helped to create certainty and regulated the supply of developable land, thus reducing risk for investors and developers. Deregulation and the move towards a more free market-based approach in the 1980s sought to free up supply-side constraints, although this created uncertainty and risk for new development as well as for existing investments and users. In addition, deregulation and greater centralization failed to account for the political impacts of reform: planning controls were popular with the traditional, conservative-minded constituency that had elected the Conservatives. One role of planning was to manage markets, providing certainty and information for the actors involved including local communities. There is an irony, therefore, that it was the successive Labour governments of Tony Blair that provided the forms, language and processes for planning that were to prove far more successful in rolling out neoliberalism. This was achieved by combining a market-supportive role for planning with wider social and environmental objectives. It was the social dimension and the lack of wider support and legitimacy that was missing from the crude, deregulatory approaches of the 1980s and 1990s. In the 2000s planning was again given a range of purposes that drew upon the theories and language of the left, particularly the planning community, giving it legitimacy beyond the narrow confines of developers and investors to include a wider society concerned with the environment and social inclusion. Third Way planning was not some 'middle way' between liberalism and socialism but a complex package of initiatives concerned with managing and delivering growth in ways that caused the minimum of fuss and the maximum of efficiency.

In planning, this combination of legitimacy and market-based planning was to be achieved through three main mechanisms: a new politics, new spaces and scales, and a new ethos. In this chapter I focus upon the new ethos of planning widely labelled as spatial planning. I begin with a brief overview of the emergence of spatial planning as a new ethos in 2002–04 and how it sought to shift planning from a public mechanism concerned with trade-offs and antagonisms between growth, environmental protection and social objectives to an approach that eschewed trade-offs and instead sought 'win-win' outcomes in classic New Labour ways. This shift was not simply a naive attempt to 'square the circle' but a deliberate tactic to deliver growth and place planning at the heart of Labour's local government modernization agenda against a Treasury-led inclination to deregulate.

Yet the spatial planning era was always a temporary fix: the weight of expectations that a consensus-based approach could deliver new development that was socially inclusive *and* environmentally sensitive was always going to be exposed as idealistic and unrealistic. What the experiences of spatial planning highlight, however, is the experimental, ephemeral and resilient nature of neoliberal spatial governance. Spatial planning was a distinct era and ethos for planning that followed attempts to roll back planning in the 1980s and centralize it in the 1990s. We can see the subsequent approach of localism from 2010 as a successor ethos that is itself temporary and experimental. Significantly, the 'blame' for each successive failure is laid at the door of planning itself: it was not the credit crunch and subsequent recession that were blamed for the decrease in housing supply in the late 2000s but state interventions in markets and spatial planning in particular. The argument from the right was that it was not lax regulations that led to financial meltdown but too much state control, including planning. What is overlooked is that some of the changes of the

2000s, particularly the new regime of development planning introduced at the same time as spatial planning, were actually beginning to have an impact, e.g. on issues such as increasing housing supply. Nevertheless, when the credit crunch came a scapegoat was needed in order to draw attention away from the inherent crisis of capitalism.

This is not to say spatial planning was blameless or an innocent bystander. Far from it. The ethos of spatial planning began to crack under the weight of its inherent tensions and enormous expectations before the shift to localism in 2010 (see Chapter 9). However, the shift from one planning ethos to another was not simple or clean. Spatial planning had legacies and consequences that lingered long after New Labour had been removed from office. The first is the damage on planning as an activity, process and profession. There is an important distinction that needs to be made between spatial planning as an ethos, i.e. a set of beliefs and ideals that help to shape the application and objectives of planning, and the tools and processes of planning itself. Ideally, one would expect an ethos to influence all aspects of an activity, thus providing a coherent purpose and basis for acting that is reflected in the tools and processes. As I go on to discuss, spatial planning and the new system of development planning which were introduced simultaneously even though they were actually quite independent of each other. The new system of development planning introduced in 2004 under Labour – RSSs and LDFs – provided an understandable evolution of planning with the introduction of a strategic, target-driven tier at the regional level and a suite of flexible development documents locally. While by no means perfect there was at least an attempt to evolve the tools of planning and give it a more strategic role in coordinating development and growth at the regional scale. Spatial planning, as an additional, overarching ethos, provided an added layer of complex and confusing objectives for this change making it less likely, if at all, that the new system of regional strategies and LDFs would be successfully rolled out and effectively implemented. Spatial planning was championed by a range of interests as an attempt to head off the divergent and seemingly irreconcilable demands for deregulation, social inclusion and climate change adaptation and mitigation. That spatial planning failed to achieve these aims undermined the credibility of and trust in planning. The second legacy is the excuse that the failure provided for more radical reform of planning, an excuse that was a useful front for the more ideological driven austerity-driven changes and politics from 2008 onwards.

From New Right to New Left

The Labour Party had little interest in planning while in opposition. The internecine battle over the future of the party in the 1980s combined with an understandable focus upon high-profile areas such as health, education and welfare overshadowed what little interest there was in land use planning. Planning, if it was considered at all, was perceived by the party as a largely middle-class concern with protecting rural Conservative voters from new development or an irrelevance to the declining fortunes of urban areas. When in government from 1997 the attitude towards planning was largely one of continuity from the outgoing Conservative agenda under John Major. The party's priorities focused upon education, health and demonstrating economic competence. Yet when the party was in power planning could not be ignored in the same way as it could when in opposition and some kind of policy position was needed. An early policy statement, *Modernising Planning* (DETR, 1998), summed up Labour's lacklustre attitude with its focus on speed and efficiency, achieving higher housing densities and reusing brownfield land, objectives that echoed the approach of the Major governments from 1991 onwards. The attitude that planning was a supply-side constraint on economic growth and development, characteristic of the 'Treasury view', continued as RDAs were established from 1998 in the English regions to emulate the success of the Scottish and Welsh development agencies. Planning was nowhere to be seen in Labour's otherwise ambitious agenda for the public sector other than to be blamed for being unreconstructed and in need of 'modernization', whatever that meant. Any connection between planning and Labour's election manifesto pledge (Labour Party, 1997) to safeguard the environment and develop an integrated transport policy to fight congestion and pollution was absent. As the dominant Third Way philosophy of New Labour put it, 'what counts is what works. The objectives are radical. The means will be modern' (ibid.: 1). Judged by the subsequent amount of change, or 'modernization' from 2002 onwards, planning could be considered not to have been working. But in the early days of Labour planning was very much the Cinderella of policy.

Change emerged slowly and came about largely as a consequence of other concerns, chief among which was the realization of the role that planning played in high-profile and electorally sensitive policy areas. Two early concerns of the Deputy Prime Minister, John Prescott, who was responsible for planning at the time, helped to bring planning closer to the top of Labour's agenda. One issue was that there had to be a 'step-change' in new housing provision in order to tackle the historically low levels of building and the problem of affordability. The second issue concerned urban areas including some of the nation's largest conurbations, many of which had been in long-term economic decline and were considered concentrations of social problems. Neither issue was new but it was a reflection of how marginalized planning had become that it was not seen as being clearly linked or part of any government approach. Instead, in what would be a characteristic of Labour's approach to policy an arm's length body was established to provide 'expert' solutions. The Urban Task Force report chaired by Lord Rogers was established in 1998 and mandated to think holistically about urban areas and policy. The underlying view of Rogers was that cities were more than physical manifestations of economic forces; they were places where social and economic consequences and inequalities were played out as well as having a key role to play in addressing environmental issues such as climate change. But the important argument of Rogers that caught the imagination of New Labour was the link between the party's progressive social objectives and the economic success of urban areas. Making the connection between the economic, social and environmental echoed the 'win-win' philosophy of New Labour. The Urban White Paper that followed the Urban Task Force report in 2000 (DETR, 2000a) started to make the link to planning though in a way that still regarded planning as sitting outside the issues, unproblematically implementing policy through reactive regulation of new development.

The ideas from the Urban White Paper were conveyed through a revision to the 1992 national Planning Policy Guidance (PPG) Note 3 Housing (DETR, 2000b) in March 2000. The revised PPG 3 sought to encourage planning to increase development density, reuse brownfield land before greenfield, focus on design quality and integrate transport choice into plans. There was no overall vision or new ethos for planning but simply a series of new considerations to incorporate into a reactive, decision-making process. It is also worth noting that though minimal, these changes did not originate from within the government or from Labour Party policy but from an inquiry of experts. Yet planning at least had begun to have a role in Labour's agenda.

The Urban White Paper was not the only influence on planning in the first Labour government, however. While there was a slow but growing realization within the government that planning was if not a key then certainly a component of some significance in delivering wider policy objectives, there remained another, more familiar, agenda. True to form the Treasury was actively pursuing its long-standing obsession with deregulation. Three Treasury-commissioned inquiries in the early days of New Labour all highlighted how planning controls increased business and consumer costs and decreased competitiveness (McKinsey Global Institute, 1998; DTI, 1999; Better Regulation Task Force, 2000). To complement these inquiries a range of think tanks and business organizations continued to push the notion that planning controls inhibited growth and added to business costs (CBI, 2001). For these bodies planning remained a negative, regulatory tool reflective of a bygone era of 'command and control', state regulation and rationing which was out of kilter with the needs of a modern globalized economy. Such anti-planning views were reminiscent of, if not identical to, those that had helped to shape the deregulatory approach of the 1980s. For those ideologically opposed to planning or any kind of market regulation the attempts to deregulate planning during the 1980s had not been given enough time to demonstrate the benefits. The new business-friendly Labour Party gave such views serious consideration, particularly given the desire to develop its credentials as being substantially distinct from 'Old Labour'.

These tensions between an emerging role for planning on the one hand and an antipathy towards it on the other were to remain a recurrent theme within the government. More immediately the tension was temporarily resolved in favour of the Treasury's agenda by the appointment of Stephen Byers as Secretary of State for Transport, Local Government and the Regions and Lord Falconer as planning minister following the 2001 general election. Both epitomized New Labour and brought a radical and critical perspective to planning. Critical views were not uncommon in the party and elsewhere, given the high-profile planning issues at the time that included the long-awaited decision on Terminal 5 at Heathrow following a planning process lasting eight years. A Green Paper published in 2001 provided the first coherent statement on planning under Labour. *Planning: Delivering a Fundamental Change* (DETR, 2001) was accompanied by a suite of other proposals concerning compulsory purchase powers, major infrastructure, planning obligations and planning fees. The approach was to continue the theme of improving speed and certainty in planning, a theme that could have come from any planning minister of the previous twenty years or more. The underlying understanding of planning was of a bureaucratic process rather than as one having a positive, market-enabling function. As such planning could be made to work in ways that minimized any impact on the market itself by being made to work faster and by being much clearer and upfront about the objectives it was trying to achieve. To realize this Byers proposed replacing local plans with a new kind of plan, known as an LDF. Furthermore, a new tier of plans, RSSs, were to act in both a coordinating and target-setting capacity. RSSs would set region-wide targets for housing and employment growth as well as identifying the infrastructure needed to achieve such growth. These targets would in turn inform the new, local system of LDFs which, rather than being one 'plan', would be a suite of documents, parts of which could be updated and changed quickly and cheaply as necessary. LDFs would be delivery focused and conform to regional targets. Other changes included replacing negotiated and time-consuming planning obligations with a fee, introducing a national planning framework for major infrastructure and the introduction of BPZs within which planning permission would be granted in advance for a range of developments. Within local government more generally a range of performance targets had been introduced under the Best Value regime as well as investment in IT to help to disseminate best practice and manage planning applications electronically. The agenda was very much one of speed and certainty. Planners may not have liked the direction it was taking, but at least it was a direction though one that was nothing like the 'biggest shake-up of planning in fifty years' that Byers promised (DTLR, 2001: 1).

From land use to spatial planning

The 1980s and 1990s had been lean times for planning in the UK. Constant criticism and reforms, however ineffective, had led to an embattled, inward-looking and residualized practice largely concerned with regulating land and property in an ill-defined and variable public interest. The role of planners and planning was to draw up land use plans and take decisions on proposals to develop in accordance with those plans. There had been a number of attempts to reform the separate functions of plan making and decision taking – fundamental and distinct characteristics of UK planning – through zoning-based approaches and other mechanisms such as the expansion of the Use Classes and General Permitted Development Orders. However, these had been at the margins and mainstream practice maintained the separation of plan and permission characteristic of the UK approach to planning. This separation had advantages and disadvantages. The main advantage was that it maintained flexibility and allowed the decision maker – the planner or local planning authority – to take into account a range of factors, of which the plan was one, in determining development rights. The flipside of flexibility is uncertainty. Decisions also did not need a plan, although without a plan there was an even greater lack of certainty about the outcome, the lack of a strategic overview of decisions and possible inconsistency between different localities. The separation of plan and permission was predicated upon having a plan. The problem was that plan making was slow and expensive. During the 1980s the then Conservative government had even discouraged authorities from making plans. Instead, decisions on planning applications were to be made 'on their merits' (DoE, 1986). As it was possible under the UK system to take decisions on proposals in the absence of a plan (or at least an up-to-date plan) so plan making was not a priority for many cash-strapped local authorities. The result was incrementalism and 'planning by appeal' as applicants submitted multiple, similar applications for the same site, appealing to the Planning Inspectorate against the refusal of planning permission. The result was a planning system that was narrow in its scope and horizons, reactionary and lacking a strategic perspective. Morale among planners was low and the profession struggled to attract new applicants. For Ambrose (1986) the question was 'whatever happened to planning?' Byers' proposals in the Green Paper reflected the (accurate) view that planning was 'slow, ponderous and uncertain' (DTLR, 2001: 1). The Green Paper proposals for planning were focused on making the system quicker and more certain for those involved, particularly businesses and developers. For planners, it was more of the same. The previous two decades had been characterized by such language and attitudes within central government. If planning was slow, uncertain and costly the government's solution was to reduce and streamline it rather than to seek to reform it into a more positive role, despite the experiences of the New Right.

Yet Labour's proposals were not the only view on the future of planning. As the Conservatives had found to their cost in the late 1980s there was a growing environmental awareness among the public in general and the rural middle class in particular, the very areas that Labour had successfully courted in 1997 and whose support they needed to retain power. For the Conservatives, the attempts to deregulate planning had been abandoned in the early 1990s in the face of such opposition. This 'pro-planning' constituency was a loose coalition of self-interested, anti-development NIMBYS combined with environmental campaigners who saw planning controls as a means to help to address climate change. This more supportive view of planning was shared by others. The House of Commons Select Committee on Transport, Local Government and the Regions was highly critical of the pro-development Green Paper in its report in 2002 (HoC, 2002) while the Royal Commission on Environmental Pollution called for planning to be reorientated better to address environmental issues and protection (RCEP, 2002). The Select Committee agreed with the analysis in the Green Paper but argued that the reason that planning was slow and reactive was that it was under-resourced and lacked direction and vision. These two bodies were not alone in seeing fundamental problems with Labour's proposals. Responses from business were lukewarm at best. There was particular concern about the proposed new development plans, Local Development Frameworks, envisaged by the government as being quicker and cheaper to prepare and update. Instead of a single document LDFs would be a suite of documents, parts of which would not need updating while other parts could be monitored and updated as and when required. Concern was expressed that the introduction of a new system of development plans would cause upheaval and delay and that greater attention should be paid to making the existing system work. In retrospect, the concern that introducing a new system of plans would lead to delay and uncertainty was proved correct. Yet this anxiety was overtaken by events in May 2002 when Byers was moved and the Department of Transport Local Government and the Regions was subsumed within a newly created Office of the Deputy Prime Minister (ODPM) under John Prescott. Prescott had a much broader vision for planning and the public sector and was far less enamoured with the 'less is more' view of regulation common within parts of New Labour. Prescott had commissioned the Urban Task Force and followed it through with the Urban White Paper. For him planning and the public sector were more than regulators. An opportunity to reshape the ongoing planning reform agenda had arisen with the appointment of Prescott.

This opportunity was seized by a coalition of interests including the planning profession itself. The new planning would reflect the rhetoric and aspirations of 'old' and New Labour seeking to be progressive, business-friendly and concerned with growth. It would be underpinned by the language and ideas that had been developing in the wake of the breakdown of structuralism and Marxism and the embrace of postmodernism, namely post-structuralism: a planning agenda for the globalized, networked society of new times which would wrap the market-based approach within the language and progressive notions of the left. The label spatial planning emerged to distinguish this planning for new times and provide a discourse that helped to define the problems, issues and solutions. It is worth pointing out that the term spatial planning is bound up with a variety of understandings. There is a long history to some notions of spatial planning and many claim that it can be traced back to the origins of the UK planning system in the late nineteenth century (Allmendinger, 2011). There is also the claim that spatial planning has continental European origins, both in practice and as a Euro-English term that provided a collective term for a variety of planning practices. However, spatial planning, as it emerged and was used in the era after 2002 in the UK, has a much more specific meaning. This confusion of understandings and lineage, whether deliberate or not, served a useful purpose in giving the term a 'back story' and allowing different interests to sign up to the 'new planning' agenda. Such strategic confusion was a characteristic of spatial planning that was to continue throughout the 2000s and prove to be one of its major weaknesses.

The different understandings and definitions of spatial planning were neither reconciled nor helped by the range of ideas that influenced and shaped it. The first influence on the notion of spatial planning was the view, echoing the concerns of relational geographers, that the global spaces of networks and flows required a more flexible and strategic understanding of the nature of space and role for planning. Planning had always looked beyond territorial units and engaged with wider, more strategic issues but the new times of globalization and networked societies pointed towards a less inwards and more outward-looking approach:

> Planning decisions should no longer be constrained by artificial local administrative areas which are often arbitrary and potentially constraining to ensuring the most effective dialogue. Planning must be better related to coherent areas at the local, regional and national levels, in terms of socio-economic geography and natural regions. For example, the areas within which people search for jobs and homes or natural watersheds and river catchments ... This requires a more flexible approach to 'planning areas' dependent upon the issues being addressed – different regions for different issues.
>
> (RTPI, 2001: 5)

Planning needed to be strategic both in the sense of thinking beyond territorial and sectoral boundedness. How this was to be achieved within the UK context of elected local authorities with the legal responsibilities to plan was unclear (see Chapter 8).

The second influence came from notions of collaborative planning and deliberative governance (see Chapter 3), both of which were gaining traction as progressive and inclusive alternatives to representative democracy within academic and some policy circles. The gap between the everyday realities of planning and the holistic, deliberative, inclusive and progressive underpinnings of collaborative planning was, to say the least, wide. Yet collaborative planning and its advocates had a clear normative agenda concerned with equity, social justice, democracy and sustainability – traditional centre-left progressive tenets. According to collaborative advocates, planning should not be apolitical but actively seek to create a better, fairer and just world. Third, there was the mapping of this planning for new times onto New Labour's agenda and language. A number of rich reinterpretations of planning emerged echoing the language and themes of New Labour, particularly around notions of inter-dependency, governance, progress, scalar flux and consensus. For Healey, a new politics of space was emerging from governance rescaling, a shift from man-agerialism to entrepreneurialism in state-market relations, the emergence of public-private partnership-based experiments, new policy spaces and the possi-bility of a new collaborative mode of policy making (Healey, 2006a). For Healey, spatial planning was 'a strategic orientation which emphasizes the spatiality of policy interventions and emphasizes the qualities of places' (2006b: 527).

Spatial planning and its more strategic focus and orientation had come about as a response to new times. Planning was about 'place making', connecting and coordinating the various elements of what constituted places and people's lives. If Labour could distance itself from the past and distinguish itself through the label of *New* Labour then planning could do the same with *spatial* planning. The Royal Town Planning Institute (RTPI)'s *New* Vision for Planning (emphasis added) drew heavily on the New Labour lexicon:

> There is a growing recognition that we are all part of increasingly inter-dependent communities – residential, work-based, regional, national, global. This is giving rise to more complex relationships which need to be managed if we are to create a society of equity and opportunity, to develop an economy that responds to growing demands and to safeguard an environment that can support us and the generations as yet unborn.
>
> (RTPI, 2001: 1)

This aspirational and inspirational language was a far cry from the anti-planning rhetoric of the previous two decades. Planners were used to working within a much narrower, almost piecemeal remit.

The fourth influence on spatial planning concerned giving planning a more positive role in change. Planning was to be repositioned from regulation to partnership, from reacting to change to promoting and working with developers and landowners. As part of this repositioning traditional, 'command and control' styles of planning were contrasted with the new spatial planning emphasizing the differences in outcomes, skills, and ethos. This trick of portraying 'old' and 'new' planning was one that had been deployed by academics in their crude portrayal of a modernist planning at sea in a postmodern world (e.g. Sandercock 1998). A narrative around spatial planning as genuinely distinctive emerged, painting a simplistic and misleading image of 'old style' land use planning and contrasting it with spatial planning to emphasize the change. Table 6.1 provides a clear example of how the Planning Officers Society presented the positive and progressive language and ethos of spatial planning contrasting it with the narrow and limited nature of land use planning. This contrast was as stark as it was misleading. In many parts of the country the 'straw man' of land use or regulatory planning would not be recognized (see Allmendinger, 2011, ch. 5), yet the counterpoint provided a useful device in helping to 'win the argument' that there was a significant difference between 'old' and 'new' planning. However, the distinctions raised clear expectations with little indication of how spatial planning would actually deliver and achieve what amounted to a seismic shift in practices and resources. Normally irreconcilable objectives that were the daily concern of land use planning such as environmental protection, economic development and social inclusion would apparently be reconciled under spatial planning. How this would be achieved and why such a reconciliation had escaped planning in the past was glossed over. As I go on to discuss in the next

Table 6.1 Planning Officers Society contrast of land use and spatial planning

Land use/regulatory	Spatial
Legal framework	
Scope prescribed by statute and case law	Scope significantly broader, though to be prescribed (see below)
Boundaries are familiar	Boundaries to be established
Institutional	
Plan could be prepared in isolation from other agencies	Requires a collaborative approach with a range of agencies
Compatible with silo council organization	Predicated on council having an integrated approach to strategy and delivery
Plan owned by the council	Council leads preparation on behalf of local strategic partnership and a range of agencies owned by a wider community
Planners could be peripheral to the council but still prepare the plan	Expects planners to be engaged in corporate strategy and policy making
Content	
Vision not mandatory	Shared vision required
Objectives constrained to land use	Scope for diverse and more fundamental objectives
Site specific and defined areas for operation of policies	Can contain non-site-based policies
Requirement for general conformity with higher level planning strategy	General conformity with regional/London-based strategy continues, but now also the requirement to use the Community Strategy
Process	
Process generally only of legal concern	Process ongoing and important in itself
Consultation with communities focused on proposals	Early and ongoing engagement with communities, focused on needs, concerns and problems
Consultation with agencies on proposals	Requires consensus with agencies on strategy, integration and delivery
Monitoring a limited suite of data	Monitoring performance on delivery of objectives across the board
Implementation	
Delivery mainly through development control by the local authority	Delivery through a range of channels and range of agencies
Focus on allocations and what gets built (outputs)	Focus on the delivery of objectives and all the elements which go together to achieve them (outcomes)

Source: Planning Officers Society, 2005.

chapter, it was particularly significant that the question of whether it was desirable to seek consensus over competing objectives was not discussed.

Finally, the need for spatial planning to neutralize the Treasury agenda of deregulation was still being promulgated through business and development interests. It transpired that the dominant and crude 'burden on business' view of planning from within the Treasury was open to revision. The key to a change of view, as the CBI realized, was the role of housing affordability in future growth and competitiveness and, in particular, in any move for the country to join the euro. The cyclical nature of the housing market was identified as an impediment to economic convergence with the euro in 2003 (HMT, 2003). In order to smooth out the peaks and troughs of the housing market and the wider effects of house price inflation upon the economy there was need to increase housing supply. Yet this new focus for the Treasury emerged against the more traditional backdrop dominated by the view of planning as a barrier to growth. As the CBI put it in its evidence to the House of Commons Select Committee on the 2001 Green Paper: 'In every respect, in every survey we conduct, every business we talk to … planning is always at the top of the agenda as a fetter on the productivity enhancement and the job creation in British business' (HoC TLGR, 2002: HC476-III). This perspective was reinforced by the HBF, which called the system overly complex and inconsistent: 'Plans are too long and inflexible and preparation timetables are too lengthy' (Memorandum to the House of Commons Transport, Local Government and the Regions Committee, Planning Green Paper, Thirteenth Report of Session, 2001–02, 17). The BPF added that the current system was failing everyone, and was 'overly plan-hierarchical, bureaucratic, unnecessarily complex, slow and inconsistent' (ibid.: 47).

Spatial planning sought to address the deregulatory instincts of the Treasury, arguing that a new approach to planning would not only deliver more housing and improve affordability, it could also do so in ways that were coordinated and integrated with other sectors such as transport and education. This argument had some success within the government though the Treasury itself, while mollified, was not convinced and proceeded in its own attempts at planning reform, announcing the Barker Review of Housing Supply in April 2004. The Barker Review's terms of reference went wider than planning and included the ability of the house building industry to respond to demand (Barker, 2003). However, the planning system was given equal billing as the focus of the inquiry. The timing of the Treasury-led review was curious given the reform of planning going on elsewhere in government. It also managed to add to the confusion over the government's intentions for planning – were the reforms aimed at facilitating spatial planning or were they more akin to Byers' original deregulatory intentions? Such confusion did little to help planners charged with implementing a new development planning system and working towards the new ethos of spatial planning.

The result was that a range of views emerged on what spatial planning 'was' (Allmendinger, 2011: 91–94). For some, spatial planning amounted to little more than a rebranding exercise emphasizing and focusing on how planning was an important facilitator of growth. For others, it was a 'back to the future': spatial planning was putting a label upon what progressive authorities had been doing for some time (e.g. Goodstadt, 2009; Peel and Lloyd, 2007). Others still emphasized the experimental nature of New Labour thinking that sought to create policy laboratories in an inherently fluid and unstable context.

However vague and contested, the notion of spatial planning captured the attention of the government as a way of appeasing the different demands on how planning should be reorientated and reformed. The shift from the attitude in the 2001 Green Paper began to focus more upon 'softer' reform rather than widespread 'harder' institutional and systemic reform. The difference in language and intention from within the government on the purpose of reform and the new role for planning under John Prescott was stark:

> Too often the culture of planning is reactive and defensive. We want a culture which promotes planning as a positive tool: a culture which grasps the opportunities to improve the experience of planning, for those affected by its decisions, whether businesses, community groups, individual members of the community or planning professionals.
>
> (ODPM, 2002: para. 6)

Yet the phrase 'spatial planning' does not feature in the 2002 House of Commons Select Committee's report (HoC, 2002) or the RTPI's submission to the Select Committee. Nor does the notion of spatial planning appear in the Deputy Prime Minister's 2002 announcement on how the government was going to proceed with the 2001 Green Paper (ODPM, 2002). The government intended to proceed with the proposals to create LDFs and RSSs, regarded as necessary for speeding up planning and creating certainty as part of a clear pro-business agenda, but with a new, broader purpose to which this new system would be put to work. *Planning: Delivering a Fundamental Change* (DTLR, 2001) had evolved into *Sustainable Communities: Delivering through Planning* (ODPM, 2002). The 2001 Green Paper was based upon a more traditional view of planning as a 'necessary evil' of land use regulation that *could* be beneficial but needed to be controlled and monitored:

> Getting planning right means that our goals for society are easier to achieve. Good planning can have a huge beneficial effect on the way we live our lives. It must have a vision of how physical development can improve a community. But, some fifty years after it was first put in place, the planning system is showing its age. What was once an innovative emphasis on consultation has now become a set of inflexible, legalistic and bureaucratic procedures. A system that was intended to promote development now blocks it. Business complains that the speed of decision is undermining productivity and competitiveness. People feel they are not sufficiently involved in decisions that affect their lives. So it is time for change.
>
> (DTLR, 2001: Foreword)

The 2002 statement, by contrast, brought into the positive, proactive and spatial understanding of planning a wider remit than merely business interests:

> An effective planning system is essential to delivering the step changes we need to tackle the challenges of ensuring that everyone has the opportunities of a decent home, and the quality of life that goes with that. An effective planning system is essential to delivering our objectives for living communities; for urban and rural regeneration; for improving the country's infrastructure; and for achieving truly sustainable development. Without an effective planning system we risk constraining the economy, at a cost to everyone in the UK ... We want planning to rediscover its purpose, to be a strategic, proactive force for economic prosperity, social cohesion and environmental protection.
>
> (ODPM, 2002: paras 1, 14)

Yet these two very different visions and understandings from 2001 and 2002 were to be achieved through the same proposed means, i.e. the introduction of RSSs and LDFs. This was despite the fact that RSSs and LDFs had originally been envisaged as a means through which planning could be speeded up and greater certainty created and were now vehicles through which spatial planning, a very different notion however it was defined, could be achieved.

This shift in purpose had not gone unnoticed. During the passage of the Planning and Compulsory Purchase Bill there was a debate within Parliament on the purpose of the changes to planning with some cross-party and back-bench concern over what was being proposed. Given the origins of the changes in 2001 and 2002 it was possible for different emphases to be read into the reforms. For some the reforms sought to address regulatory burdens; for others they were about social inclusion, environmental protection, housing affordability or public involvement. This resulted in some confusion:

> It makes me suspect that they [the government] see the legislation as a vehicle to advance the new Labour project – whatever that might be – rather than to make sensible use of the country's land. We will discover that as time goes by.
>
> (David Wilshere MP, *Hansard*, 9 January 2003, Standing Committee G: Col. 016)

There were questions and amendments tabled during the passage of the Bill that sought greater clarity about the purpose and the role of the new arrangements, particularly with respect to the objectives of RSSs, their relationship to the proposed LDFs and the powers of the Secretary of State in directing future change in planning.

The provisions of the Bill and the debates in Parliament were paralleled with the emerging ethos of spatial planning elsewhere and outside Parliament. The RTPI was pushing the notion of spatial planning as a new form of planning and sought to lobby MPs as the Bill proceeded reassuring them that spatial planning could achieve all their wishes. In its *New Vision for Planning* (2001) the broad proposition was that spatial planning was more than land use planning but it was still not clear what it actually was:

> Our focus is on the location and quality of social, economic and environ-
> mental changes. In developing a New Vision for Planning we therefore use
> the term 'spatial planning'. We do so to emphasise that planning is as much
> concerned with the spatial requirements for, and impacts of, policies – even
> where these do not require a 'land-use' plan – as it is with land use zonings.
> The interrelationships, for example, of governmental policy can only be
> properly demonstrated by consideration of their aggregate impacts for
> specific places. 'Spatial planning' operates at all the different possible scales
> of activity, from large scale national or regional strategies to the more
> localised design and organisation of towns, villages and neighbourhoods.
>
> (2001: 2)

Calls for greater clarity were met with more and longer definitions and descriptions. Such calls continued after the Planning and Compulsory Purchase Bill received Royal Assent on 13 May 2004. Building upon the RTPI's definition Baroness Andrews, then Junior Minister for Planning, stated that the 2004 Planning and Compulsory Purchase Act 'establishes a process it [the government] calls 'Spatial Planning'... It facilitates and promotes sustainable and inclusive patterns of urban and rural development. Rather than operating through a narrow technical perspective, spatial planning should actively involve all members of society because everyone has a stake in the places in which they live, work and play' (quoted in RTPI, 2007: 6). The symbiosis between government and profession was further highlighted by the common language on the notion of spatial planning presented to local authorities and planners:

> Spatial Planning goes beyond traditional land use planning to bring together
> and integrate policies for the development and use of land with other
> policies and programmes which influence the nature of places and how they
> function. That will include policies which can impact on land use, for
> example by influencing the demands on, or needs for, development, but
> which are not capable of being delivered solely or mainly through the
> granting or refusal of planning permission and which may be implemented
> by other means.
>
> (ODPM, 2005: 1)

Further backfilling of the definition and notion of spatial planning was also achieved through a series of reports and commissioned research on 'good practice'. An industry grew up around advice and guidance from consultants and academics (e.g. DCLG, 2006a; 2006b) as well as an explosion in national guidance, strategies, reviews such as the Egan Review (ODPM, 2004) and the creation of a host of new semi-independent advisory bodies such as the Planning Advisory Service, Planning Portal and ATLAS, the Improvement and Development Agency (IDeA), Planning and Regulatory Services Online (PARSOL). At the same time the Treasury-driven counter-narrative regarding the role of planning as a constraint on competitiveness and growth was ongoing and drew upon its own reviews and evidence (e.g. Barker, 2004, 2006). While not exactly at war with one another the two distinct views on the purpose of planning created confusion. The Treasury charge against planning led to an inquiry by the ODPM Housing, Planning, Local Government and the Regions Committee entitled *Planning, Competitiveness and Productivity* in 2003 that sought to counter the view, specifically from the CBI, that planning was a burden on business. It concluded that the view was based too much on anecdote and not facts:

> The evidence that we have received suggests that businesses generally support the planning system and seek a number of changes in implementation, which do not necessarily require legislation. The best local authorities already run their planning departments in proactive, responsive ways and if the resources are put in place, such approaches can be adopted by others.
>
> (HoC ODPM, 2003: 5)

It is noticeable that the CBI and other industry groups subsequently toned down their general criticisms of planning and began to focus more upon the speed of decision making, an issue that the government addressed through the Planning Delivery Grant initiative from 2003 (Allmendinger, 2011: ch. 6).

One common way of trying to pin down spatial planning was to contrast it to what went before in an attempt to change attitudes and behaviour but not prescribe action. The Planning Officers Society attempt was typical of this approach (see Table 6.1), seeming to be an attempt by its members to be clear in their own minds about what spatial planning actually was as much as a way to help planners understand it. Another approach to communicating the nature of spatial planning was to rearrange a number of positive, proactive adjectives into new albeit similarly vague definitions:

> A successful planning framework is one that is layered, integrated, and dynamic. Spatial planning is multidimensional, linking development to place, time, and the agents of change. An important principle of spatial planning is that it avoids narrow, exclusive and disjointed practices. It is outcome-focused, but also programme-based.
>
> (UCL and Deloitte, 2007: 11)

None of these approaches and definitions really got to grips with the notion or the upshot that spatial planning was all things to all people, its scope and professional, sectoral and territorial boundaries being fuzzy. It was broadly agreed that spatial planning was not land use planning though there was far less agreement about what it actually was. One consequence of this confusion was a lack of understanding from planners themselves over what was expected: if planners were to become the facilitators of progressive, consensus-based spatial visions in order to create sustainable places they were either unaware of their new incarnation, particularly if they were dealing with the increasing number of planning applications, or unclear what it meant. The reality of planning practice remained more prosaic and less romantic than the aspirations espoused by the government. This relationship between development plan making and development control was a particular issue. There was an assumption within the government and the RTPI that spatial planning as an overarching ethos would naturally encompass development plan making and development control, if not replace them both. Decisions on individual planning applications would naturally 'flow' unproblematically from consensus-based spatial visions, particularly given the strengthening of the statutory link between development plans and decisions in section 38(6) of the 2004 Act. Yet the statutory basis and ethos of development control, which broadly fell within the remit of the 1990 Town and Country Planning Act, was largely left untouched by the changes introduced to development plan making in the 2004 Planning and Compulsory Purchase Act. The connections between the two arms of planning were largely left to the imagination of planners. Planners still had statutory responsibilities to determine planning applications though the criteria against which such proposals would be determined were changing through the explosion in central government planning guidance that sought to explain and backfill the notions of spatial planning and the implementation of the new system of development plans enabled in the 2004 Act. A range of new Planning Policy Statements (PPSs) were published, underpinned by spatial planning notions and replacing the older-style PPGs to further the scope of planning into new or expanded areas that were felt to fall within the ambit of spatial planning. As the Barker Report pointed out in 2006, these new or expanded areas of responsibility went far beyond the traditional remit of planning to include, inter alia, air quality, crime prevention, gambling, noise and health. By 2006 central planning policy guidance ran to over 800 pages (Barker, 2006: 69). As well as expanding the scope of spatial planning to include new areas and considerations the driver behind the expansion was also the need to explain the new system of plans. The two purposes fed each other.

As part of the changes to development plans and the ethos of planning the purpose or objective of planning was also changed in national planning guidance to become the delivery of sustainable development. This was to be achieved through an ethos of spatial planning and the vehicle would be the new system of development plans, LDFs and RSSs along with a plethora of other plans and strategies such as Community Strategies. Community Strategies (after 2007 known as Sustainable Community Strategies) had been introduced in 2000 to promote economic, social and environmental well-being within individual areas. They were envisaged as the 'plan or plans' within which other local plans and strategies would sit, enabling coordination and integration across different sectors and regulatory regimes. PPS 1 *Delivering Sustainable Development*

(ODPM, 2005) was the keystone government guidance on planning. The objectives for planning as a whole were set out as broad and progressive:

> Planning should facilitate and promote sustainable and inclusive patterns of urban and rural development by:
>
> - making suitable land available for development in line with economic, social and environmental objectives to improve people's quality of life;
> - contributing to sustainable economic development;
> - protecting and enhancing the natural and historic environment, the quality and character of the countryside, and existing communities;
> - ensuring high quality development through good and inclusive design, and the efficient use of resources; and
> - ensuring that development supports existing communities and contributes to the creation of safe, sustainable, liveable and mixed communities with good access to jobs and key services for all members of the community.
>
> (Ibid.: para. 5)

If plans were to be given a new and expanded role then it was also one that had to be coordinated with other plans and strategies, particularly the new Community Strategies. '*Planning is a tool for local authorities to use in establishing and taking forward the vision for their areas as set out in their community strategies*' (ibid.: para. 11, emphasis added).

Planners were simultaneously trying to grapple with a new system of planning and a new and less than clear ethos for planning against a backdrop of significantly increasing development activity and a complex context of relationship with the Community Strategies. While well intentioned, the host of new planning guidance managed to generate even less clarity: the more the government tried to explain and prescribe via PPSs and accompanying best practice and technical guidance the more uncertainty was created. In an environment of almost overwhelming guidance prepared by different parts of government over a period of time it was possible to find competing arguments to support a range of positions. Spatial planning was a key mechanism in tackling climate change (DEFRA, 2005; ODPM, 2005), an inclusive and integrative process, a brake on economic development and competitiveness (Barker, 2004, 2006) and a tool of social inclusion and urban renaissance, to name a few objectives and aspirations for spatial planning. How such objectives translated into policies in local circumstances, particularly when top-down targets in regional spatial strategies and performance monitoring around housing were emphasizing speed and certainty, was never satisfactorily resolved.

One way in which local authorities sought to reconcile these multiple objectives was through shifting the 'onus of proof' to the applicant. The abstract and open nature of expanding central guidance about spatial planning provided little in the way of assistance on development decisions. How could a proposal for a new urban housing extension be evaluated and determined against objectives such as sustainability when it was not at all clear what sustainability meant? The common approach was to require developers to demonstrate how their proposals met the tenets of central guidance and objectives. This was achieved through a growth in supporting information requirements: when an application for planning permission was submitted there would be a requirement to submit a wide range of supporting information including a Design and Access Statement, Affordable Housing Statement, Air Quality Assessment, Biodiversity Survey and Report, Economic Statement, Environmental Statement, Flood Risk Assessment, landscaping details, Noise Impact Assessment, Planning Statement and Statement of Community Involvement. The above list is by no means exhaustive. Each of these accompanying statements and assessments was required to demonstrate how the proposal met the objectives of planning and local circumstances. National and local lists of supporting information requirements were published and risk-averse local authorities who were themselves unsure about how to assess proposals against the new planning ethos required applicants to provide as much information as possible. From 2005 the number of supporting documents increased substantially. One outcome was a business boom for planning consultants. Another was to add to the barriers and costs of submitting a planning application.

The cost of supporting information requirements was substantial (Allmendinger, 2011): the number of statements submitted increased almost sixfold at a cost of around £140,000–£180,000 for a development of around 20 dwellings at 2009 prices. This was on top of design fees and planning obligations. The actual impact of such information was less than clear. As concluded by the Killian Pretty Review (established to look into the issue): 'The volume of material associated with applications can be sometimes be huge, and we suspect, from our discussions with stakeholders, that substantial parts of some documents are subject to only minimal scrutiny and assessment' (Crouch, 2008: 51).

The wider implications were also significant. The growth in supporting information requirements had arisen from the need to interpret the meaning of spatial planning and sustainability. The transfer of this interpretation to applicants for planning permission and also those putting forward sites for inclusion in LDFs amounted to an admission of failure on behalf of public planners. However, there were two other implications. First, the submission of a range of assessments and studies to demonstrate that a proposal or site met the objectives of spatial planning and sustainability turned a political exercise into a technical one. The 'experts' employed to undertake such assessments about environmental impacts, noise, traffic, design philosophy, etc. provided expensive and lengthy documents that almost inevitably justified the proposal. It was difficult to challenge such assessments given the ambiguity of what they were seeking to demonstrate, the division of assessments into multiple documents (e.g. design, environment, noise, health, etc.) and the lack of sufficient expert knowledge and resources within local authorities and communities fully to engage with the content. Local authorities that required such information often had to pay for consultants to interpret and assess them, thus further distancing common understandings into the realms of a small cadre of experts. This displacement ended up, as the Killian Pretty Review concluded, in a 'tick box' exercise whereby local authorities required supporting information and interpretations even though these did not actually help to shape outcomes.

The second consequence was that mentioned above, a shift in the 'onus of proof'. There were two rather uneasy presumptions within the planning process at the time, a long-standing presumption in favour of development and a newer presumption in favour of the development plan. The essence of these was that proposals that conformed to the development plan should normally be allowed. Yet under the new planning ethos even if a proposal conformed to the development plan the applicant would still need to 'prove' or at least demonstrate through the submission of supporting information that it achieved or at least addressed a range of new objectives.

Impacts and evaluations

One natural response to the above analysis is that the new ethos of planning provided a range of barriers to growth and housing delivery. Developers have long held that increasing transaction costs in the form of supporting information requirements and making development riskier through uncertainty over what would and would not constitute sustainable development or spatial planning was a 'barrier' to development. Yet the figures in Table 6.2 highlight that during the era of spatial planning, roughly spanning 2004–08, housing supply increased substantially, particularly from the private sector and housing associations. This joint increase is to be expected given that much of the affordable housing delivered is as a proportion of private development through planning agreements. However, the point is that spatial planning presided over an era of significant increases in housing supply.

There is, of course, a question of cause and effect. Did spatial planning as an ethos lead to this increase? There are two dimensions to the answer. The first concerns the influence of the general economic situation and availability of development finance and the second concerns the influence of the new system of development plans that was introduced alongside spatial planning. Disentangling these influences is not easy and any attempt to do so will inevitably be based on individual perspectives of the role of planning. The HBF and the CBI, for example, have long argued that planning placed a significant constraint upon housing supply and continued to do so during this period (Barker 2004, 2006). Yet the figures in Table 6.2 point to a different story. The fall-off in housing delivery from 2007–08 onwards cannot be linked to anything other than the credit crunch and subsequent recession and the necessary increase in future housebuilding has been squarely linked to the availability of finance (HoC CLG, 2012: para. 5). What we can say is that during an era when finance was available the planning system as a whole reacted by, at the very least, facilitating development.

Table 6.2 Housing supply in England 1990–2011

Year	Private enterprise	Housing associations	Local authorities	Total
1990–91	132,500	14,580	12,960	160,030
1991–92	132,050	15,970	7,110	155,130
1992–93	115,910	23,970	2,580	142,460
1993–94	116,050	30,210	1,450	147,710
1994–95	125,740	31,380	850	157,970
1995–96	123,620	30,230	760	154,600
1996–97	121,170	24,630	450	146,250
1997–98	127,840	21,400	320	149,560
1998–99	121,190	18,890	180	140,260
1999–00	124,470	17,270	60	141,800
2000–01	116,640	16,430	180	133,260
2001–02	115,700	14,100	60	129,870
2002–03	124,460	13,080	200	137,740
2003–04	130,100	13,670	190	143,960
2004–05	139,130	16,660	100	155,890
2005–06	144,940	18,160	300	163,400
2006–07	145,680	21,750	250	167,680
2007–08	145,450	23,110	220	168,770
2008–09	108,010	25,510	490	134,020
2009–10	89,540	25,180	370	115,080
2010–11	81,980	22,760	1,310	106,050

Source: HoC CLG (2012): para. 4.

The evidence points to the ethos of spatial planning having far less of an influence on housing delivery than the target-driven approach of RSSs and LDFs. Indeed, it was the housing targets in RSSs that caused many local authorities and communities to object to the post-2004 planning reforms while developers focused their attention and criticisms upon spatial planning. This would suggest that it was the development planning changes – originally envisaged as a deregulatory, pro-growth reform – rather than spatial planning, which was more concerned with repackaging growth as sustainable, that were significant.

The confusion and ambiguity around spatial planning was a dimension of this impact. As environmental groups and local communities took seriously the intentions of inclusive, socially balanced and environmental development local authorities had to deal with the practical implications of what it meant in practice. The overall picture is that planning authorities largely ignored what they considered to be extraneous and just got on with the process of finding sites for housing. Spatial planning as an ethos had little impact on the process of planning or planners themselves. As one analysis put it:

There is (still) a major failure to take account of neighbouring communities (administrative boundaries still rule); there is a lack of integration in terms of the link between plans and investment; and there is a long way to go to engage effectively with communities.

(Goodstadt, 2009: 8)

The RTPI, a strong proponent of spatial planning, also notes that there was not wide buy-in to the ambiguous: 'it is apparent that amongst key participants including planners, councillors, senior local authority and other public sector managers there is little common understanding what this means in practice' (2007: 1).

Conclusions

The ambiguity about the nature of reform and the notion of spatial planning reflected deeper tensions within the heart of the Labour government about the role of the state, regulations and markets. There is little doubt that spatial planning originally emerged as a reaction or opportunity and that the confusion over what it was and what it meant for planning reflected such tensions. However, it became something that both the pro and anti planning camps could sign up to as its purpose became understood and growth began to be emphasized. Spatial planning was originally 'an uneasy combination of different aspirations' (Inch, 2012: 1043) but its ambiguity and vacuity became its major strength in the eyes of the government. Its outward face was of sustainability, consensus, inclusion and partnership but spatial planning developed into a vehicle to achieve growth management through carefully choreographed processes that displaced and deferred opposition and antagonism, as I go on to discuss in more detail in the next chapter.

Yet it was the failure to deliver these wide, ambitious and irreconcilable aspirations that eventually led to the discrediting of spatial planning, and it was the events in the financial markets of 2007 and 2008 that finally led to its demise. As a growth management ethos spatial planning was replaced by an ethos of austerity and the re-emergence of the language of planning as a supply-side constraint. The hopes of advocates of planning as more than a regulatory mechanism were lost. However, as far as planning authorities and planners were concerned spatial planning was largely a distraction. Some in Parliament at the time that the 2004 Act was making its way through Parliament felt so too:

Conservatives do not believe that there is much wrong with it [the planning system] that could not be put right. The two aspects that are fundamentally wrong are that it is too slow and that planning authorities do not have enough staff with sufficient expertise. It would be entirely possible and better to reform the present system than to conduct the root-and-branch reform proposed in the Bill. No Government can introduce an entirely new system and get it right first time. The Bill proposes fundamental change, and I guarantee that members of the Committee will one day be back in another Committee Room on another Corridor discussing another planning Bill to amend this one. It would be better to try to amend the existing system, but the Government have introduced the Bill, and we must debate it.

(Clifton Brown, *Hansard*, 9 January 2003, Standing Committee G: Col 005).

It is tempting to compare the above sentiment with the approach taken five years later by the Conservatives that heralded the shift to localism, but the point here is that whatever the ethos, planning as a local authority activity continued largely unaffected. There was nothing in the ethos of spatial planning that could not have been implemented through the erstwhile regime. Indeed, many authorities and planners claimed to have been planning in a spatial way long before the 2002–08 era and continue to do so. Yet this 'business as usual' view misses the point of the changes given the overall argument of this book. Spatial planning was a distinct though ephemeral growth strategy that matched the characteristics of the era and reflected the New Labour orientation towards 'win-win' solutions. Of course, there was nothing 'wrong' with planning but it has to be constantly redefined and reshaped to meet the needs of the present and to respond to the perceived drawbacks of the previous regime; hence there followed the distinct eras of neoliberal spatial governance discussed in Chapter 5.

7 A new politics for planning

[Alliances] open up the opportunity for new styles of collaborative consensus building, to replace adversarial politics and competitive interest conflict. Through consensus building, coordination of different governance efforts could be achieved, with benefits for efficiency and effectiveness of urban region governance.

(Healey, 1997: 236)

To operate a system of land use allocation which assumes that all decisions can be made consensually is to delegitimize opposition.

(McClymont, 2011: 240)

Introduction

As discussed in the previous chapter spatial planning provided a new growth-supportive ethos for planning. This fresh disposition with its emphasis upon positive-sounding and inclusive concepts such as delivery, growth, strategy, partnership and networks had a range of dimensions. One corollary was the emergence of new spaces and scales of planning. Another consequence, discussed in the previous chapter, was a new ethos for planning. Spatial planning encouraged planners to consider functions and relations beyond territorial spaces, linking diverse issues and influences into fluid and fuzzy strategies that loosened their links to the accountability and transparency of local plans and strategies. Another dimension was an accompanying new form of politics for planning. Spatial planning was underpinned by a range of tactics or strategies that sought to depoliticize growth through seeking consensus around development. In this chapter I shall focus upon the politics of spatial planning and neoliberal spatial governance before turning to the new spaces and scales of planning in the next chapter.

The basis of this new politics for planning has already been outlined. In a classic Third Way view, conflict was something that had been transcended and belonged to the past, to the 'old politics'. New Labour's big tent emphasis on 'joined-up thinking', 'policy integration' and the modernization of public services eschewed conflict and privileged, if not assumed, agreement. Spatial planning reflected this approach and was founded on the idea that there was a consensus on growth and development waiting to be uncovered. Disagreement and conflict would be marginal and consensus, which could be achieved through dialogue, was the 'natural order'. This was a significant shift in the underlying assumptions for planning and the role of planners notwithstanding the established view that planning was always concerned with legitimizing market-driven outcomes. This shift in the politics of planning as a necessarily related dimension to spatial planning has been largely overlooked. Planning, as it was envisaged in the post-war era, was based on the acknowledgement and acceptance that there would be winners and losers in the process. The role of planning was balancing different and sometimes irreconcilable interests in the (vague) search for an overarching public good. Spatial planning, on the other hand, sought the triple bottom line of 'win-win' seeking to fuse opposites into a holistic, unifying outcome. If economic growth was the way in which social and environmental improvement would be achieved who could be against it? Spatial planning involved a repositioning of planning away from an arena where difference and conflict were acknowledged, and resolution was a possibility not an inevitability, to a process for managing conflict and reaching consensus. As I go on to argue, such a view was, at the very least, misplaced. Conflict and disagreement (i.e. the political) could not be managed away through the politics of spatial planning. As communities and groups across the country demonstrated the political was, if anything, heightened in an era of growth, particularly in relation to increased housing supply. Conflict was very much still in evidence. Rather than a post-conflict ethos for growth, spatial planning ended up obfuscating, deferring and displacing conflict, leading many to seek to challenge decisions outside of planning, typically through the courts. The outcomes from this era, particularly with regard to the role and reputation of planning and planners, have been various though highly damaging for planning and planners. In this chapter I focus upon how planning's credibility and reputation was significantly and irreparably damaged through its politicization and capture as part of a programme of neoliberalism, ultimately giving the incoming coalition government formed in 2010 a ready excuse and justification for further reform. Spatial planning confirmed the view of some that planning and planners were never 'neutral' and the public interest was always skewed towards private interests. For others, the role of spatial planning laid bare the contemporary nature of governance in an era of neoliberalism. A further and related consequence was that spatial planning undermined the idea of planning as a profession. Despite the continued claims to the contrary from the professional institute, spatial planning gave further credence, if any was necessary, to the view that planning was not neutral or apolitical but deeply embedded within the contested struggle for power and influence. Ironically, spatial planning may have helped to expose the lie that planning was neutral and also to hasten greater honesty about the role and status of future planners.

While there was a clear shift towards spatial planning from 2002 onwards, there are, however, different views on the significance and the role played by planners during this era. Were planners dupes, innocents and simply 'acting on orders', or more active partners in the shift and its consequences? There are broadly two views in response to such questions. On the one hand there are those who argue that spatial planning and its consequences were a well-intentioned though poorly thought through attempt to create a new and positive role for planning for new times. Planning needed to evolve and meet the challenges of the twenty-first century, including climate change and environmental stewardship, health, economic growth and social justice and cohesion. The consequences and failures of spatial planning were more due to 'cock up' than 'conspiracy'. As the previous chapter established, there is evidence to support this view, particularly given the shift in 2002 from a 'deregulatory' to 'spatial' approach with the same legislatory framework. The implications and impacts of introducing a new, vague ethos combined with an under-resourced profession and a new system of development planning was not thought through. There was also a further dimension to the 'cock up' understanding of an inadequate or misguided theory underpinning the approach: ambiguity and confusion also derived from a naivety over the underlying assumptions about Third Way ideology and its translation into spatial planning. Such post-1989, 'big tent', 'beyond left and right' politics assumed, wrongly, that fundamental conflict was a characteristic of the Cold War era and differences of views in the post-ideological twenty-first century would be slight and manageable. Experts and professionals could explore and propose solutions and once people came together to discuss issues it would be clear that fundamental differences could be managed and overcome. Science and scientific approaches and assessments would produce answers to any 'tricky' issues or 'wicked' problems pointing to how environmental, social and economic conflicts could be reconciled.

The alternative to the 'cock up' view sees spatial planning and its consequences as a product of a more fundamental logic and tactic of neoliberalism. Rather than a confluence of a well-intentioned and progressive agenda of the 'new left', spatial planning and the post-2002 reforms were the product of a contested power struggle to embed market-based forms of governance more deeply. The planning profession colluded and provided the reassurance that 'the public interest was safe in their hands'. Ambiguity with regard to decision-making arenas and to concepts such as sustainable development was a deliberate tactic and reflected a particular growth model whereby difference and conflict could be displaced and masked behind positive pro-growth notions. These ideas were presented as 'obvious' and pitched at such an abstract level as to be difficult to disagree with – who could be against development if it was sustainable? Any difference of views that arose would then be about means, not ends, options would be controlled and managed, and the public interest redefined to focus upon choices within a pro-growth umbrella. The role of planning under this approach was to uncover and facilitate the 'natural' consensus that underlies the multitude of lifestyle differences of an individualistic society.

Both the 'cock up' and 'conspiracy' views paint in broad strokes but the balance of evidence falls firmly on the conspiracy view, particularly when other factors and reforms are taken into account. For example, the strengthening and deepening of the target-based culture, particularly within development control during the same period reinforced the notion that there were few political questions to be addressed undermining the notion of consultation and development quality. That spatial planning as a new ethos failed is not in doubt. The phrase has now largely been eradicated and wiped from the lexicon of planning save for a small core of diehard, recalcitrant academics and practitioners. However, much as planners would like to forget it and move on, more reflection and understanding are necessary regarding the extent to which spatial planning was merely a temporary episode in neoliberal spatial governance, an episode that has been subsequently repackaged and repeated. It is the evolutionary, experimental and disposable nature of contemporary planning practices that should concern us.

What is also largely overlooked is the extent of this failure, why this occurred and what it tells us about the nature of spatial planning and governance. The outcomes of spatial planning not only failed to achieve the objectives for growth but actually started to impede growth. Those charged with making sense of this ambiguity and translating it, including local communities and other stakeholders found this form of abstract principles less than helpful particularly when it came to having to reconcile competing objectives. This led to the government 'backfilling' by producing guidance and best practice on what spatial planning should be and how concepts such as sustainable development, which was the new purpose of planning, should work in practice:

> The Government set out four aims for sustainable development in its 1999 strategy. These are:

- social progress which recognises the needs of everyone;
- effective protection of the environment;
- the prudent use of natural resources; and
- the maintenance of high and stable levels of economic growth and employment.

> These aims should be pursued in an integrated way through a sustainable, innovative and productive economy that delivers high levels of employment, and a just society that promotes social inclusion, sustainable communities and personal well being, in ways that protect and enhance the physical environment and optimise resource and energy use.
>
> (ODPM, 2005: 4)

It was unclear what such entreaties actually meant in practice to communities that had to decide if a new housing development would lead to social progress, environmental protection and economic growth. If a proposal met some of these objectives and not others then was it sustainable development? How should the objectives be weighed? Was environmental protection more important than economic growth? Such trade-offs had been part and parcel of planning, a planning that understood that decisions and outcomes would normally, if not inevitably, be a compromise and only exceptionally a consensus. The upshot of spatial planning was that communities were disenchanted and disillusioned when the promise of consensus building did not match up to the *realpolitik* of planning decisions.

A final dimension of the new politics of spatial planning concerns complicity. While partnerships between the public and private sector emerged in the 1990s as a way of creating synergies leading to 'better' outcomes the role of partnership-based governance as part of spatial planning took on a new role and significance. From the early 2000s partnerships reflected a shift towards creating a shared sense of purpose: if planning authorities, developers and the community were partners in an endeavour then who would oppose change and, significantly, in what arena would any opposition be channelled? Partnership-based governance redefined the public interest to being an inclusive one based on who was involved rather than what was being proposed. If you were not a 'partner' then you were not part of the public interest.

This chapter will focus upon how spatial planning as an ethos for planning introduced a new form of politics, one that has been labelled as being part of the 'post-political condition', a condition that aims at depoliticization and attempts to depoliticize issues through a range of tactics and strategies. It is through such tactics and strategies of depoliticization that consensus is likely.

New times, the Third Way and the emergence of the post-political condition

As discussed in Chapter 3, the rise of collaborative, inclusionary and discursive approaches to and understandings of planning sought to adapt practices of land use control to new times from the early 1990s. Such a shift remained largely abstract and in the realms of academia. It was the opportunity afforded by Labour's Third Way philosophy and the emergence of spatial planning that adopted and modified collaborative approaches and assumptions into a new politics for planning. Planning was by no means alone in this shift based on the understanding that antagonistic politics were a thing of the past. Yet antagonism, protest, challenge and public dissatisfaction characterize if not dominate current discussions and practices of planning in the UK. The high-profile cases of Heathrow's Terminal 5 (eighty-six months from application to decision) and Dibden Bay Container Port (forty-three months from application to decision) (Barker, 2006: 63) grab the headlines. Such highly visible and nationally news-worthy contestations can draw attention away from the far more numerous though no less controversial local planning issues. One indication of the continued contested nature of local politics and planning is the increasing incidence of judicial review. The number of judicial reviews has been on a steady upward trajectory rising from 160 in 1975 to 11,200 in 2011. The proportion of planning-related challenges has mirrored this rise. Beyond development control there is also evidence of a lack of engagement in other planning processes and issues, particularly plan making. The focus on contestation within planning, particularly from bodies such as the CBI, is normally to do with delay and the cost to the economy. More overlooked are the wider, social costs of contestation, and in particular the credibility of a planning system that seeks consensus and dialogue and yet is subject to indifference from the public. Clearly, consensus around planning issues is not the norm. Yet public participation and involvement remain an important and statutory element of planning. Politicians and planners still place great emphasis on public involvement and the need for communities to be involved in planning decision making.

How can these two seemingly contradictory elements – the move towards greater consensus-based involvement in politics and decisions and the increase in contested decisions – be understood and explained? One emerging approach is linked to the idea that there is a new politics associated with neoliberal govern-mentality and spatial governance. For some we are living in a 'post-political era' of governmentality where 'debate, disagreement and dissensus [have been replaced] with a series of technologies of governing that fuse around consensus, agreement, accountability metrics and technocratic environmental management' (Swyngedouw, 2009: 604). According to this view contestation and political choice did not suddenly disappear with the collapse of the Eastern European socialist states. Instead, Žižek (2002a) argues that 'end of history' understandings of new times are a shallow veneer beneath which there remain deep divisions and antagonisms. Such antagonisms arise from the consequences of neoliberalism: nationalism, ethnic violence and terrorism are not the remnants of some outmoded form of antagonistic politics as Giddens and Beck would argue, but reflections and consequences of contradictions within capitalism. According to this view, the gap between the goal of consensus-based politics, including collaborative approaches to planning, and a growing dissatisfaction with and challenge to decisions reflects an ongoing depoliticization of society. Depoliticization is an answer to the problem that the issues facing modern societies are now either uncontested and marginal or else so intractable as to be beyond the realm of politics. And depoliticization is a set of managing strategies or tactics that shift decision making from the sphere of the contested politics into the sphere of managerial or technocratic solutions. The decline of politics and the depolitici-zation of society find expression through falling voter turnout, decline in party membership, the lack of choice between the main political parties and voter trust, for example. We therefore experience a circular situation whereby the problem – a lack of political engagement – requires a solution that lends itself to further disengagement.

However, depoliticization is not universally perceived as retrograde or unde-sirable. On the contrary, such a shift is regarded by some as necessary in order to govern and manage modern, open and networked societies in which there is a more pluralized, differentiated public. The fragmentation and globalization of society means that mass party, class-based affiliations and politics are a thing of the past: there is such a thing as too much democracy, particularly when democratic processes paralyse policy making and decision taking. For example, Hay (2007) argues that, far from being insidious, depoliticization is an inevit-ability: our expectations of politics and the political are out of kilter with reality. If we imbue politics as a process of deliberation or as a mechanism for the provision of collective goods with high expectations then we are bound to experience disappointment. What modern politics needs to do is filter those issues and decisions that are suitable for deliberation and those that, instead, are difficult and intractable and need to be approached in new ways. Depoliticization seeks to find solutions to such intractable issues through other means. In other words, depoliticization is not inherently a 'bad thing', even though there is a dominant, normative view within academic literature that highlights the

> disavowal of the democratic obligations of a government to its citizens in a democratic polity. It is a convenient mechanism for disarming opposition, sweeping under the carpet potentially contentious issues. And it is a technique that is likely to prove both especially useful and particularly insidious where the chosen reform trajectory is certain to prove unpopular.
>
> (Hay, 2007: 92)

A variety of global and national non-governmental and governmental bodies as well as a range of think tanks argue that depoliticization is a welcome trend (Hay, 2007: 92). The basis for this view is that in seeking to be open, transparent and legitimate modern governments are now subject to intense lobbying from interest groups that makes areas of public policy overtly political and antagonistic. Furthermore, politics now seeks to make policy based upon focus groups and 'celebrity politics' through media opportunities and presentation. Rather than taking the 'right' route in the wider public interest politicians are now lobbied to serve particular interests over others. The result is a damaging short-termism in politics, a volatile disaffected electorate and the emergence of new avenues of political engagement.

The argument goes that taking away or depoliticizing decisions from politicians and handing them back to the realm of 'experts' in a 'politics free zone' will lead to 'better policy'. Hay quotes a speech made by Lord Falconer, the former Minister for Housing, Planning and Regeneration, to the Institute for Public Policy Research in 2003:

> What governs our approach is a clear desire to place power where it should be: increasingly not with politicians, but with those best fitted in different ways to deploy it. Interest rates are not set by politicians in the Treasury, but by the Bank of England. Minimum wages are not determined by the Department of Trade and Industry, but by the Low Pay Commission. Membership of the House of Lords will be determined not in Downing Street but in an independent Appointments Commission. This depoliticisation of key decision-making is a vital element in bringing power closer to the people.
>
> (2007: 93)

This approach does not perceive depoliticization as undesirable but embraces and facilitates it as a way to save politics from politicians. The distinction between politics and the political that anchor studies of post-politics is openly acknowledged as are the deep-seated, antagonistic and distributional issues that form the ontology of the political domain. The facilitation of the depoliticization approach is founded upon the view that democratic politics is not the best way in which such divisions are to be resolved and collective decisions and public goods provided: it is politics that is 'broken' through its openness and accountability. Depoliticization is a way of addressing division and antagonism not, as the second modernity theorists would argue, because there are no 'big choices' left but because traditional politics is not the best way to address them.

Notwithstanding the more sympathetic reading of depoliticization and the normative arguments that advocate more, not less, depoliticization another, more left-leaning academic reaction to the notion that we are entering a new period of modernity and associated politics following the 'end of history' has been negative if not hostile to such trends (see, for example, Buller and Flinders, 2005; Burnham, 2001; Flinders, 2004). Rather than celebrating and exploring the implications of new times there has been a focus on the difference between the promise of greater involvement and collaboration and the reality of increased contestation. Critics claim that depoliticization and the decline of politics have been accepted too readily and even facilitated by powerful interests because they suit a neoliberal agenda. New avenues for involvement and participation such as Freedom of Information legislation have been delivered and facilitate individual consumer-based politics but do not challenge or even reverse the decline of politics. The result of this mismatch has been a growing political disenchantment characterized by hostility towards politics and politicians as the term 'political' has taken on a pejorative meaning as 'underhand' or 'self-serving'. For some it is the loss of antagonism and confrontation that underpins this disenchantment (though the evidence for a causal link is open to debate, see Hay, 2007). For others, there has been the emergence of what Crouch terms post-democracy: 'while elections certainly exist and can change governments, public electoral debate is a tightly controlled spectacle managed by rival teams of professional experts in the techniques of persuasion, and considering a small range of issues selected by those teams' (2004: 4).

There are a variety of different alternative and critical interpretations linked to a range of 'posts': post-democratic (e.g. Crouch, 2004), post-ideological (e.g. Žižek, 1989), or post-political era (e.g. Mouffe, 2005). Others have foregone the 'post' prefix and instead have focused upon the 'hollowing out' of democracy in recent times (e.g. Marquand, 2004). For those who are less willing to accept depoliticization as a necessary or even positive attempt to 'save politics', depoliticization amounts to a form of neoliberal politics, one that is market-supportive and does not challenge the precepts of market-based governance.

The widespread use of the prefix 'post' in such analyses and characterizations refers to something following 'after' politics, democracy or ideology and pre-supposes that some other system existed before. Similarly, the characterization of planning as 'post-political' (e.g. Allmendinger and Haughton, 2011a; Haughton *et al.*, 2013) implies that at some point in the past there was a 'political planning', a state to which we presumably could return. However, as Crouch (2004) points out, 'post' as it is used in such analyses implies more of a continuum or punctuated evolution than a clear break. There will still be clear traces of the previous era, particularly as it is in the interests of those who benefit from the change to portray continuity and familiarity. Yet there will be significant and identifiable differences as well as continuities, even if those differences are difficult to discern. This more gradual shift reflects the experiences of planning, as I explain further on. Nevertheless, there is a confusing and, at times, frustratingly disparate variety of views on the causes and implications of depoliticization and the nature of the era of 'post-politics'.

This confusion partly arises from the varied nomenclature employed. The terms 'post-democracy', 'post-politics' and 'post-political' tend to be used interchangeably, although they represent different interpretations of a broad and diffuse phenomenon. For Rancière (1999) and Žižek (1999), for example, depoliticization concerns a shifting of the political, not its eradication. Thus, for them politics is not eradicated but shifted to other arenas and times. Both point to different strategies of displacement of the political involving the abolition of the political by politics (and vice versa). Five different forms of such political displacement are advanced: archipolitics, para-politics, meta-politics, ultra-politics and post-politics (Žižek) or post-democracy (Rancière). It is the latter post-politics or post-democracy that map most closely onto the deliberative, consensus-based politics characteristic of such movements as the Third Way and Big Society programmes. The analysis of political displacement posits a world devoid of conflict and antagonism and characterized instead by consensus. Displacement of the political is a tool or characteristic of neoliberal governance that seeks to reduce fundamental political differences to consensus-based politics through a variety of techniques (Marchart, 2007: 161) including, from a planning perspective, partnership forms of governance. It is this displacement of the political and the variety of strategies through which it is achieved, particularly in planning, that is of most interest. However, before exploring these techniques there is a need better to understand the distinctions between politics and the political.

Politics and the political

The 'new politics' of planning and neoliberal spatial governance is founded upon consensus and professional, expert management that seeks to avoid contestation, and instead manage difference and deliver growth. Yet antagonism has not been eradicated and remains a feature of planning-related issues rather than the process of planning itself. Instead, difference and antagonism now find expression elsewhere, through legal challenges or other avenues or arenas (Žižek, 1999). How have society and planning been depoliticized and how can we understand the techniques and tactics of such a post-political era? One starting point in understanding this new form of politics concerns the distinction between politics that operate at the ontic level and the political that is ontological. Politics, or the *'practices of conventional politics'* (Mouffe, 2005: 8, emphasis in the original) has encroached upon or sutured the political, or the way in which society is instituted:

> By 'the political' I mean the dimension of antagonism which I take to be constitutive of human societies, while by 'politics' I mean the set of practices and institutions through which order is created, organizing human coexistence in the context of conflictuality provided by the political.
>
> (Ibid.: 9)

Or, as Swyngedouw (2011) puts it, the political refers to a shared public space of living together without any foundational assumptions or basis. Politics, on the other hand, is the power-play between political actors and the everyday choreographies of policy making within an existing institutional and procedural configuration. This brings us to a related common characteristic of post-political critiques, that of the post-foundational thought concerning politics, the political and antagonism (Marchart, 2007; Mouffe, 2005; Žižek, 1999). The ontic-ontological distinction between the politics and the political echoes the lack of any pre-given entities and the inherently and irreducibly antagonistic nature of the political:

> Politics, then, in the forms of the institutions and technologies of governing, and the tactics, strategies, and power relations related to conflict intermediation and the furthering of particular partisan interests, contingently institute society, give society some (instable) form and temporal, but spatialised coherence (and in a 'democratic' polity does so in the name of the people).
>
> (Swyngedouw, 2011: 9)

Such a distinction between politics and the political in its current usage can be traced back to Carl Schmitt (see Marchart, 2007; Mouffe, 2005) and has formed the post-foundational understandings of Badiou, Mouffe, Rancière[1] and others. The distinction is subtle but important to grasping the critique of the post-political condition. In post-foundational thought politics is 'split from within' (Marchart, 2007: 7–8) releasing something essential in our understanding about its nature. Politics, at the ontic or empirical level of everyday practices remains a discursive regime, social system or form of action. On the other hand the political, which exists at the ontological or fundamental level, is distinct and contingent. The political has no pre-social given:

> On the one hand, the political, as the instituting moment of society, functions as a supplementary ground to the groundless stature of society, yet on the other hand this supplementary ground withdraws in the very 'moment' in which it institutes the social. As a result society will always be in search for an ultimate ground, while the maximum that can be achieved will be a fleeting and contingent *grounding* by way of politics – a plurality of partial grounds.
>
> (Ibid.: 8, emphasis in the original)

This is why many post-political theorists base their understanding upon a *post-* rather than an *anti-*foundational perspective: post-foundational theory does not assume the absence of any ground but the absence of an ultimate ground. Anti-foundational theory echoes the 'free for all' relativism of postmodern pluralism whilst post-foundational theory accepts the existence of *some* grounds. In other words there are both a plurality of contingent foundations that temporarily ground the social and an impossibility that such foundations are permanent and can be grounded (Marchart, 2007: 15).

The distinction between the two fields of politics and the political provides the fulcrum of post-political critiques. The political opens up the opportunity of alternatives and possibilities through its lack of grounding. Politics, on the other hand, is 'an always contingent, precarious and incomplete attempt to institutionalize, to spatialize the social, to offer closure, to suture the social field, to let society coincide with community understood as a cohesive and inclusive whole' (Swyngedouw, 2011: 9). This ontic level of politics includes totalitarian moments, exclusive operations, marginalizations and silences and, under the post-political critique, a colonization of the political, suturing the gap between politics and the political (ibid.). The ontological basis of the political and its lack of grounding is smothered with the politics of the singular, e.g. 'the people', 'the community' or all-inclusive notions such as 'partnership', 'governance' and 'consensus'. Such colonization includes processes and institutions, technological management techniques and the deployment of 'experts' to determine options and alternatives as particular procedures post-politics. Thus, society can 'come into being' through politics in the sense of allocation of resources and common goods. However, under the post-political condition this distinction between the political and politics has been 'managed out' through a consensual mode of governance and the colonization of the political by politics.

Yet it should be remembered that post-politics refers to a specific form of depoliticization or displacement. Rancière (1999) and Žižek (1999) highlight different forms of political displacement or how politics abolishes the political (Marchart, 2007: 160–161). 'Arche-politics' is a politics of nostalgia built around the internalization of a set of values framed by a common self-identity. Citizens are completely embedded in their political community and no debate between communities is possible (Sharpe and Boucher, 2010). Dissent or disagreement, by definition, puts someone outside of the community. Politics is grounded upon and reflects a 'common' notion of a good society or other 'super-historical truth' (Marchart, 2007: 160). 'Parapolitics' concerns radical democratic politics whereby disagreement and dissent are tolerated within the rule of law. The political disappears within a politics of competition and antagonism is replaced by the logic of the market and consumer choice mediated through political institutions. 'Meta-politics' is 'beyond' or 'before' politics and concerns how politics does not and can never reflect a social reality that can only be uncovered through science. Difference and antagonism are merely a 'side show' or delusion. Uncovering universal, 'scientific' laws allows enlightened intervention and the real reshaping of people's lives. 'Ultra-politics' involves the dominance of the political as difference and antagonism over politics whereby the political adversary is to be destroyed. Ultra-politics is Žižek's description of right-wing, populist politics or fascist regimes whereby politics becomes about 'them and us', thus demonizing a group within society. Finally, 'post-politics' seeks to displace politics through the projection of a world without conflict where consensus is already established or where it can be established through the deployment of various strategies of politics such as deliberative democracy. Under post-politics political struggle is neutralized by technological management:

> In *post-politics*, the conflict of global ideological visions embodied in different parties which compete for power is replaced by the collaboration of enlightened technocrats (economists, public opinion specialists...) and liberal multiculturalists: via the process of negotiation of interests, a compromise is reached in the guise of more or less universal consensus. *Post-politics* ... emphasizes the need to leave old ideological divisions behind and confront new issues, armed with the necessary expert knowledge and free deliberation that takes people's concrete needs and demands into account.
>
> (Žižek, 1999: 198, emphasis in the original)

As Marchart puts it:

> These diverse figures of displacement all lead with regularity to the same result. They all seek to put the play of the political difference to a halt, thereby either reducing the political to politics or hypostatizing politics into the political.
>
> (2007: 161)

The significance of these different strategies of political displacement is considerable. The first consequence is that they give rise to a specific as opposed to a more general use of the term post-politics as a colonization of the political. Rather than or in addition to the more generalized notion of depoliticization we have a specific form of the post-political which is '*predicated upon the disavowal of antagonism through the progressive inauguration and institutional arrangement of consensus*' (Swyngedouw, 2011: 10, emphasis added).

The second consequence, as far as the experiences of planning are concerned, is that the different forms of political colonization or displacement open up the possibility of different strategies and regimes of post-politics, perhaps fusions, overlaps and 'borrowing' between different forms. This is a point I return to further on in this chapter when I explore the different post-political strategies and planning. However, the more general point to make here is that such a displacement of the political has a number of implications including leaving those who disagree or want to have their voices heard little choice but to express themselves through alternative, often violent or insurgent means. This constitutes another common theme concerning the evacuation of politics from the public sphere, the colonization of the political by politics through the deployment of experts and bureaucrats.

Post-politics, planners and the police order

The post-political displacement of politics through the deployment of the notion of consensus has been the focus of many analyses, particularly given the links with Third Way thinking (see, for example, Badiou, 2009; Mouffe, 2005; Dikeç, 2005; Rancière, 1999, 2001; Žižek, 1999). A number of political philosophers have challenged the notion that, in the words of Swyngedouw (2009: 604), the social is the foundation of the political and, more fundamentally, the need to recover the political from politics and its obsession with governing, management, accounting and process:

> There is much talk today of 'dialogue' and 'deliberation' but what is the meaning of such words in the political field if no real choice is at hand and if the participants in the discussion are not able to decide between clearly differentiated alternatives?
>
> (Mouffe, 2005: 3)

The challenge to post-political strategies has taken a number of forms. For Rancière, 'politics proper' is contrasted with 'the police' or the ways in which choice is presented as no choice or in Margaret Thatcher's infamous phrase, 'there is no alternative'. Politics only happens when an alternative challenges this presupposition. Rancière's position, like that of many contemporary French political philosophers, derives in part from the consequences of the protests of Paris in May 1968. For Rancière, the protests highlighted the importance of understanding the difference between the actual reactions of workers and Marxist conceptions of what those reactions should have been. In particular, Rancière highlights the way in which workers rejected the partitioning of their lives by would-be representatives, most notably Marxist theories of class struggle and consciousness. For him, the overall lessons concern artificial partitions and representations that seek to homogenize individuals into groups:

> In many cases, we have a tendency to interpret as collective practice or class 'ethos' political statements what are in fact highly individualized. We attach too much importance to the collectivity of workers and not enough to its divisions; we look too much at worker culture and not enough at its encounters with other cultures.
>
> (Rancière, 1983)

This lack of a pre-given in the experiences and activities of workers prefigures and grounds Rancière's subsequent non-foundational approach and focuses his attention on what he termed the partition of the sensible. This partition of the sensible and management of the political is part of the post-political condition and the police order managing what is counted, heard and unheard as part of politics (Rancière, 1999). The partition of the sensible refers to what is thinkable or possible as well as the sharing out of spaces so as to create a shared or common understanding. Such partitions are presented as consensus within post-political regimes though actually amount to the prevention or suppression of dissensus, or the attempt to render invisible or inaudible alternative voices or options. For Rancière, politics is about equality or the freedom to say or partake on equal terms in the face of a managed politics that excludes or partitions what can be included and said: 'equality is the very premise upon which a democratic politics is constituted; it opens up the space of the political through the testing of a wrong that subverts equality' (Swyngedouw, 2009: 605).

Enforcement of consensus and the partition of the sensible is undertaken by 'the police', or the means by which society imposes the distribution of the sensible. In the sense used by Rancière the police refers to a range of mechanisms, processes or actors, including planners, who limit participation and frame issues:

> The police is thus first an order of bodies that defines the allocation of ways of doing, ways of being, and ways of saying, and sees that those bodies are assigned by name to a particular place and task; it is an order of the visible and sayable that sees that a particular activity is visible and another is not, that this speech is understood as discourse and another as noise.
>
> (Ibid., 1999: 29)

Politics and the police are essentially different worlds with different logics: the former is based upon the equality of the members of a community and the latter upon inequality. Inequality, or the ability to participate on equal grounds, is 'naturalized' and made to look 'normal' or acceptable by the police:

> Politics consists of reconfiguring the distribution of the sensible that defines the common of a community, by introducing into it subject and new objects, in rendering visible those who were not, and of making understood as speakers those who were only understood as noisy animals.
>
> (Ibid., 2004: 38)

Following Foucault, the police order includes various elements of self-regulation or the subliminal ways in which individuals frame their own decisions and the ways in which governments shape such decisions. However, not all police orders are 'bad':

> I propose to reserve the term *politics* for an extremely determined activity antagonistic to policing: whatever breaks with the tangible configuration whereby parties and parts or lack of them are defined by a presupposition that, by definition, has no place in that configuration – that of the part that has no part ... political activity is always a mode of expression that undoes the perceptible divisions of the police order by implementing a

basically heterogeneous assumption, that of the part who have no part, an assumption that, at the end of the day, itself demonstrates the contingency of the order, the equality of any speaking being with any other speaking being.

(Ibid., 1999: 29–30, emphasis in the original)

The police order is necessary for collective action and decisions. Where the police order presupposes inequality and imposes a taken for granted social hierarchy through a partition of the sensible then it limits equality. The partition of the sensible provides Rancière with a position from which to approach depoliticization and post-politics as forms of consensus that seek to suppress, manage and police alternatives shifting political to managerial issues based upon neoliberal tenets of commodification and economic rationality (Baeten, 2007). In relation to planning and the environment politics should be concerned with dissensus in the production of spaces – the meeting of the police and equality, restaging and rephrasing social issues, police problems, etc. (Swyngedouw, 2009: 607).

In the post-1989 'end of history' era the notion of 'political realism' is often deployed by politicians to invoke the necessity of unpopular or unpalatable decisions. The presentation of options as, in effect, no option through appealing to the idea that 'reality' dictates a particular decision (as in 'the reality of our economic situation requires...' or 'globalization means that we cannot....') normalizes certain options and eliminates the political, presenting a single possibility in the place of many (Rancière, 1999). The use of 'realism' to manage conflict is a particular strategy of the police: under the post-political condition everything is politicized and can be discussed but only in a non-committal way and as a non-conflict. Absolute and fundamental choices are managed away and politics becomes something that can be practiced without division or separation (Rancière, 2004).

Yet the political is never eliminated – it is simply displaced. When a group moves from the invisible to the visible it challenges the consensus, the self-evident divisions and the police order and, instead, asserts its equality. For Rancière, politics and the police are two different orders. The police seek to normalize inequality by presenting the exclusion of some groups as acceptable. Politics, on the other hand, is founded on the principle of equality. 'Doing politics' or the political is a third space whereby the police and politics overlap challenging, however fleetingly, what is not said and who is not included. Consensus politics seeks to justify inequality while politics is founded upon it. Consensus in this interpretation is a democratic problem, not the answer to democracy's problems, since it renders fundamental disagreement almost invisible, in arrangements choreographed by experts and managers that render them largely apolitical:

The folly of the times is the wish to use consensus to cure the diseases of consensus. What we need to do instead is repoliticize conflicts so that they can be addressed, restore names to the people and give politics back its former visibility in the handling of problems and resources.

(Rancière, 1999: 106)

Politics proper re-emerges when the police order is challenged and the natural order is 'interrupted' by the 'institution of a part of those who have no part' (ibid.: 11).

From the above we can point to three main dimensions and characteristics of the depoliticization of planning that help to frame our understanding and direct attention to the way in which the new politics of planning has been operationalized. First, post-political strategies seek to colonize politics via the political. Second, in post-politics fundamental choices are managed and politics becomes something that is practiced without division and through consensus. Finally, while the police order presents what is 'acceptable' – the division of the sensible – politics is never eradicated, only displaced.

Depoliticization, post-politics and planning

The depoliticization of planning through post-political strategies has been an ongoing project constituted through a range of tactics and tools. Like neoliberalism some of these have been more successful than others, leading to evolution and reform in the approaches and strategies. How has this been achieved in planning? One of the main strategies of depoliticization has been the shift towards *managerialism and technocracy*. As I argued above, it would be misleading to claim that spatial planning heralded the beginning of depoliticization. While for Žižek (2002b) the ultimate sign of post-politics is the growth of the managerialist approach to government that deprives government of its political dimension, there is a tradition within planning stretching back to the rational comprehensive and systems approaches that dominated practice and policy in the 1960s and that echoes an understanding of depoliticization as a way of governance by experts (Allmendinger, 2009). Public Choice Theory interpretations of planning also posit a more depoliticized form of planning, emphasizing the need for a rule of law and reduction in discretion. A more accurate view would be that the period from the early 2000s witnessed an intensification that could be viewed as a new form of politics of planning. One must also be wary of falling into the trap of imagining politics to be totally absent. As Rancière and others point out, politics will always resurface. Thus there are still clear instances of planning becoming overtly 'political' and subject to very public debate as with the publication of the National Planning Policy Framework in 2011. Yet it would be difficult to deny that there has been a growth in expert managerialism within planning throughout from the 2000s onwards. As discussed above, the role of expert knowledge is often presented as 'independent' and 'non-political', thereby endowing it with greater credibility and objectivity, presenting it as a nucleus around which other political interests and demands can collaborate and co-operate. Experts, consultants and policy researchers combine to frame the understandings around which political debates are centred in ways that are presented as problem-focused and non-political. Expert 'know-how' and delivery is given a primacy that systematically excludes others and which others feel compelled to follow. The upshot is that politics focuses upon solving problems defined and framed by experts and planners. This leaves those who wish to challenge the role of experts little choice but to use other arenas such as the courts as a means of challenging 'the police order' to use Rancière's phrase.

One clear example of the growing use of expert knowledge is the significant increase in technical supporting documentation and studies in planning from the mid-2000s (Allmendinger, 2010, 2011). Some of this growth, such as the requirements for the Strategic Environmental Assessment and Environmental Impact Assessment, did not originate from the UK government but from the EU. Much of the growth did emerge from Westminster, however, through the need to demonstrate that a particular development met the various, vague and shifting elements of sustainability. A plethora of studies and analyses were required to accompany proposals including traffic, health and crime assessments. While the impact of this growth in expert supporting documentation was to displace politics into the realm of policy experts and managers such as planners, it was ultimately counter-productive owing to the uncertainty, delay and cost to developers.

An accompanying shift that has helped to facilitate a post-political planning has been the growth in performance indicators and performance-based management. Local authorities have been encouraged to work within set time limits, and nationally determined performance indicators and to use incentives and rewards to meet such targets. Measures such as the Planning Delivery Grant, introduced in 2003/04, rewarded those authorities that met Performance Indicators (see Allmendinger, 2011, ch. 6). Such performance-based measures and incentives amount to what Raco sees as '*the re-definition of temporal frames of decision-making and political intervention*' (2014: 153, emphasis added). The relationships between time and the political are complex and can be strategically structured to limit the scope of conflict and demands. Performance measures and incentives create policy time frames in order to limit flexibility and debate: short time frames are used by state agencies to limit the length of time faced by individuals and groups to mount challenges to policy programmes.

A second tactic of post-political planning involves consensus and fuzzy concepts, that is the underlying assumption that there is a consensus that growth and development are a 'good thing' and largely uncontested. There has been an 'off and on' 'presumption in favour of development' within planning policy for many decades. A presumption in favour of development differs from a consensus around development, however, in that the presumption-based approach largely concerns the 'onus of proof', i.e. it falls to the local planning authority or objector to say why something should not go ahead rather than the applicant having to demonstrate why it should proceed. Spatial planning framed the extent and degree of any disagreement to the details rather than the principles of change. This was achieved through the accompanying shift in the objectives of spatial planning. Under erstwhile regimes planning operated in the public interest balancing various economic, social and environmental concerns. Under spatial planning, as discussed above, planning sought to achieve sustainable development. In post-political planning agreement was sought through appealing to universal themes that seem to command agreement as a result of their broadly progressive if non-specific framing: 'It is as if in late capitalism "words do not count", no longer oblige: they increasingly lose their performative power' (Žižek, 1994: 18).

A third tool of post-politics concerns what has been termed the (hyper)pluralization of policy-making structures (Raco, 2014). Broader questions of accountability are obfuscated through post-politics by incorporating a hyper-diverse range of actors directly into the delivery and management of welfare systems. This leads to a fragmentation of power among a range of bodies so that decision-making processes and structures not only become more complex but also more difficult to understand for citizens, social groups and even professionals and experts working in policy fields. Such a pluralization goes hand in hand with the strategic replacement of decision making into a plethora of bodies and regulatory agencies working on multiple scales.

Such strategies have three specific impacts upon the political; deferring the political; displacing the political; and dispersing the political. *Deferring* the political puts off the point of conflict until some future time – possibly never. This can be achieved through the deployment of vague and positive objectives, e.g. sustainable development or through partnership-led approaches that are predicated upon consensus and being part of progressive process. Consultation is managed and the level of generality, not actually engaging with the detail, just the catchwords and slogans. *Displacing* the political shifts conflict to other arenas, fuzzying where accountability and the political actually sit. This can involve the displacing of the political into technological or managerial arenas managed by 'experts' who identify the 'problems and 'issues'. There is no concrete forum where the political resides. *Dispersing* the political refers to the ways in which the political is fragmented and diluted from an immediate or physically affected community to new, undistinguished communities, such as the 'public interest' or 'future generations'. This 'opens up' the political to selective interests and influences that planning seeks to 'balance'.

A new politics for planning?

The examples of the use of deferral, displacement and dispersal as post-political tools of planning depoliticization highlight how we can interpret the ways in which planning has shifted through the lens of post-politics. What we need to understand better is what has happened in practice and whether experiences amount to a new politics of planning. The broad oeuvre of post-politics and the literature on depoliticization has provided a basis for analyses of contemporary planning practice in the UK, particularly the experiences of planning over the past two decades or so (see McClymont, 2011; Allmendinger and Haughton, 2011a; Raco, 2011; Allmendinger and Haughton, 2012; Haughton *et al.*, 2013, Raco, 2014; Allmendinger 2011). There is a normative dimension to such studies and they broadly explore what they see as the negative consequences (for alternative, more supportive interpretations see Innes and Booher, 2010). What the more critical perspectives highlight is how the consensus-based spatial planning ethos of New Labour drew upon the analysis and arguments of the collaborative planning movement (see McClymont, 2011). The arguments against the erstwhile conflictual approach to planning were threefold; the time taken to deliberate leads to consultation fatigue and does not deliver social justice; its antagonistic nature is intimidating and puts off those who would otherwise engage; and the system favours those with the resources. These are broadly the arguments used by collaborative planning advocates (see Innes and Booher, 2010). In her analysis of development control McClymont argues that the shift towards a more collaborative, deliberate and consensus-based approach to planning characteristic of the 2000s has had a range of undesirable consequences, however well intentioned such a shift was. One such consequence has been to label those who oppose development as 'enemies', undermining and devaluing their legitimate input into planning decisions. Another related impact has been the way in which consensus-based approaches have led to the stifling of alternative ideas and futures: 'Instead of bringing to the fore competing interpretations of how the area should develop, this process has stifled dissent and criticism, excluding as illegitimate those attempting to maintain alternative versions of the area's future' (McClymont, 2011: 251–52).

I have argued elsewhere (Allmendinger, 2011; Allmendinger and Haugton, 2015) that the shifts towards more collaborative approaches in the 2000s were counter-productive and led to perverse impacts. Drawing upon two examples of urban regeneration I found that a consensus-based approach founded on the principles of sustainable communities and urban renaissance did not lead to conflict-free development but simply deferred and displaced such conflict while undermining trust and confidence in planners: 'Communicative planning was supposed to respond to the issues that emerged over social engineering and collaborative planning was to be overtly consensus based, but neither have solved the top-down tradition of planning' (Lees, 2014: 12).

Such studies confirm the broad depoliticization thesis, though this is an area that is only recently receiving attention (Metzger *et al.*, 2015). Other forms of depoliticzation justify further attention, particularly in relation to informal policy and planning. One dimension of the new politics of planning concerns the emergence and growth of informal processes and spaces of planning. I cover the new planning spaces in the next chapter but here I want to draw attention to the emergence of informal planning and policy processes and governance as a characteristic of depoliticization under New Labour. One area that has not received much attention is the extent to which planning has been depoliticized through the growth in informal planning and policy processes. There is a subtle distinction here between technical and managerial processes of political displacement on the one hand and informal processes on the other. Technical and managerial processes of depoliticization exist within formal or statutory processes of planning and policy making, e.g. environmental impact assessments, retail impact assessments, employment land studies, etc. all inform statutory plan making and decision taking. Informal planning operates 'behind the scenes' and involves shaping agendas and outcomes before statutory processes.

Two forms of informal planning and policy making stand out. The first concerns new informal planning arenas for decision taking. As part of the move to 'open up' planning to cross-cutting issues with broad appeal such as sustainability, new instruments and strategies were created. Local Area Agreements (LAAs) and then MAAs along with Community Strategies provided one new form, and UDCs or their equivalent for the Growth Areas another. These new spaces and scales of planning fuzzied the sector and physical boundaries of input into planning and plan making: the land use or spatial plan for an area was linked much more closely to other plans and strategies. One consequence was that for those wishing to engage in issues around growth and development there was no clear locus – plans and strategies were self-referential and related to each other, making accountability and transparency difficult to pin down.

The second form of informal political displacement concerns the increased use of arm's length, 'neutral' arenas for policy consideration and formulation in the form of commissioned policy reviews. The more high-profile reviews included the McKinsey report on productivity in the UK economy (1997–98), the Rogers review of urban regeneration (1998–99), the Barker review of housing supply (2003–04), the Egan review of skills for sustainable communities (2003–04), the Barker review of land use planning (2005–06) and the Killian Pretty review of speed in development control (2007–08). Such reviews were given a specific remit to consider policy issues around planning and growth and thereafter were implemented in part or in full. The advantage of such approaches as far as ministers were concerned included the bypassing of civil servants (though the reviews were staffed by civil servants), the consideration of radical and controversial issues that could, if necessary, be floated and then ignored if there was a backlash and the breaking of a direct link between the reviews and direct public accountability – ministers gave evidence and could therefore distance themselves from the consideration of issues. Such reviews were a common and significant component of policy making in various governments though had a particular import under New Labour (Allmendinger, 2011).

An important element of the vagueness of policy – the fuzzy notions and inclusive-sounding catchphrases – derived from the need to reconcile multiple and competing conceptions of policy that arose from the very nature of New Labour's ambitious policy themes: climate change and economic growth; environmental protection and housing development. Such multiple and potentially conflicting objectives emanated from the unresolved objectives of different ministers and ministries as well as the underlying Third Way, big tent fundamentals of New Labour. Reconciliation was necessarily through ambiguity. Planning reflected such equivocation though also helped to deliver it through providing a

ready-made ethos. The alternative to acquiescence might have been fundamental reform and deregulation, an alternative that the Treasury and many in
business were pushing for.

Conclusions

The post-politics and depoliticization literature has something significant to say
on the experiences of and changes to English planning over the past two decades.
As a broad approach and understanding it helps to make sense of the changes
experienced by planning, changes that I would argue amount to a new politics of
planning. Nevertheless, the literature remains abstract, missing the nuances of
an evolving, highly complex, multi-scalar, networked public policy arena. The
term post-political remains problematic, not least because of its homogenizing
portrayal of a distinction between the political and politics. This is understandable
given that the tactics and strategies of depoliticization will vary by sector and
through time. Actual instances must be explored empirically. Yet we must
add some notes of caution and resist the persuasive argument that planning is
post-political rather than subject to post-political tendencies.

Planning practice and policy has undoubtedly changed but some elements
remain consistent. Similarly, while there are widespread outbreaks of 'politics
proper' there are statutory points at which comprehensive public involvement
and politics take place. Technical/managerialist techniques of environmental
assessment, for example, have grown in use and sophistication but largely as a
response to ensure that environmental issues are properly integrated into planning
decision making. This is not to say that expert-driven, technical assessments are
politically neutral or that they all exist to serve progressive ends. The widespread use of retail impact assessments from the mid-1990s, for example, and
their focus upon quantitative measures of demand and supply have been
roundly and repeatedly criticized for not allowing local planning authorities the
ability to resist new retail floorspace that would compete with 'local' shops.
The nationally imposed, economically driven algorithm of retail need specifically excluded other factors as material to any decision, including the desire of
local communities to protect existing retailers from competition. Similarly, the
widespread introduction of quantitative indicators of performance for local
planning authorities backed up by financial incentives privileged speed of decision making over quality of decisions. Such performance targets and incentives
created a wide range of perverse outcomes though another impact was to
reduce decision making within planning into a binary rather than an analogue
range of decisions around 'acceptable' and 'unacceptable' (Allmendinger, 2011).

The assenting views on depoliticization point to the longer-term trends and
changing nature of politics as being inevitable and even desirable for new times.
The problem for planning and planners is not just how to reinvent new forms
of political engagement but how to pick and choose which issues will be the
focus of such engagement. This may be something that planning has been good
at for some time. Yet the consequences of such selective engagement remain

clear: the high-rise slums, urban motorways, and soulless peripheral estates of the 1960s and 1970s. Spatial planning sought to manage the political through a range of tactics and strategies yet the political kept emerging, challenging the displacement, deferral and transfer of politics.

Whether planners will be given the discretion to re-engage is open to question. One consequence of the shift to the new politics has been the impact upon planners themselves. Public confidence and support for planning along with respect and trust in planners has undoubtedly diminished. This diminution has helped to justify some of the changes introduced by the coalition after 2010 and has added succour to the portrayal of planners by the Prime Minister as 'enemies of enterprise'. Yet as with space/scale and ethos the politics of planning are only temporary: 'The postpolitical, by disavowing division and foreclosing radical disagreement, generates deadlock and is bound to fail politically as its negotiated technical compromise will find itself confronted with the "return of the political", the re-emergence of conflict' (Oosterlynck and Swyngedouw, 2010: 1582).

The re-emergence of the political came in numerous forms under New Labour, from challenges to the ambiguous nature of empty, positive phrases such as urban renaissance to the reaction against top-down targets for regional planning. Change began with the credit crunch of 2008 and the emergence of 'austerity politics' but it was under the coalition and the emergence of localism that the next era of politics was to begin, as I discuss in Chapter 9.

Note

1 Rancière's conception and terminology is confusingly different from others who engage with this topic. He labels politics 'the police' and retains the term 'politics' for a disruption of 'the police' or the consensus. Nevertheless, the distinction remains and echoes the difference between politics and the political.

8   New spaces and scales

Introduction

The spaces and scales of planning, typically reflected in plans and strategies, have evolved, ebbed and flowed over time reflecting the priorities and philosophies of different governments and cultures of planning. The central and local scales have been more resilient than others. Meanwhile, some spaces, such as local plans or whatever nomenclature is apposite for the time, have also endured. Yet under neoliberal spatial governance various scales and spaces have either emerged or disappeared, and some have had formal statutory significance while some have been more informal with temporary arrangements. This chapter explores how, despite this historic evolution, spaces and scales have begun to take on a new role and character, helping to deliver and facilitate growth-led planning in a variety of ways. Such ways include masking, fuzzying or displacing the political realities of such growth by breaking the link between what I will go on to describe as more traditional territorial space and the more amorphous and fragmented new spaces of neoliberal planning.

One distinction between the spaces and scales of neoliberal spatial governance and the more historic changing nature of the spaces and scales of planning, concerns purpose. We can see how new spaces and scales of planning emerged during the immediate post-war era in response to the perceived need to provide a more strategic overview through the introduction of structure plans or to create 'spaces of delivery' around new towns. This restless search for the 'perfect' assemblage of spaces and scales was always continuous because no ideal model exists. Yet the search was underpinned by a progressive desire for functionality: what are 'natural' or useful planning spaces, how do we identify them and how do they map on to accountable, local democratic processes and legitimacy? The more contemporary reshaping of planning spaces and scales has included such a desire for functionality but also for other, more disruptive and deceptive purposes. One problem in distinguishing between these two broad approaches to the changes in spaces and scales is that there are legitimate questions about how planning should be organized. During the debate on the Planning and Compulsory Purchase Bill that heralded the start of the spatial planning era in the early 2000s, questions were asked about the nature of the proposed new regional planning spaces. Regions were being introduced in the Bill as a new scale and space of planning and as a way of providing greater sectoral coordination, overcoming perceived local resistance to new development, particularly housing, and enabling a more 'spatial' form of planning. During the debates on the introduction of regional planning there was an objection to the nature of space itself:

> There is no such thing as a natural region of the south-east. We could have a long debate about whether other bits of regions could be described as natural, but the south-east region – the one in which my constituency will have the misfortune to lie if the Government do not see sense – is artificial. It exists only for administrative purposes.
> (David Wilshere MP, *Hansard*, 9 January 2003,
> Standing Committee G: Col. 017)

One response to the above would be that there are, of course, a range of spaces and scales depending upon the place (e.g. neighbourhood, city, region) or sector (e.g. housing, transport, health). Part of the natural tension within the practice of planning concerns the need to look beyond territorial spaces and their boundaries and beyond planning's necessary territorial 'fix' to the less clearly defined but important networks, relations and multiple spaces beyond. However, another response would be that regional planning was introduced specifically to help to impose a pro-growth agenda by seeking to overcome the narrow, territorial, silo-based attitude of some local spaces, a view that has some credence given the backlash against regional planning by many local authorities and their eventual abolition by the coalition government in 2012. A more practical response, and one that emerged in retrospect, is that the regional space did not 'exist' as far as functional planning is concerned. RSSs were, in fact, merely 'containers' for a suite of sub-regional strategies that mapped onto more natural or functional spaces, e.g. cities and their hinterlands. Many such cities, particularly the smaller ones, have no territorial space beyond the city boundaries making planning and spatial governance difficult and less effective. The latter point raises an important issue at the heart of any discussion of spaces, contemporary planning and neoliberal spatial governance, one that concerns visibility.

David Wilshere's natural focus was upon the visible manifestation of planning, in this case the region. As regards regional planning, from 2004 there was a clear and overt target for those opposed to the consequent loss of control and influence of local spaces and scales. Yet this was a distraction. Many new planning spaces do not derive their use, impact or legitimacy from statute but emerge and are used precisely because they can be denied and abandoned if necessary. Such 'soft spaces' have grown in number and significance in recent years and are a characteristic of neoliberal spatial governance.

If distraction is one characteristic of neoliberal planning spaces then another is competition. The hierarchical trickle-down form of planning more typical of the immediate post-war era has given way to fragmented, multi-scalar and spatial assemblages of competing, overlapping and temporary spaces and scales.

Such new planning spaces jostle with each other, emerging, disappearing and competing for attention and duration. The purpose of such spaces has also changed (as discussed in Chapter 6). Whereas previously planning spaces sought to impose a consistent, uniform and hierarchical land use regulatory framework they now comprise a patchwork of overlapping, multi-scalar, localized practices. New planning spaces are multi-performative, seeking to promote, shape, coordinate and facilitate change and deliver growth beyond local jurisdictions yet needing to fall back upon the legislative powers and democratic legitimacy of local political processes.

The upshot is that planning now comprises a multitude of spaces, some of which are what we might think of as 'formal', statutory or 'hard' spaces based on territories, e.g. local authorities and regions., and some of which are more 'informal' spaces that overlap, overarch or work within territorial plans and strategies. Such extraterritorial or 'soft' spaces help to fulfil specific functions such as providing strategic coordination and delivering complex developments across different sectors and administrative boundaries. However, these spaces lack the territorial legitimacy and sanction of more formal hard spaces but seem increasingly to perform an important, even critical, role in spatial governance. This situation has been helped if not actually encouraged and facilitated by planning doctrine and its embrace of more strategic, relational understandings of and approaches to space and planning (see Chapter 3). Post-structuralist understandings of space highlight its relational nature emphasizing non-territorial, open and porous spaces comprised of networks and flows that are characteristic of a globalized world in which boundaries, particularly national boundaries, mean very little (e.g. Amin, 2004; Massey, 2005). Such a view combines with a normative rejection of territorial, bounded space as somehow repressive. This relational perspective has been influential in planning, helping to underpin the shift towards a more strategic, collaborative and relational form of planning and the move from regulation to 'place making' (Healey, 2007).

Recent empirical studies have begun to question this understanding and normative preference. They highlight that planning comprises relational *and* territorial spaces, with the latter forming the basis of legitimacy and accountability in planning (Haughton *et al.*, 2010; Haughton and Allmendinger, 2010). It is clear that planning operates in both territorial and relational spaces, 'opening up' the issues, sectors and spaces which planning engages with and then 'closing' them down into a territorially sanctioned and legally defined space. Territory provides the space within which planning is bounded but not fixed. Yet there is more to the new spaces and scales of neoliberal planning than a greater open and strategic attitude. The soft spaces discussed above provide more than an attempt to 'think relationally and act locally' (McCann and Ward, 2011). In some forms these new planning spaces seek to avoid and obfuscate difficult issues and questions by displacing politics. Such spaces can also disrupt existing spaces and spatial practices, providing impetus to change and an experimental challenge to the status quo. In short, the new spaces of neoliberal planning are hard and soft, territorial and relational, progressive and regressive.

One 'way in' to make sense and frame these shifts is to consider these changes from three different understandings of the nature of space from the perspective of a material practice such as planning from the perspective of notions of space, rationalities of planning and sovereignties and accountabilities of planning (see Table 8.1).

Notions of space. I have already outlined three broad kinds of space as far as planning is concerned. Territorial space is the jurisdictional space by which the administration and politics of planning are bounded but not fixed. Territorial space and the bundle of legal and political roles, rights and responsibilities that are linked to it 'close' planning by facilitating intervention and allocation through democratic processes of land and property rights, i.e. zoning, and then sanctioning development. Relational space, on the other hand, is open, porous and comprised of dynamic and varied actor networks (see Chapter 3). Relational space is always open and becoming contingent, emergent and contested. Relational space is extraterritorial, 'opening' planning up to issues and influences such as gender or globalization and the impacts of networks beyond the local. As far as planning is concerned the main difference between territorial and relational spaces is that of longevity or permanence: territorial spaces are what Massey (2005) would term a 'temporary permanence'. The third notion of space – soft space – is an attempt to bridge the two through material practices. From one perspective soft spaces challenge the crude characterizations of territorial spaces as 'static' and relational spaces as progressive and dynamic, and imply an interplay between the two. From another perspective soft spaces represent

Table 8.1 Understandings of space and planning

	Territorial space	*Soft space*	*Relational space*
Dominant notion of space	Bounded, 'inward-looking' though with coordination and strategy with other territorial spaces where necessary, e.g. travel to work areas.	Disruptive and experimental, overlapping and multiple. Functional.	New spatial imaginaries. Deliberate fuzzying of territorial and sectoral relations and ties.
Typical rationalities of planning	Land use. Reactionary based upon land use allocations, 'predict and provide'.	Pragmatic and opportunistic. Temporary alignment and building blocks, e.g. bidding for funding. Delivery.	Spatial planning. Consensual and collaborative, partnership-based governance.
Sovereignty	Largely territorial, legal and jurisdictional. Hierarchical, 'trickle down' and transparent.	Building block or bespoke. Selective displacement of sovereignty and accountability.	Fuzzy. Pooled and prevailing displacement. Sovereignty and accountability displaced.

attempts at spatial governance, recognizing and embracing relational challenges within a territorially dominated polity. Functional planning spaces such as sub-regions that cross territorial borders or the pooling of territories into new spaces to create more strategic planning units provide temporary alignments of space for a particular length of time or issue such as transport or economic development.

Rationalities of planning. Different spaces of planning have varied rationalities. Territorial space and planning tend to be associated with and characterized by more traditional 'predict and provide' reactionary land use rationalities of planning. Each jurisdiction of planning is required to fulfil its statutory functions in determining future need, undertaking public participation and allocating land in a plan or strategy over a period of time and then deciding on development proposals to meet the requirements of the plan. Relational spaces naturally involve a relational rationality that seeks to break out of such procedural and territorial constraints and engage with new spatial imaginaries and notions such as place making rather than regulation. Processes are more open and inclusive with a breakdown of the distinction between 'the planner' and 'the planned'. The outcomes can be unanchored to territory, i.e. a strategic vision that cuts across and is not necessarily directly related to territorial spaces. Relational rationalities, also known as strategic spatial planning or spatial governance, bring with them new skills and knowledge about governance, partnership, collaboration and emergence, but crucially are reliant upon territorial spaces of planning if they are to deliver. Finally, soft space rationalities of planning are more pragmatic and opportunistic, melding the necessity of territorially tethered powers with the opportunities afforded by more outward-looking and non-sequential rationalities. Soft space rationalities provide temporary and bespoke approaches to address functional or specific issues pushing forward the limits of a land use focus into new issues, for example, climate change or social inclusion, while maintaining an anchor to territorial planning.

Sovereignties and accountabilities of space. The final dimension that helps us to frame and comprehend the new spaces and scales of planning concerns where sovereignty and accountability of space and planning lie. Territorial spaces maintain sovereignty and, within the UK context at least, sovereignty is nested and hierarchical. In other federal jurisdictions sovereignty is shared though clearly defined. Accountability of space and planning is relatively clear and transparent as decisions affecting the territory are sanctioned by bodies that map onto them and are based upon legally defined powers. Relational spaces break the link between space and accountability, fuzzying sovereignty through a pooling and displacement of politics. The 'where' of space in planning is shifted and ruptured and left to planners to determine who and what are included and which issues and scales are significant. Finally, soft spaces can be assemblies of bespoke 'building block' sovereignties that create functional spaces by 'joining together' existing territorial spaces. At another level such spaces can be less accountable cross-boundary assemblies of vague and fuzzy sovereignty that deliberately provoke and challenge other special rationalities and notions. In such cases politics can be displaced, sometimes deliberately so.

The changing nature of planning space

Planning space in the English context has been dominated by territoriality. The authority 'to plan', both in creating a land use plan and determining the right to develop, is one granted through statute to legally defined local planning authorities, usually lower-tier or unitary authorities. In some 'two-tier' areas the planning authority for functions such as minerals and waste is the County Council, although such areas are also territorially defined. There is provision for joint planning boards whereby two or more local planning authorities can mutually undertake planning functions. At various times there has also been a hierarchy of planning functions as higher-tier authorities have also been required to produce more strategic plans. Such territoriality is complemented by a traditional, hierarchical embedding of planning spaces as central government produced national policy, statutory instruments and circulars that provided top-down guidance on the objectives and processes of planning with which local territorial spaces had to conform. For example, greater coordination and integration was achieved during the post-war era through the introduction of an enhanced central role in setting national policy and priorities. At various times an intermediate scale, loosely defined as the region, was introduced in order to bridge the relational, non-place-specific national policy and the more territorial local planning authorities.

This pared-down outline of the territorial, hierarchical basis and functions constitutes the core of English planning practice though it has not been a static approach. The spaces of planning have changed and evolved to meet perceived needs of different eras and challenges. In Figure 8.1 these spaces are represented as ovals of differing sizes with the size reflecting the significance of that planning space. Thus in the pre-Second World War era the local, statutory spaces dominated within what would now be regarded as a more minimalist central policy framework.

Figure 8.1 seeks to provide a simplified and stylized impression of how the spaces and scales of English planning have evolved. It represents the main changes in an attempt to highlight two points. First, up until the 1980s the spaces and scales of planning were relatively stable and largely involved a hierarchical, central-local division of government. From the 1980s onwards this stability broke down, particularly from the 2000s when there was an almost frenzied approach towards the creation and destruction of planning spaces and scales. There was some change, particularly around the time of local government reorganization in the early 1970s but the turning point was reached in 1979 and was followed by the various changes introduced by the Thatcher governments throughout the 1980s. A range of new experimental and disruptive spaces of planning were introduced while other spaces and scales were downplayed. Second, an important set of new planning spaces emerged from the early 2000s

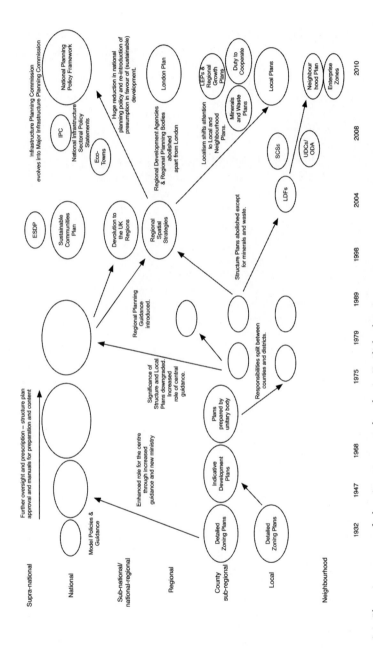

Figure 8.1 Changing nature of planning spaces and scales in English planning
Note: This is an updated version of a diagram from Haughton and Allmendinger (2010). Key: IPC (Infrastructure Planning Commission), ODA (Olympic Delivery Authority), RDA (Regional Development Agency), RPB (Regional Planning Body), SCS (Statement of Community Involvement), LDF (Local Development Framework), REPC (Regional Economic Planning Council), ESDP (European Spatial Development Perspective), UDC (Urban Development Corporation), LEP (Local Economic Partnership).

onwards heralded by New Labour's decision to reorientate planning towards a spatial approach. The two phases of change – the 1980s and the 2000s – both unsettled and reformed the formal scales and spaces of planning and assumed that practice would follow. The reforms of the 1980s (covered in Chapter 4) were deregulatory, experimental and insurgent and sought to downgrade and 'hollow out' structure and local plans while priming other spaces such as EZs and UDCs with public subsidies and 'light touch' planning regimes. The changes to planning spaces in the 2000s sought to facilitate growth and better coordinate it through a target-driven approach that aimed to look beyond territorially anchored land use planning towards a more coordinative spatial approach. This new ethos, called spatial planning (see Chapter 6), encouraged cross-sectoral thinking and working.

A major difference between the two approaches of the 1980s and 2000s, which were only twenty-odd years apart, was the changing nature of government and governance. The reforms of the 1980s were built on a hierarchical, top-down, linear understanding of planning and government – the 'Westminster model' of central policy 'flowing' to those in local authorities who would be charged with implementing it unproblematically in the light of local circumstances. By contrast, the post-2000 reforms, were designed to deliver growth against the backdrop of a globalized, fluid world of regions in which the levers of control had become fewer and less effective. These latter changes to the spaces of planning were more about suturing and coordinating in a fragmented world of public and private actors, seeking to fuzzy and break down the boundaries and barriers between sectors and focus upon issues. If there were major differences then there were also major similarities. Both approaches ignored or failed to recognize that planning, planners and localities did not necessarily or even ordinarily do what those in Westminster wanted. There are two broad ways of interpreting this. One view is that different outcomes 'on the ground' were a deliberate attempt to thwart the government's intentions. In the case of the Thatcher reforms there is significant evidence to support this proposition (Allmendinger and Thomas, 1998). The other view is more 'cock up' than 'conspiracy' and would see the different outcomes as a consequence of a range of factors including confusion, complexity, lack of clarity, inadequate understanding of the issues and the relation to the policy itself. As I argued in Chapter 6 in relation to the ethos of spatial planning there is evidence to support this view in relation to the reforms under New Labour.

In terms of the consequences of reform for the spaces of planning it will be clear from Figure 8.1 that planning spaces became congested if not confusing for planners on the 'inside' as well as others trying to engage with the processes of planning. If the idea was to reshape planning to achieve some given ends – deregulation or coordinated growth – then something was awry. The relatively enduring territorial spaces of planning were where change could be effected yet it was here where it was most difficult to encourage and facilitate new thinking.

Reform of territorial spaces was and has always been politically difficult, locally unpopular and very expensive. One outcome in both eras was the emergence of a host of alternative planning spaces or interpretations of planning space – working around the problem. The problem itself was very real. During the 1980s the undermining of structure and local plans and the privileging of focused spaces of deregulation and growth led to local authorities and planners simply subverting the government's intentions: simplified planning zones ended up as anything but simple or as a space of deregulation (Allmendinger and Thomas, 1998). Local plans continued to play a significant role in the minds and decisions of planners despite central government intentions. In relation to Labour's objectives in the 2000s the problem was not so much one of opposition from local planners – after all, the ethos of spatial planning and Labour's policies more generally had a central role for planning and planners – but one of delivery, or 'making things work'. The upshot was broadly the same. Alongside new statutory spaces of planning there emerged other new informal spaces and practices.

The observation that there are both formal and informal spaces of planning is not a new one. What differentiates the periods of reform from 1970 onwards and the era of planning as a form of neoliberal spatial governance is the sheer extent and complexity of planning spaces – both formal and informal. It is these informal or soft spaces that have become the focus of much recent research in planning and spatial governance. Soft spaces represent a growing characteristic or tool of spatial governance both in the UK (Haughton *et al.*, 2010; Allmendinger and Haughton, 2013) and continental Europe (Allmendinger *et al.*, 2015). Soft spaces have been defined as 'informal or semi-formal, non-statutory spatialities of planning and regeneration, with associations and relations stretching both across formally established boundaries and scalar levels of planning and across previously entrenched sectoral divides' (Metzger and Schmitt, 2012: 265–266).

From relatively pragmatic and humble beginnings soft spaces have emerged as a mainstream tool of English planning which fulfils a range of functions. Some have come about to suture or bridge scalar or territorial 'gaps', and help to coordinate the plans and strategies of multiple public and private actors (e.g. the Thames Gateway). Others emerged to help to create extraterritorial, functional planning areas for housing, economic development or environmental issues. Some were introduced to bypass and avoid lengthy, expensive and risky statutory processes while at a more development site level soft spaces have been used to help to coordinate and deliver large regeneration schemes (Haughton *et al.*, 2010). In all, soft spaces help to deliver and overcome impediments to development and growth and stand alongside the formal or 'hard' spaces of planning as and when necessary.

Figure 8.1 shows formal or 'hard' spaces of planning while Figure 8.2 superimposes some significant soft spaces onto this. The four broad soft spaces identified are very much a narrow snapshot of activity and spatial governance. Sitting alongside and above a number of territorially anchored, regional hard spaces are more fluid, aspirational and fuzzily defined meta-regional soft spaces. The Northern Way and Thames Gateway strategies sought to provide multi-

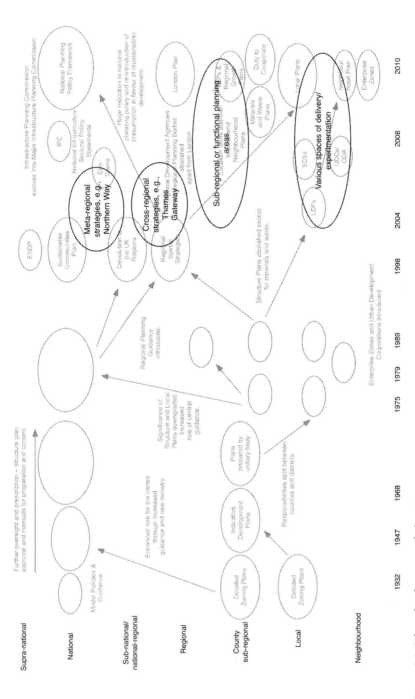

Figure 8.2 Selected soft spaces of planning

sectoral and spatial coordination without the panoply of formal procedures, delay, expense and accountabilities that would be required if they had been statutorily created. Such flexible, fleet of foot and ultimately disposable governance spaces fulfilled an important function and role in the government's growth agenda. At the sub-regional level various soft spaces emerged to create new functional areas opening up territorial planning to more relational dimensions and helping to coordinate growth across administrative boundaries. At the site or neighbourhood scale the needs of particular areas of growth required delivery bodies or spaces to provide the necessary holistic approaches to complex development. Spaces emerged that focused upon helping to visualize and promote large schemes that often crossed territorial boundaries and involved multiple sectors. While the ultimate statutory authority to plan remained anchored in territorial spaces, the 'heavy lifting' of planning was being undertaken elsewhere, sometimes out of the public gaze.

These four are not the only examples of a dynamic and fluid process of spatial creation and destruction. The result of the dynamic, multiple and functionally varied hard and soft spaces of planning is a complex and congested spatial governance landscape. The tools of spatial governance are becoming increasingly flexible and varied, drawing upon a range of different spaces and spatial imaginaries, shifting between territorial, relational and soft spaces depending on need.

Neoliberal spaces of planning

The complex and dynamic hard and soft spaces of planning reflect and help to facilitate neoliberal spatial governance. Cutting through this complexity to some degree can identify seven current types of planning spaces (see Haughton and Allmendinger, 2010).

New formal or statutory spaces of planning. The history of planning is replete with new statutory or hard spaces of planning, a recent example being neighbourhood plans which were introduced in the Localism Act 2011. However, one of the more significant recent episodes affecting new hard spaces of planning concerns regional plans. Following devolution in the late 1990s, a new range of statutory spaces was created in the UK. For English planning, the main consequence was the reintroduction of regional planning, which remained in place until, with the exception of London, it was revoked by the coalition government in 2010. These new regional state spaces were created to help to deliver strategic coordinated planning, providing additional spatial sensitivity by generating informal sub-regional plans as part of their approach. Although such sub-regional plans were 'soft' they highlighted the symbiotic though complex relationship between hard and soft spaces. It is worth noting that while the hard spaces of regional planning were abolished the softer sub-regional spaces were then given greater weight and significance, though not necessarily upon the same boundaries, by the coalition via LEPs (see below).

Informal or soft spaces of planning. Soft spaces emerge for a number of reasons and can be used to create new spatial imaginaries intended to help to shift attitudes, coordinate public and private actors and garner support for proposals (Haughton and Allmendinger, 2015). Within the category of soft spaces three distinct types can be identified. The first form of soft space could be termed *bottom-up functional.* Statutory plans and planning spaces often map uneasily onto development opportunities or functional planning areas, e.g. travel to work or housing market areas. One way in which local authorities seek to address this is to prepare plans and strategies better to reflect such functional geographies at various scales, alongside though sometimes outside of formal plans. Examples include the growth of new sub-regional planning spaces (see below). The second form of soft space, *bespoke delivery spaces*, can be distinguished from the first in terms of motivation. Formal or statutory plans are characterized by the lengthy preparation times, inflexible preparation processes and problems of coordination across territorial boundaries. Working through informal plans and strategies allows planners to deliver development on different terms and over shorter timescales than through statutory plans and strategies. Research on the Thames Gateway highlighted examples of where the authorities were 'going through the motions' of statutory plan making while focusing attention upon informal, delivery-focused shadow and master plans (Allmendinger and Haughton, 2009). *Top-down functional spaces* are the third category of soft space and emerge from central concerns in order better to coordinate planning or promote a particular issue or viewpoint such as economic development. The exact nature of the space is usually left to localities to determine but such spaces include functional planning areas such as housing areas or travel to work areas, coordination such as LAAs and growth such as LEPs and City Deals. Localities can be invited to bid for central funds through such spaces thereby incentivizing areas to develop them, as was the case with City Deals.

Fuzzy spaces. The hard boundaries of most territorially anchored statutory plans and strategies do not sit well with the needs of more relational, networked forms of space and governance. While soft spaces are one approach to deal with this mismatch, another is the ambiguity through 'fuzzy boundaries' to enable flexible policy responses or to mask politically sensitive proposals. Examples include the six areas created in the Wales Spatial Strategy, and the initial city-region proposals of the Northern Way (Haughton et al., 2010, Heley, 2013). LEPs sometimes also fall within the fuzzy category, since some have overlapping boundaries. Another recent manifestation of this is the neighbourhood plan. These plans emerged post-2010 and have no fixed or defined boundaries as they represent self-defined communities that again can overlap.

Spaces of emancipation. Alternative planning spaces have a long history in planning and there is tradition of local actors coming together to create their own visions and strategies, sometimes to counter those of local government, sometimes to take the initiative and sometimes to act as delivery vehicles. Historic examples would include Coin Street Community Builders in London and the

Eldonians in Liverpool while more contemporary examples include the current push on neighbourhood planning under the auspices of the localism agenda (see Chapter 9).

Private planning spaces. Alternatives to public plans and strategies are rare but seem to be growing. There are a handful of examples of large landowners preparing planning schemes either independently (e.g. Slough Estates) or on behalf of public authorities (e.g. large planning or development briefs). The number of such spaces has been on the increase encouraged largely by the falling resource issues within local authorities. Since 2010 the creation of LEPs has provided another dimension to encouraging the emergence of 'private planning spaces', most remarkably the Atlantic Gateway in the North West (Dembski, 2012). The Atlantic Gateway was a new spatial imaginary to provide coherence to large parcels of land within a single ownership between Manchester and Liverpool. The introduction and evolution of LEPS is providing another fillip to privately planned spaces. Privately led LEPS are increasingly being encouraged to feed into and possibly take the lead in growth-related planning matters, particularly housing targets within local plans even though the boundaries of LEPS are wider than those of single planning authorities. The possibility of such privately led planning spaces becoming more dominant is growing as local authorities are subject to austerity-driven shrinkage and encouraged to look to such bodies for input.

National spaces of delivery. Following a number of high-profile, lengthy and costly planning inquiries concerning major infrastructure and projects, new national spaces of delivery and governance arrangements were introduced in 2008 through the Infrastructure Planning Commission (IPC, now Major Infrastructure Planning Unit). Distinct policy frameworks were developed for different sectors with spatial implications and steers. The scope of national spaces of delivery is flexible and open to future revision allowing adaption to future delivery needs to include sectors such as housing and growth through new settlement proposals.

Transnational and other transboundary spaces. A range of new macro-regional strategies instigated and encouraged by the EC are emerging as inter-governmental initiatives aimed at reinforcing international cooperation. The Baltic Sea Region was adopted by the European Parliament in 2009. Subsequently, the Danube, the Alps, the Mediterranean and the North Sea strategies have followed and have reached various stages ranging from preparation to adoption. England and Scotland are (marginally) involved in the emerging North Sea strategy though others may emerge. The lack of financial, institutional and legislative backing for such regions has not impeded their development. If anything, these 'missing' elements have been an advantage in allowing the strategies to adapt and be rolled out flexibly, meeting the varying needs of different member states and the different political, legislative and cultural differences across member states.

These seven kinds of planning space fulfil a range of functions and roles, some intentional and some unintentional (Table 8.2).

Table 8.2 New English planning spaces and characteristics

Types of new planning space		Examples of new planning spaces						
		Regional Spatial Strategies 2004–12 (except London which continues)	National Planning Policy Framework 2012	Enterprise Zones (two main eras – 1980s and 2010s)	City regions/sub-regional plans (on and off throughout the 1990s and from 2010 onwards)	Local Enterprise Partnerships (2011–)	Neighbourhood Plans (2011–)	Infrastructure Planning Commission/Major Infrastructure Planning Unit (2009–)
New formal or statutory spaces of planning		✓	✓					✓
Informal or soft spaces of governance	Bottom-up, functional				✓		✓	
	Bespoke delivery space			✓				✓
	Top-down, functional	✓		✓	✓			✓
Fuzzy spaces						✓		
Spaces of experimentation and disruption				✓		✓	✓	
Private planning spaces				✓		✓	✓	
National spaces of delivery			✓				✓	✓
Spaces of political displacement or deferral		✓	✓		✓	✓	✓	✓

Note: Key: ✓ primary role, ✓ secondary role.

The multiple functions of contemporary planning spaces can be seen in the following four recent examples:

- *Regional Spatial Strategies*. Introduced in 2004 and abolished in 2012 (apart from London) RSSs provided a new strategic tier under spatial planning. While territorially linked to existing administrative boundaries there was a degree of fuzzyiness as the strategies themselves were containers for a number of sub-regional plans and strategies. There was also significant political displacement between the different sub-regional plans and the RSSs with the latter often used as a justification for housing and development targets in the sub-regional strategies.
- *Enterprise Zones*. Originally introduced in the 1980s as bespoke delivery vehicles aimed at promoting growth through reducing supply-side constraints EZs actually promoted development through significant fiscal incentives. However, the portrayal and promotion of 'planning free zones' was disruptive and helped to 'win the argument' that planning controls were a 'burden on business'. In the later incarnation from 2010 onwards EZs are linked to LEPs, the private sector-led partnerships aimed at determining growth priorities and policies for an area. LEPS and EZs constitute business-led planning spaces. Such spaces have a maximum lifespan of ten years.
- *Neighbourhood plans*. As part of the discourse of localism neighbourhood planning constitutes a new planning space, the boundaries of which are fuzzy and determine a particular community. Neighbourhood plans can overlap and have specific concerns. Yet neighbourhood plans need to conform with local plans though can challenge or resist existing thinking and policies. This allows for such plans to be both disruptive spaces and also spaces of political displacement. The latter comes from the simultaneous introduction of a national presumption in favour of sustainable development. The suggestion of localism and neighbourhood plans does not match the reality of a pro-development planning framework.
- *Infrastructure Planning Commission/Major Infrastructure Planning Unit*. Established under Labour following concerns about delays in planning for major development proposals, the IPC created new nationally determined planning spaces for major energy, transport, water, waste and waste water proposals. Such spaces were concerned with delivery through expedited procedures separate from local processes. The creation of a non-departmental public body guided by national policy on each sector displaced the political and provided new, functional though fuzzy spaces within existing territorial spaces. The IPC was absorbed into the Planning Inspectorate and renamed the Major Infrastructure Planning Unit in 2012.

The above examples highlight how new planning spaces have multiple characteristics, often presenting one face to the outside and undertaking other significant functions. These are complex spaces and interactions that do not lend themselves to easy presentation or characterization. Below, I provide a more in-depth exploration of one new space of increasing significance to growth and development in order to highlight the complexity and multifarious nature of new planning spaces.

New sub-regional planning spaces

It is possible to illustrate some of the issues affecting new spaces of planning through the emergence of what is beginning to appear as a privileged scale and space of English planning in the guise of the sub-region. In the English experience sub-regions are broadly at a scale lower than the region though higher than individual authorities, helping to 'fill the vacuum' of formal strategic planning through, for example, providing cities with functional planning hinterlands. It has long been recognized that sub-regions have a key role in planning though in recent years there has been a growing recognition of the role of the sub-region as a space and scale for economic growth. While RSSs, Regional Strategies and RDAs were an early victim of the coalition government such bodies actually covered a number of functional sub-regions. Many of these sub-regions have continued to exert a strong influence upon planning subsequently regardless of the abolition of the statutory scale of regional plan. This is partly because such spaces provide useful functional scales and partly because of the growing endorsement of sub-regions on the part of the government. While the perceived significance of sub-regions preceded the coalition government, particularly with the publication of the Treasury's *Sub-National Review of Economic Development and Regeneration* (HMT, 2007) and the creation of Local Area and MAAs under New Labour it is the emergence of LEPs, the 'Duty to Cooperate' and the Heseltine Review (Heseltine, 2012) that has underscored the recent importance of the sub-region. However, such movements were pushing at an open door as far as sub-regional planning is concerned. Local authorities have been developing various sub-regional planning arrangements to help to coordinate and provide strategic input into plans. The result of these two broad movements towards the sub-region is a coalescence of overlapping, multi-functional planning spaces that engage with existing plans and strategies in a variety of ways. The ethos of localism (see Chapter 9) encourages and facilitates this situation. Sub-regional spaces of planning take two main forms:

- *Conjoint planning spaces.* Usually comprised of joint partnerships between territorial authorities in which statutory plan-making powers have been fused resulting in the ability jointly to adopt a single planning document. Single plans are backed up by the full or partial pooling of institutional and administrative arrangements, e.g. joint planning committees. Such arrangements can be short-lived or long-lasting and depend upon continued political support and alignment. The central government can facilitate and encourage conjoint planning spaces through City Deals, for example, that can be predicated upon such arrangements.

- *Conjoint policy spaces.* A second tier of sub-regional spaces involves cooperation between territorial authorities. There are some joint policy outputs, though plan-making functions remain coordinated but separate. Such an alignment of policy usually seeks to provide a strategic overview and can be achieved through the pooling of some resources in the creation of joint planning units though each authority retains responsibility for the interpretation and can, through their individual plans and decisions, comply or depart from the joint policy framework.

While there are clear functional justifications for sub-regional planning driven by growth and development there is also an austerity-led influence. A joint evidence base and single plan has undoubted cost savings for local authorities under financial pressure. What is also clear is that City Deals, LEPs and austerity all point towards the growing significance of sub-regional planning arrangements rather than 'harder' and costlier local government reorganization.

Conclusions

The growth in overlapping, complex and opaque spaces and scales of planning, including soft spaces, raises a host of consequent issues for planning. This phenomenon is not confined to the UK, however. Other countries and planning systems are experiencing similar challenging and disrupting reforms and changes. While a feature of planning throughout history, the increasing complexity of spaces and scales of planning is a characteristic of neoliberal spatial governance. Early incarnations of neoliberalism sought to reduce and deregulate – planning was a barrier to growth and the market. As it became clear that planning actually had a necessary, positive and supportive role to play in helping to legitimize market decisions and create confidence through reducing risk then the old paradigm of 'more' and 'less' planning gave way to a more sophisticated approach, one that had implications for the nature of planning space. The more visible and statutory duties of planning – plan making and decision taking – were not only the focus of growing environmental awareness, demands for greater participation and delay; they were also no longer appropriate or functional spaces. This twofold problem of visibility and redundancy has been tackled not through deregulating planning or changing the territorial spaces of local planning authorities but simply shifting or displacing the spaces of planning. There has been a range of new spaces and a change in the nature of existing ones to more informal, fuzzy, less visible and transboundary arenas. This shift has not only been welcomed by the profession but actively encouraged by it. The ethos of spatial planning encouraged planners to 'think relationally' across sectors and to take on broad new challenges such as climate change in ways that engaged with the global and the local as a form of 'place making'. There is little mention in spatial planning of territorial spaces and territorially sanctioned functions of planning such as development control.

However, the rise and rise of new planning spaces and the complexity of relations between spaces – formal and informal – has shifted the focus of attention, raising the question 'where can planning be found?' or 'where does planning actually sit?' Such questions have profound and serious implications for planning, particularly in an era characterized by public involvement and localist demands for a 'say'. Soft spaces provide a useful displacement of planning and antagonism though this will always only be a temporary situation as communities and other interests realize that formal statutory planning processes and visible 'hard spaces' are only part of the story of contemporary planning. Yet putting aside the more deliberate displacement, the unintended implications of spatial and scalar fluidity are also serious for the proper functioning of planning. The connections and coordination of the sheer number of new hard and soft planning spaces at different scales as well as other sectoral spaces such as transport provide a hurdle to effective planning and the drive to further reform and simplify.

9 Localism, the Big Society and austerity planning

Introduction

The election of the coalition government in 2010 confirmed the rejection of Labour's ethos of spatial planning with its perceived top-down, target-driven culture. In its place the coalition introduced its own themes, centred on localism and the Big Society, both of which were supposed to turn top-down into bottom-up, thus reinvigorating communities to take ownership and responsibility for planning. Neighbourhood plans would be at the vanguard of localism, empowering communities and providing local solutions to local problems. As the Conservatives' policy statement on planning prior to the general election set out: 'if we enable communities to find their own ways of overcoming the tensions between development and conservation, local people can become proponents rather than opponents of appropriate economic growth (Conservative Party, 2010b: 1).

Localism sat alongside the Conservatives' other ethos of the Big Society, an ethos that emerged partly as a response to the individualistic 'nasty party' image of the 1980s but also as a way of shifting the responsibility and cost of public services from the state to voluntary, charitable and community bodies. The Big Society ethos was more diffuse than the simpler principle of devolution away from Whitehall and Westminster. Drawing upon a range of characteristics, though never really being clear on what it was, the Big Society became a tapestry of loose associations: 'You can call it liberalism. You can call it empowerment. You can call it freedom. You can call it responsibility. I call it the Big Society' (David Cameron, quoted in Norman, 2010: 195).

As well as a lack of clarity over the nature of the Big Society the relationship between localism and the Big Society, particularly in areas such as planning, was never clarified despite some attempts to portray localism as the means towards a Big Society model. Inevitably, the result was confusion: were planners meant to be implementing a new, bottom-up form of planning, devoid of central control and input, or were they seeking to help to assemble and facilitate a non-state-dominated approach to planning and regulation?

The lack of clarity allowed those charged with actually undertaking planning to read rather different interpretations into the approach. Yet the coalition's preaching about localism seemed at odds with what else the government was actually doing in practice, compounding the confusion over the new ethos for planning. With regard to localism, two stories about changes to planning appeared in the same week and made for rather depressing reading for those who expected localism to mean, well, localism.

> Planning authorities have been banned from considering whether renewable energy plants would be a better fit for their communities, if they receive an application for a fracking mine.
>
> (*Observer*, 3 August 2013)

> Communities secretary Eric Pickles at the weekend announced that the government's 'streamlined' suite of planning guidance ... would include new guidance on change of use. This would make it clear that the public should be able to rent a single parking space without planning permission, he said, provided there is no public nuisance to neighbours or other substantive concerns.
>
> (*Planning*, 5 August, 2013)

Clearly, localism had come up against the more traditional preference for a one-size-fits-all centralism. As for the Big Society, the overall impact was little better. The rather nebulous nature of the concept meant that planners simply ignored it, not knowing what it meant for planning, particularly against the backdrop of austerity-driven measures post-2008: what or who would take up the reins of planning in this Big Society?

So if the new ethos for planning was not about communities making decisions for themselves then what was it about? Alongside localism and the Big Society and sitting rather uncomfortably with both, planners were told that planning would also be deregulated, 'freeing up' the entrepreneurial spirit and helping to bring the country out of recession. This more traditional Conservative concern gained greater prominence particularly during the credit crunch and recession as planning took on its more familiar guise as a convenient culprit for the country's economic woes. The coalition repeated this view of planning as a 'burden on business' while simultaneously championing localism: 'The Government is to re-write the planning rules to speed up development and inject new life into the flagging economy as David Cameron attempts to seize back the political initiative following a bruising summer' (*Independent*, 2 September 2012).

The view of planning as an impediment and the idea that it needed to be deregulated is familiar to planners. In an assessment of the Thatcherite atmosphere and approach to planning during the 1980s Thorne compared the anti-planning rhetoric of the time as being like 'the Vicar in Church, repeatedly railing against sin' (1986: 28).

Did this third ethos for planning fare any better than localism and the Big Society? As with localism deregulation did not translate well, if at all, into action. Compared to the rhetoric of freeing up growth and jobs, it was almost comical that the single flagship deregulatory change to planning was a temporary relaxation of permitted development rights to allow rear house extensions of up to 8 m in depth. In addition to the mismatch between rhetoric and reality there was widespread local resistance and criticism of this move, even on the part of some Conservatives who felt that the changes went too far. While various small-scale initiatives were introduced to portray ministers as 'doing something', the biggest impact of the deregulation or 'less is more' ethos for planning reform was rhetorical, 'winning the argument' that the recession was due to too much rather than too little regulation. Thus, the criticism of planning helped to feed the mistrust of planners and of planning necessary to justify the notions of localism and the Big Society.

This is not to claim that these three approaches to and understandings of planning were deliberate, compatible and coherent. They were sometimes compatible, sometimes in tension with each another and at other times distinct and irreconcilable. They represented different worldviews that in turn reflected the different perspectives of ministers and departments on the role and purpose of planning. The three approaches were deployed to different audiences and used to support distinct narratives about planning and spatial governance. As with neoliberalism more generally, there was also a competitive or experimental element between these narratives, a search for a successful way to reshape planning. In criticizing Labour's spatial planning ethos the Conservatives and the coalition had to have an alternative.

One way to understand this complex environment of ideas and themes under the coalition would be to argue that it was a deliberate electoral strategy to present different faces to different audiences, pleasing everyone and being vague. There is undoubtedly some truth in this. The Conservatives had been out of power for thirteen years and attempts to win elections through shifts to the political right in the interim had failed to persuade enough voters to back the party. The party needed to win votes in the political 'middle ground' and embrace issues such as the environment. However, this understanding of the origins of a multifarious strategy only goes so far. Two more factors need to be taken into account. The first is the extent to which the different approaches and underlying philosophies reflected deep-seated differences within the party over the role of the state and regulation generally and planning in particular, tensions that echoed those in the 1980s (Chapter 4). The second was the wider context of the recession and the genuine feeling within the country at the time concerning the future of capitalism and the need for an active *dirigiste* state to rescue it. This was, after all, the period when major banks had been nationalized in an attempt to stem economic meltdown (Gamble, 2009).

In fact, localism, the Big Society and deregulation were a confusing and confused reaction to the unprecedented state of the nation and the lack of a clear sense of what to do about it. There was no easy or clear solution or ideological 'quick fix', so a risk-averse strategy covering a number of possibilities emerged. Planning was at one of its periodic points of change – how would it evolve and emerge anew and what combination of these approaches would constitute the next era of neoliberal spatial governance? For planning, the shift in ethos and policy from 2008–10 at the start of the recession under Labour was heightened by a range of announcements and manifesto pledges from the Conservatives as the major parties tried to tackle the fallout from the financial crisis and recession. Following the general election in 2010 this uncertainty continued and there was a lack of clarity over policy generally in a difficult and constantly changing political and economic context. The wider backdrop of a rapidly worsening economic situation and a dramatic fall-off in development activity provided yet more influences and inputs into planning policy. Legal challenges to the proposed abolition of regional strategies from a large developer and a concerted backlash against the draft National Planning Policy Framework (NPPF) added to this febrile situation. One reaction from planning and planners was simply to 'get on' with things, retrenching into core statutory roles, rolling forward ongoing work within the erstwhile planning context. For others progress ground to a halt as some authorities used the uncertainty as an excuse to halt work and resist any residual development activity that had not been throttled by the recession. It is no exaggeration to portray the period 2008–12 as a 'lost era' for English planning.

Yet this era of uncertainty and the more risk-averse and unresolved approach of the coalition gave way to traditional Conservative convictions as it became clear that economic recovery would return, capitalism would survive and the blame for the recession had been successfully pinned upon too much rather than too little regulation, including planning. As a consequence the balance between the three themes of localism, the Big Society and deregulation began to shift and to be clarified from 2012. It was neither easy nor straightforward to do this. This chapter charts the changes in planning under the coalition and how this era of neoliberal spatial governance firmed up and coalesced from a miasma of uncertainty and a genuine feeling that the recession and financial meltdown might herald the end of neoliberalism.

Localism, the Big Society and deregulation

Like New Labour, the Conservatives under David Cameron initiated a general policy review following his election as party leader in 2005. On the assumption that the traditional arguments between left and right about economic management had given way to a consensus in the 1990s, the focus of the review was on social issues or 'compassionate Conservatism' as it was called at the time. Cameron's six policy reviews were undertaken against a backdrop of strong economic growth and all reported just as the Northern Rock bank was encountering problems in the spring of 2007. The result was that the reviews were largely overtaken by events and the Conservatives were faced with the need to reconfigure policy to account for the new economic realities emerging from the implications of sub-prime mortgages and the credit crunch. The abruptness of the shift led to confusion and contradictions and a return to more traditional 'knock-about' politics, with the Conservative opposition blaming the then Labour government

for the economic situation and lambasting 'big state solutions' while simultaneously supporting 'big state' bank bailouts. Beyond the confusion about economic
policy the themes from other policy review areas were a heady mix. On the one
hand there were underlying traditional Conservative themes of personal
responsibility, fiscal prudence and a natural distrust of 'big ideas' and ideology.
On the other hand there were new ideas and themes around social entrepreneurship, pluralism in service provision, environmental issues and a New
Labour-like pragmatism and eclecticism about the source of policies. Issues that
had split the party, such as Europe and immigration, and that had appeared to
make the Conservatives 'look nasty', such as welfare, were deliberately avoided.
It is therefore no surprise that the resulting electoral strategy reflected this
combination of confusion in economic policy combined with traditional and
new themes. The outcome was a suite of approaches characterized by vagueness,
risk aversion and popularity. Planning was no exception to this.

The lineage of the Conservative and subsequent coalition's approach to
planning post-credit crunch can be found in a discussion paper from one of the
many right-leaning think tanks that were seeking to influence Conservative
thinking in the run-up to the 2010 general election. This discussion paper needs
to be read in the context of a party 'feeling its way' towards a policy position in
unprecedented times at the beginning of the economic crisis, a situation that
had emerged primarily due to housing-related personal borrowing. There is a
tradition of outsourcing policy and drawing upon external thinking in policy
formulation going back to the development of Conservative Party policies and
ideas in the 1970s and 1980s from bodies such as the Adam Smith Institute, the
Institute of Economic Affairs and the Centre for Policy Studies. These bodies
could 'think the unthinkable' and float proposals allowing them to be 'tested'
through public reaction. In the context of the late 2000s and the recession the
ability to gauge the reaction to ideas was felt to be even more important. One such
'think piece' that floated (though with encouragement from some within the
party) a range of ideas to inform Conservative thinking on planning was *Our
Towns, Our Cities: The Next Steps for Planning Reform*, which was published
in 2009 by the Bow Group, a conservative think tank founded in 1951. *Our
Towns, Our Cities* provided a far-reaching critique of Labour's approach to
planning within the broad ambit of emerging Conservative thinking at the time.

Although there were the usual deregulatory critiques and proposals from a
range of right-leaning think tanks that sought to influence Conservative policy,
Our Towns, Our Cities provided a more nuanced, pragmatic and risk-averse
understanding of the reforms to planning introduced by Labour based in part
on interviews with stakeholders and the perceived need to be cautious about
proposing anything that might prolong the recession. While accepting that some
of the reforms under Labour had been positive, the gist of the critique centred
on four issues: the use of central targets and performance management; the link
between growing local antagonism towards development and top-down regional
planning; national planning guidance as complex and excessive; and the overall
failure of Labour's planning mechanisms and ethos to deliver new housing and

economic growth. There was also a wariness about being too radical in the context of the recession and further undermining investment and growth. According to the Bow Group, reform of Labour's approach should be based upon evolution rather than revolution: 'a future Conservative Government should not make a fundamental overhaul (of planning), but focus on practical reforms to the system to support our towns and cities and assist in the economic recovery' (2009: para. 1.1).

There would be no 'bonfire of controls' but instead changes that sought to provide a system that was more accountable, that would lead to better outcomes particularly for the environment and be streamlined while not creating uncertainty, particularly for investors and developers. However, if *Our Towns, Our Cities* was underpinned by a theme it would be a shift away from what its authors saw as a 'one size fits all' ethos towards much greater local flexibility of approach. Thus, the Bow Group put forward the triad of decentralization of control, an increased emphasis upon local solutions and some deregulation, three themes that were to be echoed in the Conservatives' subsequent approach. To this end *Our Towns, Our Cities* called, inter alia, for the dismantling of regional planning, greater freedom for communities to determine planning policy that suited their circumstances, and a streamlining of environmental regulations and central planning policy. As if to make a connection to the Thatcherite past there was also a proposal to reintroduce enterprise zones, that archetypal New Right planning tool of the early 1980s. *Our Towns, Our Cities* sought to tick lots of boxes and constituencies in a cautious, pragmatic and reflective way. Reaction was, as expected and hoped, neither wholly positive nor negative, but cautious (Allmendinger, 2011).

The broad analysis and many of the proposals from the Bow Group found their way into Conservative policy a year later in the party's *Open Source Planning* (Conservative Party, 2010b), a manifesto that contained a similar wide-ranging critique of the planning system that had evolved under Labour. Echoing the Bow Group's analysis and proposals the broad thrust of *Open Source Planning* was that the centralized, top-down approach to planning underpinned by targets and performance measures had not delivered economic growth and housing development largely because such an approach had alienated local communities. In its place *Open Source Planning* proposed a decentralized ethos that would provide the incentive and the powers required for local communities to address growth and development issues in ways that reflected local characteristics and priorities. In place of antagonism, a locally led approach, it was suggested, would lead to communities being proponents rather than opponents of development. *Open Source Planning* focused upon three broad categories of change.

The first was a series of proposals that would enable the localism agenda to be implemented and allow neighbourhood groups to come together to specify what kind of development they wanted in their area. The notion of neighbourhood, like localism and the Big Society, was left deliberately open, but such groups would prepare their own neighbourhood plans that would lead to a 'fundamental and long overdue rebalancing of power, away from the centre and back into the hands of local people' (Conservative Party, 2010: 2). Neighbourhood plans would be accompanied by financial incentives to persuade communities to accept more development. For a period of six years the Conservatives proposed that the government would match the increase in council tax and business rates that would result from new development and pass this on to communities (it is worth noting that the terms 'communities' and 'neighbourhoods' are used here in the way that *Open Source Planning* used them, distinguishing between neighbourhood plans and community benefits). Communities would also receive a share of any planning obligations negotiated on the back of new development (ibid.).

The second main change involved dismantling Labour's spatial planning. *Open Source Planning* pledged to abolish the regional tier of planning and nationally prescriptive planning guidance would be substantially reduced and reorientated towards the localism agenda. To counter any charge that the new localist approach was atomistic and uncoordinated, a 'duty to cooperate' was proposed that would require coordination between adjoining local authority areas on issues such as housing, employment or infrastructure to ensure that 'functional planning' prevailed. A 'duty to cooperate' helped to address any suggestion that the Conservative approach to planning was silo-based though in doing so this created a tension with the notion of localism – what if two adjacent authorities came to very different conclusions about the priorities for planning in their 'functional' area? In addition, the Conservatives pledged to reform Labour's recently introduced approach to national infrastructure by abolishing the Infrastructure Planning Commission and using private bills to facilitate schemes through Parliament. According to *Open Source Planning* this approach would introduce greater public scrutiny.

The third main change sought to appeal to the deregulatory instincts of the party though also provided a further challenge to the notion of localism. *Open Source Planning* proposed the introduction of a 'presumption in favour of sustainable development' that echoed the Thatcherite 'presumption in favour of development'. This shift in emphasis in the nature of planning as a decision-making process was fundamental. Rather than the applicant for planning permission having to demonstrate that permission should be granted, the new emphasis shifted the burden to the local planning authority to demonstrate why permission should not be granted. *Open Source Planning* argued that it was 'right and proper' for the system to have 'a predisposition in favour of sustainable development' (Conservative Party, 2010b: 11).

Like other changes that were announced in *Open Source Planning* the presumption in favour of sustainable development was then tempered. It transpired that the presumption in favour of development would sit alongside the existing presumption in favour of the development plan, as was currently required under the 2004 Planning and Compulsory Purchase Act:

A presumption in favour of sustainable development will give the planning system an inbuilt bias towards the creation of appropriate new houses, offices, schools, shops and other development. Our emphasis on local control will allow local planning authorities to determine exactly how much development they want, of what kind and where. But unless they use their local plans explicitly to rule out particular types of development in specific areas, the planning system will automatically allow applications to be approved.

(Conservative Party, 2010b: 11)

Thus the notion of simplifying planning and making the system clearer and more market orientated was partly undermined by the perceived need to appeal to different constituencies and put safeguards in place, hedging policy by allowing talk of radical change. The inclusion of 'sustainable' in the presumption in favour of development was another example of this hedging – what did 'sustainable' and 'unsustainable' mean in this context?

The overall result, as with the notion of spatial planning under New Labour, was a complex 'layering' of inputs and priorities: the new planning system would seek to give greater control to local areas except in the circumstances when it was decided that planning was too important to be left to neighbourhoods to decide. Not only would local authorities be incentivized to get on and adopt a development plan but the changes altered the nature of the plan itself. Spatial planning – that proactive, coordinating and integrating approach to planning that sought to facilitate development through a combination of targets and broad reassurances about the nature and benefits of growth – was truly 'dead' under the Conservatives' proposals. Local plans would now become negative, land use control documents ruling out developments that the new presumption in favour of development would otherwise permit. On paper this system met the Bow Group's aims for an evolution rather than revolution of planning though the perceived need to appease and appeal to different constituencies led to the possibility that different proposals would neutralize each other.

Reaction to *Open Source Planning* was, at best, mixed. Those championing greater decentralization welcomed the notion of localism but questioned the remnants of centralism and deregulation, while business groups and developers took the opposite view, worrying that localism could allow some communities to avoid development. Much of this agenda survived the Coalition Agreement following the general election (Cabinet Office, 2010) and began subsequently to inform planning policy. Along the way other related changes and proposals also emerged as the coalition tried to appear as though it had a strategy for economic recovery, including the introduction of business-led LEPs. The recession had other effects on planning policy too. The full scope of the public sector retrenchment and expenditure cuts began to grow in importance as it became increasingly clear that the deficit would not be cut as quickly as hoped. In addition, the influence of 'events' such as the recession, and the voices of bodies such as the CBI began to develop in significance, influencing policy and proposals as the recession continued. What also became clear was what was *not* included in *Open Source Planning*, particularly regarding the existence of the IPC which the Conservatives had previously committed to abolishing, and the role and significance of the proposed NPPF, the details of which had been left to develop subsequent to the election.

The post-2010 landscape for planning was directed by four broad influences. The first influence was the nascent and embryonic proposals in *Open Source Planning*. If reaction to the proposals had not been overwhelmingly positive neither had it been damningly critical. This guarded response, which was a product of the vagueness and hedging in the document itself, provided enough encouragement for the Conservative Party to proceed. The second influence was the growing realization that public sector cuts would need to be more severe than initially envisaged. The institutions of planning, mainly local authorities, would be a major focus for such reductions. As development activity fell away the authorities' planning function began to look vulnerable. A survey of eighty-one local authorities in England and Wales in 2013 revealed that cuts of an average of 10 percent were anticipated in planning budgets, with 75 percent of those surveyed expecting to cut their planning budget in the next twelve months (Haughton and Allmendinger, 2013). Third, as the recession went on longer than expected the balance of reform shifted more towards the deregulatory aspect and away from the notions of localism and the Big Society. Planning was advanced less as a way of helping to secure growth as it had been under spatial planning and more as an impediment to growth, echoing the broader argument that too much rather than too little regulation had caused the recession. Finally, the shift from what were rather stark themes and ideas in opposition to the need to develop a set of policies and reconcile obvious inherent tensions inevitably led to an evolving, fissiparous and complex mix of policy influences and themes. At the time of the general election it was not clear how planning would evolve and which of the influences above would 'win out'.

The party's experiences after it had begun governing in coalition with the Liberal Democrats highlight the way in which this open approach evolved into a new phase of neoliberal spatial governance. In order to show how this occurred I analyse the changes from 2010 onwards using the same framework as in Chapters 6, 7 and 8, i.e. the impact and influence of coalition governance on the ethos, politics and spaces and scales of planning.

A new ethos for planning?

Labour's spatial planning constituted a distinct era of neoliberal spatial governance comprised of a new ethos, a new politics and new spaces and scales (Chapters 6, 7 and 8). However, the era of spatial planning came to a rather abrupt end in 2008 prior to the general election and the coalition coming to power in 2010. As an approach spatial planning was concerned with growth management achieved through all-embracing, positive mechanisms that displaced the political. Displacing the political was always going to be temporary and so it transpired as opposition to development and growth began to flourish. However, the consequences and implications of the backlash against spatial planning were lost when growth came to a halt as a result of the credit crunch and subsequent recession. This coincidence meant that spatial planning was discredited and labelled a 'burden on business', conveniently taking the blame for the recession. That spatial planning failed in any case through losing legitimacy was overshadowed by the more immediate concerns of the failing economy. A new ethos for planning that constituted the next era of neoliberal spatial governance was required. Labour began the search for a fresh approach from 2008 based on a form of planning that initiated and facilitated growth rather than managed it. This constituted an abrupt U-turn as Labour shifted from the 'plan-led' growth strategy of spatial planning to the more familiar notion that too much planning inhibited growth. Similarly, prior to 2008 the Conservative Party in opposition was also developing its own alternatives as part of its attempts to create a distinct narrative around its new image of 'caring Conservatism'. Just as spatial planning was a broad umbrella concept that sought to reconcile different, sometimes competing approaches to planning, so the nascent Conservative thinking sought to provide an overarching, grand narrative that aimed for a superficial reconciliation of inherent tensions over different conceptions of the role of the state, regulation and planning. In place of spatial planning the Conservatives proffered what they termed localism, the Big Society combined with a more traditional Conservative theme of deregulation.

This approach looked eerily similar to Labour's Third Way: the notions of spatial planning, along with sustainable development and urban renaissance, labels that were all difficult to disagree with and that masked the challenging politics and choices within. Yet the impact and consequences of such 'big tent' politics, including spatial planning and its consequent politics, spaces and scales, were becoming all too clear by 2008. At some point difficult choices involving winners and losers were inevitable. The more abstract that concepts such as spatial planning or localism were, the more difficult and controversial those choices inevitably became. The big tent narrative approach – the new form of politics – simply deferred rather than replaced the political. In ordinary circumstances these lessons might have led to a rethink as the era based on the Third Way and the 'end of politics' became discredited and politically unsustainable. However, the confluence of the credit crunch and recession coinciding with the realization that spatial planning was failing to deliver conflict-free growth meant that any lessons from the emerging backlash against 'big narrative approaches' and the reasons for them were lost. The implications of this coincidence for the subsequent changes to planning were twofold. First, debate and discussion in 2008 framed the problem of a decline in house building and economic activity as one of planning regulation rather than easy credit and subsequent lack of demand for new housing. Such a supply-side interpretation was useful for those pushing for deregulation, though it was a deregulation framed within and masked by the discourses of localism and the Big Society. Second, the lessons and consequences of deploying an all-embracing, seemingly conflict-free ethos for planning were lost or at least overlooked. History, in the form of 'big narrative' approaches to planning, was about to repeat itself. The Conservatives' approach, which was subsequently adopted as the coalition's stance on planning, based around three 'big narratives', localism, the Big Society and deregulation, is explored in more detail below.

Localism

The Conservatives' traditional focus on free markets and deregulation combined with its image as the 'nasty party', was, the party leadership felt, an electoral handicap in the run-up to the 2010 general election. Such images brought to mind the conflictual politics of the 1980s and were blamed for three defeats in the general elections of 1997, 2001 and 2005. Renouncing Thatcherism clearly had not helped electorally so an alternative image and narrative was needed to persuade voters that the party had evolved and embraced new realities and issues relating to the environment and growth management, for example. Localism provided one such alternative and was broadly concerned with devolving and decentralizing decision making and responsibilities, releasing communities and neighbourhoods from the top-down, 'one size fits all' attitude of Whitehall. This policy narrative was in stark opposition to the centralized approach that was characteristic of the 1980s when, in the words of Margaret Thatcher, 'there is no alternative'.

The 2010 Conservative election manifesto included an invitation to 'join the government of Britain' (Conservative Party, 2010a: 1) and the decentralization of planning was specifically included in the Coalition Agreement in order to 'give neighbourhoods far more ability to influence the shape of the places in which their inhabitants live' (Cabinet Office, 2010: 14). Decentralization had also been an emerging theme of Labour's approach to policy post-2008. Nevertheless, it was easy for the Conservatives to contrast the centralized, target-driven approach of Labour throughout the 2000s with its emphasis, however vague, on localism.

Despite the obvious advantage of an approach that could be portrayed as the antithesis of New Labour, behind the positive and widely welcomed notion of decentralization were more traditional Conservative concerns about competition, self-reliance and the advantages of market-based mechanisms of reward. While there was a fear that the devolution of responsibility through decentralization would lead to variations in policy and service provision – a 'postcode lottery' as the media like to label it – this was increasingly seen to be not only as inevitable but desirable. As Deas puts it: 'This was a more radical, laissez-faire reinterpretation of the principle of subsidiarity, accepting not only that inter-neighbourhood disparities in governance and policy are inevitable, but that diversity breeds creativity, innovation and individual and community self-reliance' (2013: 67).

Such diversity and the loss of the traditional interventionist approach to 'problem' areas was exacerbated through the combination of public expenditure cuts and the dismantling of regional machinery such as development agencies and government offices. If local areas were to compete and innovate to promote growth then some would be at a distinct advantage in terms of starting points.

LEPs, which replaced the business-led RDAs, were to promote economic growth and regeneration through public-private partnerships. LEPs were encouraged to continue New Labour's push for planning in functional economic areas, working with multiple public and private bodies to help to deliver growth. Local, it seemed, did not necessarily mean public, democratic or accountable.

Like spatial planning the notion of localism had, in Cowell's view, 'almost limitless interpretative flexibility' (2013: 27). The thrust of localism and decentralization 'made sense' and was working with the grain of public sentiment yet the implementation and significance for planning was anything but easy. The House of Commons Communities and Local Government Committee's Third Report on localism published on 9 June 2011 concluded that the government needed to be clearer about what it meant by localism. In the words of the Committee Chair, Clive Betts, there is no generally agreed definition of the term and different government departments were adopting definitions that best suited their aims. This lack of definition, which some took to be quite deliberate and a distinct advantage, caused suspicion, if not wariness particularly from a planning profession as well as public and private bodies that were not used to working within such a vacuum.

This lack of certainty was not helped when the draft NPPF slashed central government planning policy guidance from approximately 1,000 pages to fifty. But it was not so much the reduction in content as the confusion about the new purpose of planning that the NPPF introduced that caused the problems for communities and planners. The presumption in favour of sustainable development, discussed above, underpinned the coalition's approach and provided, at the very least, a tension with the notion of localism. Speaking about the launch of the draft NPPF, the then minister for decentralization and planning policy, Greg Clark, said that 'by replacing over a thousand pages of national policy with around fifty, written simply and clearly, we are allowing people and communities back in into planning' (*Planning*, 25 July 2011). Yet the imposition of a presumption meant that localism was, at best, partial. Letting people and communities back into planning was done on the proviso that development should be allowed unless there were good reasons not to resist it.

The loss of a top-down, hierarchical approach and the possibility if not inevitability of inconsistency between areas in policy was worrying for local authorities and planners particularly in situations where issues had more than local consequences such as climate change. There is little evidence that taking away the traditional, hierarchical policy support structure would lead to a beneficial competitive and experimental policy environment as the coalition suggested. What was as significant in the changes to planning and other services at the local level were the accompanying cuts in public sector spending and the dismantling of planning apparatus such as PPSs and RSSs. A decline in development activity and a commitment to a centrally coordinated system combined with cuts in local authority expenditure forced local authorities to review planning functions and policy. Far from leading to imaginative approaches this combination of factors impacted upon the ability of local authorities to develop alternatives and instead forced a retrenchment into regulatory approaches that met basic statutory requirements.

The Big Society

If localism was 'more with less' then the 'more' would be delivered and progressed not through the state but through an army of volunteers. As Deas (2013: 66) argues, the overall desire of the Conservatives was to replace 'big government' with the Big Society, the kind of society where non-state actors delivered more of the services that had previously been the responsibility of the state. As with localism the Big Society ethos sought, in part, to dismantle the top-down state apparatus and the performance monitoring and management characteristic of the New Labour era.

David Cameron's Big Society speech on 19 July 2010 set out broad themes of empowering communities, redistributing power and promoting a culture of volunteering. Such tenets were hardly new, having been the theme of Labour minister Hazel Blears' 2008 White Paper *Communities in Control: Real People, Real Power*, which reflected the consensus across the main parties about the need for a more 'active society'. Such a consensus should have been enough to send warning signals to all about the malleability and emptiness of the notion of a Big Society. However, in the Conservatives' approach the notion of the Big Society had a particular, defensive function in helping counter the infamous Thatcherite position that there was 'no such thing as society'. In this respect the Big Society 'worked' and needed no further elucidation. Yet others attempted to take the notion further. Some right-leaning think tanks such as the Policy Exchange promoted different variants of the Big Society, some with thinly disguised libertarian political agendas that sought to reduce state influence.

The lack of definition from the government and the plethora of definitions from others meant that the translation of the Big Society concept into practical policy outcomes was to prove elusive. The notion itself was the least developed of the coalition's three tenets and it is almost impossible to find anything meaningful about what it meant for planning. Nevertheless, there was a wider, destabilizing impact of the Big Society concept upon the public sector and the role of the state:

> The desire to soften the boundary between the state, voluntary sector, and business, it could be contended, continues and extends the nascent Blairite agnosticism about the sectoral division of responsibility for service delivery but rejects the latter's insistence on measuring outputs and managing performance.
>
> (Deas, 2013: 73)

This 'softening' of the boundaries helped further to fuzzy the notion of 'public interest' and heralded market priorities regarding the purpose and tools of planning through, for example, the introduction of private sector-led LEPs. This aside, the notion of the Big Society was most useful in providing a ready answer to the question of what would fill the vacuum created by the shrinking of the state, which would come about for reasons of ideology and austerity. In this respect the Big Society helped to shore up localism and deregulation.

Deregulation

The third visible element of the coalition's approach was a more developed, traditional and familiar critique of planning controls as, to use the Secretary of State's phrase in a speech to the CBI, a 'drag anchor on growth' (*Planning*, 22 March 2011). However, deregulation and market-driven reforms were not prominent in Conservative thinking and policy development in the period between 2005 and 2008, were played down between 2008 and 2012 and only began to firm up and dominate from 2012 onwards. There is a cogent argument that localism and the Big Society, the two other visible elements of coalition planning policy, were Trojan horses for market-led reforms and deregulation. Scratching the surface of both and looking at the actual reforms as opposed to the rhetoric provided a clear, holistic picture that highlighted the extent to which localist and Big Society agendas were accompanied, infused and undermined by other changes. Where deregulation (or simplification as it was labelled) was openly advanced it was packaged as a way of supporting communities and neighbourhoods to wrestle back control through not being bound up in top-down policy agendas and targets from Whitehall. Yet the freedom such deregulatory changes engendered was only partial, and in fact was highly circumscribed. Neighbourhoods could produce plans and local authorities had greater scope to determine policies and priorities for themselves though this was within a generally permissive atmosphere of a presumption in favour of sustainable development. This tension between the desire for deregulation and the political need to ensure that communities and individuals did not feel powerless in the face of change, is familiar to successive governments. The main purpose of the deregulation agenda was rhetorical:

> One of the most significant burdens highlighted consistently during the Growth Review has been the UK's overly slow and bureaucratic planning system. Since January 2005, an estimated 3,250 pages of national planning guidance for England has been issued at considerable cost to the public sector ...
>
> The costs for business are also significant, both in time and money. On average it takes more than twice as long, 95 days, to go through the procedures to build a warehouse in the UK as the USA. Recent research by Reading University suggests that the costs to the economy associated with delays in processing applications may be up to £3 billion a year.
>
> (HMT, 2011, paras 1.25 and 1.26)

Despite some easy targets for deregulation, such as the extent of national planning guidance, there was actually little in the way of effective change. What seems to have occurred to the Conservatives is that there were other ways to change planning and promote a more business-led agenda. One approach was to introduce LEPs and make central funding conditional upon their involvement in local policy. LEPs were sub-regional, private sector-led promotional bodies envisaged by the government as influencing and shifting local planning policy agendas toward securing competitive funding. It was LEPs rather than local authorities that could bid for one of the initial twenty-one (later thirty-nine) planned EZs, an initiative that harked back to the high-water mark of deregulation in the 1980s (see Chapter 4).

A new politics

New Labour's spatial planning had sought a consensus-based approach to growth through a strategy of depoliticization involving a deferral, displacement and dispersing of the political. Spatial planning had ultimately failed to achieve its growth-led aims through the reactions against these various post-political strategies (see Chapters 6 and 7). The era since 2008 and particularly between 2010 and 2012 witnessed a different form of politics around planning that accompanied the triad of localism, the Big Society and deregulation. One significant difference between Labour and the coalition's politics of planning concerned the fecundity of influences, themes and ideas within the latter's approach. For Labour, 'spatial planning' was the 'big idea'. For the coalition, there were a number of competing 'big ideas' for planning each based upon a distinct understanding of politics and the political. This reflected the lack of agreement within the government over how to approach planning and the absence of any clear feeling over how to adapt policy to the conditions of austerity.

A second difference between Labour and the coalition's politics of planning concerned the disparity between rhetoric and action. The trinity of localism, the Big Society and deregulation were not equal in their significance as drivers of coalition policy. Localism and the Big Society, for example, acted as a kind of shield against accusations that the coalition was simply seeking a more minimal state. Ministers could draw upon deregulatory and anti-state rhetoric to business audiences concerned that greater devolution of power and responsibility to local areas might lead to resistance to growth. Deploying discourses selectively depending upon the audience was not unique to the coalition, of course. What marked the coalition's approach to planning was a combination of this selectivity combined with a rupture between rhetoric and action or policy. In other words, there was also a gap between what was being said and what was being done. While the coalition talked about the shift away from the 'big state' to the Big Society, in reality it actually embarked upon a series of centralizing initiatives and market-driven deregulations reminiscent of the later years of the Thatcher administrations in the 1980s. This gap added a further, less visible dimension to the three discourses that framed planning.

The third difference in the new politics of planning under the coalition was the role of think tanks and other external influences on policy. Think tanks played a significant role under Labour though usually provided broad directions for policy rather than detailed blueprints. However, as discussed above, there was an almost perfect correlation between the analysis and proposals in the Bow Group's *Our Towns, Our Cities: The Next Steps for Planning Reform* (2009) and the Conservatives' *Open Source Planning* (2010). Think tanks were not only providing broad policy directions but the details too.

As in the time of New Labour the coalition era was characterized by a successful reaction against this depoliticization of planning. Unlike that under Labour the reaction was national rather than merely local. I discuss this reaction later in this chapter. In the next section I focus more on the politics of planning under the coalition through the frame of deferral, displacement and dispersal.

Deferring the political. As with spatial planning under Labour the notions of localism and the Big Society introduced a new, fuzzy nomenclature for planning and spatial governance. However, the main difference, as discussed above, was that both concepts were as much a product of confusion and uncertainty as a deliberate attempt to defer the political. Yet the actual changes to planning under the coalition also undermined the rhetoric of localism, the Big Society and deregulation and ensured a level of national consistency and central control. The reintroduction of the presumption in favour of sustainable development, for example, balanced if not outweighed localism with centralism. The essence of this dual change was to allow communities a say in planning but not a fundamental one – neighbourhood plans had to conform to local plans and both existed within a framework that was pro-development. Neighbourhoods and communities could make changes and suggestions around the margins but found it difficult to actually resist development. The totality of the changes – localism and centralism – amounted to a deferral of the political, putting off contestation and disputes about development until it became clear to communities that their role and input were marginal. In this sense there is a similarity with the notion of sustainable planning and spatial planning under Labour, with ambiguity allowing disparate interests to interpret such notions in different ways. Under spatial planning it was not until the details of development became clear, usually a considerable time after the principle had been agreed, that such ambiguity was exposed. Under the coalition the full impact of the NPPF and the presumption in favour of sustainable development began to cause some discontent from 2012–13 as local authorities and communities were faced with the need to allocate land for development and introduce 'new style', 'defensive' local plans.

Displacing the political. From 2010 there was an emphasis in the coalition's approach upon neighbourhood planning backed up by financial incentives (the intention was to share some of the economic benefits of development through Section 106 and Community Infrastructure Levy income) that appealed to individual and community self-interest. This shift sought to 'collectivize' problems and solutions through the creation of new communities of 'shared fate' (Raco,

2014). In order to have a 'voice' communities were forced to take on board a share of the responsibility and even necessary resources for policies and solutions. Planning and strategy making were displaced from democratic and accountable processes and spaces to new, self-defined spaces. Communities needed to conform to processes and the production of robust evidence to support their plans and approaches. The displacing of responsibilities also displaced the political while additionally providing a subtly different role for established spaces and scales of planning. As a result local authorities started to take on planning responsibility and strategy making for neighbourhoods and communities, 'holding the ring', providing more strategic, general advice and resolving disputes.

Dispersing the political. The rhetoric of localism and the tools introduced to encourage a greater local input into planning created a patchwork of plans that were meant to help to shift responsibility to neighbourhoods and way from the centre. Housing supply and affordability – a regular issue which ministers had to deal with – could now be 'blamed' on local areas as it was now their responsibility to address such shortfalls. Yet this new approach of localism, like LEPs, was selective. Not all areas would have neighbourhood plans, and LEP coverage and approach was variable. This added a further dimension to the dispersal of the political by allowing the centre to 'blame' areas that had not assumed responsibility for addressing planning locally.

New spaces and scales

The election of the coalition in 2010 heralded a further round of spatial and scalar creation and destruction, privileging some spaces and scales and de-emphasizing others. Yet, as with the coalition's ethos of planning, there was also a mismatch between rhetoric and reality – between what the coalition said it was doing and what it actually did – that necessitates care in simply ascribing change to that which ministers would like to highlight. The main difference came down to the rhetoric of 'freeing up' localities (not necessarily local authorities) from 'central interference' while actually tightly circumscribing and limiting that autonomy.

The main change in the coalition's spaces and scales of planning was the abolition of the regional planning apparatus introduced under Labour. RSSs, Regional Economics Strategies, RDAs as well as Government Offices began to be dismantled from day one of the coalition and were blamed for alienating communities and reverting to Labour's top-down, target-driven approach to planning and housing. The Conservatives had been critical of the introduction of this regional apparatus prior to the election, preferring instead their own incentive-based approach that allowed communities to take greater control and responsibility for planning and development. Yet, as developers and house-builders pointed out, the opposition to Labour's top-down, regional approach was not simply because it imposed growth that local areas would prefer to control themselves, it imposed growth in areas that wanted no growth at all. So devolving responsibility and control to local areas would not achieve development and growth per se: more measures would be needed to actually stimulate growth.

Abolishing regional plans also threw up a number of other related issues. Regions had, in part, been justified on the basis that they would provide a strategic approach that looked beyond the local to functional planning areas. Regional plans had amounted to an aggregation of sub-regional plans that reflected such functional spaces based around travel to work or housing market areas. Such sub-regional plans 'made sense' to planners, developers and communities in helping to manage change. Thinking beyond tightly defined local authority boundaries to sub-regional spaces based on travel to work, employment and resource management-led functional spaces was a long-standing approach in planning and so it was relatively straightforward to expand such areas.

These two consequences of abolishing regional planning – ensuring development would occur and avoiding narrow local authority-based planning – required safeguards in the form of the introduction of a general presumption in favour of sustainable development, the introduction of a duty to cooperate and the creation of sub-regional, industry-led LEPs – hardly the 'freeing up' local areas had envisaged or been led to believe would occur. Some local areas also started to fill the vacuum left by the absence of regions with a host of sub-regional planning arrangements. The consequence was that new spaces and scales were introduced and emerged despite the rhetoric of localism.

The other main change in the spaces and scales of planning was the introduction of neighbourhood plans and planning accompanied through Neighbourhood Development Orders and Community Right to Build Orders. Town or parish councils were specifically targeted as the bodies to lead neighbourhood planning, though 'neighbourhood forums' (loosely defined) could also take the plans forward. Early fears of neighbourhood plans as a 'NIMBY's Charter' by developers led to the requirement that they should conform to local plans and national planning guidance.

If the new formal and sanctioned spaces and scales of planning under the coalition were focused on the neighbourhood then this largely drew attention from the emergence of informal, sub-regional spaces and the continued role of the centre in orchestrating planning despite the apparent withdrawal from such a role. Furthermore, neighbourhood plans were not as radical as some initially thought in that they provided a useful device to demonstrate the coalition's commitment to localism. Of more significance in terms of contextualizing and helping to shape the shift in spaces and scales of planning was the NPPF that had reduced the extent of national planning policy dramatically but maintained the importance of the centre in directing local planning policy.

The return of the political? The National Planning Policy Framework

While an argument can be made that there was some loose coherence or logic in them, the coalition's attempts to reconfigure planning were confused, confusing and misleading. They emerged against the backdrop of a deep recession that some at the time were claiming would herald the end of neoliberalism. Yet to argue that the changes to planning policy were confused because of the lack of clarity about what to do given this backdrop is only a partial explanation. There was confusion over how to respond to the recession from all the main parties, though the emerging Conservative policy prior to 2008 was also an ambiguous and risk-free strategy that sought to engage and appease a range of constituencies without the more recent New Right ideological underpinnings. The confusion of planning policy post-2010 was not simply a product of the tumultuous times but was also deliberately so in an attempt to mislead regarding the coalition's true intentions.

New Labour's post-political strategy was challenged when the consequences of deferring and displacing the consequences of growth – the political – became apparent. Empty phrases such as urban renaissance and spatial planning had been used to help to create a consensus around growth, a consensus that fell apart when faced with the realities of actual development. A challenge to the coalition's post-political strategy came much earlier on in its parliamentary life through the reaction to its attitude towards the role of planning and the subsequent debate on this purpose. This debate was initiated through the reaction to the publication of the draft NPPF in July 2011. The publicity surrounding the draft NPPF and the reaction of the National Trust and the CPRE combined with the active support of the *Daily Telegraph* and sympathetic coverage from other media led to frequent, sometimes daily, front-page stories on the perceived implications for new development in the countryside. One upshot was an unprecedented 10,000 responses to the draft guidance and two parliamentary inquiries, the first by the Communities and Local Government Committee (HoC CLG, 2011) and the other by the Environmental Audit Committee (HoC EAC, 2011). The draft NPPF set out the coalition's objectives for planning and reflected the three themes of localism, the Big Society and deregulation, though not always explicitly. The draft read as though it had been written by different authors, each seeking to emphasize different roles for planning. Planning was tasked with achieving social, economic and environmental objectives, the reconciliation of which would be left to local communities though within the broad steer that growth should drive and even trump the other dimensions:

> The Government is committed to ensuring that the planning system does everything it can to support sustainable economic growth. A positive planning system is essential because, without growth, a sustainable future cannot be achieved. Planning must operate to encourage growth and not act as an impediment. Therefore, significant weight should be placed on the need to support economic growth through the planning system.
>
> (DCLG, 2011: para. 13)

It was this presumption based on the feeling that the government's true intentions had been exposed that led to this reaction. One of the first of many parliamentary inquiries, the Communities and Local Government Committee, concluded that the objectives of the NPPF were essentially threefold: a stimulation in the production of local plans, the much needed reduction and distillation of the national policy context within which new plans should be developed through the publication of a concise, single statement of policy (the NPPF) and the provision of a basis for decision making in the absence of a local plan – the presumption in favour of sustainable development (HoC CLG, 2011). According to the Committee, the problem was not that the NPPF sought to achieve these objectives as there was general agreement that they were sound. The problem was that the coalition was attempting to achieve too much at the same time and that some of the objectives undermined others. The main issue for the Committee concerned the objective of reducing the amount of national planning guidance. There was broad agreement that the sheer amount of central planning guidance introduced under Labour and the expansion of objectives for planning during that period had led to confusion and had helped to slow down growth and development. Prior to the general election the coalition had promised to cut over 1,000 pages of national guidance to around fifty. This figure of fifty pages seemed to some to be a rather arbitrary number that had been arrived at without any assessment of what was needed to achieve the other objectives for the NPPF, particularly where national planning guidance was meant to help to resolve the inherent conflicts in planning between where and in what circumstances development should be permitted. The draft NPPF had, in the view of the Committee, sought to achieve one objective too many: 'The Government has set great store by the brevity and simplicity of the NPPF, but in its current form the draft NPPF does not necessarily achieve clarity by virtue of its brevity' (ibid.: 1)

According to the Committee, the result was that there was a clear disagreement between those who read into the draft NPPF a pro-development attitude and disagreed with it and those who felt that localism would strengthen the hand of communities in resisting development. Rather than speeding up the system and creating certainty the ambiguity in both the language and the brevity of the draft were likely to slow down the system and development activity. The linking of the pro-development 'presumption in favour' with the phrase 'sustainable development' was a key cause of the ambiguity according to the Committee. This leavening of the pro-development presumption with the notion of sustainability development was open to wide interpretation. In places the draft NPPF conflated 'sustainable development' with 'sustainable economic growth'. In other places there was a clear steer towards sustainability and environmental considerations.

For some, such as the National Trust and the CPRE, such a conflation and confusion sought to increase development opportunities by weakening the traditional restrictions on new development in the green belt and open countryside. In conjunction with the *Daily Telegraph* both organizations led a highly successful campaign against the draft NPPF throughout 2011 and 2012. Local opposition from rural Conservative-voting areas complemented this national campaign, echoing the problems encountered by the Conservatives in the late

1980s when the party last attempted to loosen controls on development. However, hostility to the planning reforms was not confined to rural areas. Zac Goldsmith, MP for Richmond Park in London led backbench Conservative opposition:

> It is madness to remove peoples' right to object to developments that threatens their quality of life, and the policy [the presumption in favour of sustainable development] itself represents an absolute U-turn on the Government's previous commitment to localism. If there is one lesson we should have learnt from the previous administration, it is that micro-management by the Treasury is a recipe for error, and should be resisted.
>
> (Quoted in the *Daily Telegraph*, 6 April 2013: 1)

Yet despite such concerns the government continued to pursue its discourse around reforming planning and deregulation in order to encourage economic growth, not only through the draft NPPF but also the Growth and Infrastructure Act which included further attempts at deregulation:

> It is absolutely ludicrous that it takes years to get planning decisions in this country. This country, in the current economic environment, cannot afford to wait years for development. Frankly, I am frustrated by the hoops you have to jump through to get anything done – and I come back to Parliament more determined than ever to cut through the dither that holds this country back.
>
> (George Osborne, Chancellor of the Exchequer, quoted in the *Independent*, 2 September 2012)

This frustration was shared by the Prime Minister:

> It's simple. For a business to expand, it needs places to build. If it takes too long, they'll just build elsewhere. I visited a business the other day that wanted to open a big factory just outside Liverpool. But the council was going to take so long to approve the decision that they're now building that factory on the continent – and taking hundreds of jobs with them. If we're going to be a winner in this global race we've got to beat off this suffocating bureaucracy once and for all.
>
> (David Cameron, Speech to Conservative Party Conference, 10 October 2012)

Despite attempts to win over opposition the criticisms of the National Trust and the CPRE began to garner further support as other newspapers and media outlets realized that the coalition might be forced into an early U-turn. The then minister for decentralization and policy change, Greg Clark, stated in frustration that it was not possible to make a change to 'any element of national planning policy without the CPRE objecting to it. They have objected to every change in planning policy for as long as I can remember' (BBC News,

23 August, 2011, emphasis added). The fear of a possible retreat from the draft NPPF was a concern of business so support for the coalition's reforms came from fifteen chief executives of property companies who wrote to the Prime Minister on 27 August 2011 urging the government not to back down on the NPPF and planning reform. The coalition found itself caught between two natural Conservative-supporting constituencies, unable to please both.

The constant, almost daily stream of critical stories in the *Daily Telegraph* fed by the National Trust and the CPRE continued and started to spill over into other newspapers and media. The *Telegraph*'s 'Hands Off Our Land' campaign went beyond the draft NPPF and began to highlight what it argued was a battle being fought in towns and villages against development proposals. Conservative MPs became more involved as they were lobbied by constituents fearful of the *Telegraph*'s continued and alarmist headlines. The credibility of the reforms was undermined and brought into question by this campaign. The continual criticisms and growing backbench concern finally led the government to back down and dilute some of the proposals in the NPPF, in particular being clearer on what was meant by 'sustainable development' and how the phrase was meant to promote better, not more development. Ministers stressed that there had simply been a 'misunderstanding' over their intentions in the NPPF and that they shared the National Trust and the CPRE's views on the need to protect the countryside from new development.

The government's attempts to assuage the concerns that the draft NPPF would not be a 'developer's charter' while at the same time busily persuading business groups that the coalition was trying to remove constraints on growth and reduce 'red tape' was not convincing though they did manage to stem the criticisms. Nevertheless, there were two main consequences for planning. The attempts to reform planning through the sleight of hand in the draft NNPF had clearly not worked to the point of being damaging to the government and forcing it to be clearer than it would have liked about its intentions. The headlines that spoke of a 'war on the countryside' had been harmful, alienating rural areas and vocal organizations with large membership such as the National Trust. The need to clarify the deliberate ambiguity of the draft NPPF demonstrated a return of the political.

The second consequence was a frustration at this particular approach to reform: 'if anyone comes to me with an idea for new planning legislation I am going to shoot them' (Planning Minister Nick Boles, Speech to National Infrastructure Planning Association, 9 May 2013).

This frustration was to evolve into determination as the coalition's intentions to promote growth through the shrinking of planning controls would be pursued through other means, notably LEPs.

The very public row over the ambiguity in the NPPF from bodies that were natural ideological bedfellows to the Conservatives had a significant impact on the extent and pace of planning reform. However, stepping back, one further outcome as far as the recent experiences of planning was concerned was that the debate helped to bring the political back into planning, echoing the position of Rancière (see Chapter 7), among others, that the political is never permanently foreclosed and will always re-emerge. Through the pages of the *Daily Tele-graph*, other national newspapers and media outlets there was a national debate on planning policy and reform over a period of months aided and abetted by some high-profile, critical interventions including the former poet laureate Andrew Motion (*Observer*, 1 December 2012). Occasionally, the top story on the front page of some national newspapers was planning reform. The com-ment pages on the online versions of the stories received many responses both for and against the proposals. Rather than using the ambiguity of the catch-all phrases such as 'sustainable development' wrapped within equally ambiguous and competing narratives around localism, the Big Society and deregulation to appease different factions and constituencies, the debate over the draft NPPF forced some clarity. This greater transparency was only partial in that the NPPF ultimately retained its mixed messages and remained wrapped in the competing tensions of promoting economic growth, giving greater control over planning to communities and encouraging a more active society. An exegesis of the final NPPF could still support each of these views.

Subsequently, the coalition's agenda for planning did begin to become clearer as the tension between the government's desire for deregulation and devolution was tested through some local attempts to resist development leading to what became known as 'muscular localism'. The emphasis shifted back towards the need to ensure that changes were enforced. Reluctant local authorities and communities had circumscribed if not undermined the bottom-up approach of localism. Communities had the ability to decide planning policy for themselves but only within limits. There was also a shift in strategy as the government sought to strengthen the role of LEPs in planning matters, bypassing local authorities and communities in planning reform altogether and passing on the 'blame' for a more growth-led strategy to others.

Conclusions

The coalition claimed that it had a coherent approach to planning reform:

> I see Localism as the ethos, if you like, to try to do everything at the most local level. I see decentralisation as the way you do that. If you start from a relatively centralised system, you decentralise to achieve that. ... If you do that seriously and comprehensively then I think you move from a position of a very centralised state to something we have called the big society.
>
> (Greg Clark, Minister for Decentralisation and Planning Policy, evidence to the House of Commons Communities and Local Government Committee, 2011: 12–13)

If we accept Greg Clark's argument then localism was the guiding ethos for planning under the coalition just as spatial planning was the ethos for planning under New Labour. But as I have argued above, things were not that simple. Localism as an ethos came up against two significant issues. First, the logic of localism pointed to a multitude of approaches and models for planning as well as allowing communities, if they wished, to accept less development. The coalition argued that when issues such as housing supply were devolved to local areas then communities would embrace more development, development that many areas had resisted under the top-down approach of New Labour. However, this ignored strong, entrenched, anti-development attitudes and the mismatch between local authority areas and the functional planning areas needed to plan for housing: development need in some areas could only be addressed in adjacent areas requiring cooperation across local authority boundaries. Localism encouraged an isolationist attitude towards planning and growth. Without targets and the coordinating role of regional strategies developers and landowners feared – probably rightly – that those authorities that were development averse would be able to resist pressure for new housing. When it became clear that localism might lead to less, not more, development then the Treasury and the more traditional Conservative instincts to see planning as a supply-side constraint kicked in and began to dominate. Localism became 'muscular localism' as the coalition began subtly to shift the balance towards deregulation while circumscribing localism itself with various safeguards to ensure that local areas could not avoid new development, only shape its location and coordination.

The second issue concerned the confusion created by having competing objectives and narratives for planning. The two other coalition themes – the Big Society and deregulation – were in some ways complementary and in other ways in competition with localism. Each ethos had a function in appealing to different constituencies and helping to sustain a broad appeal across pro- and anti-development interests. As happened earlier with the notion of spatial planning this deliberate lack of clarity and political displacement was exposed by the debate over the draft NPPF which highlighted the tensions between the different visions for planning.

How did we get to this situation? There is a simple and not so simple answer to this question. The simple answer is that the coalition relied upon an outdated and inappropriate understanding of the role of planning as part of neoliberal spatial governance; change was driven more by knee-jerk reactions and underpinned by ideological antipathy. The more complex answer goes back to the experimental and evolutionary nature of neoliberalism itself and how this new era provided yet more evidence of a roiling change and a search for new, better settlements, fixes and assemblages.

The failure of localism and the Big Society to deliver led to an inevitable reassessment of the coalition's approach, particularly after the general election in 2015. Yet we can analyse the changes introduced as being in some ways a continuation of spatial planning's attempts to create new spaces, politics and an ethos for planning. The coalition constituted a distinctive era for planning, though one that was eerily familiar in some ways. The nomenclature and presentation changed but the themes and objectives were consistent. Localism, the Big Society and deregulation constituted a new ethos for planning with consequential new spaces, scales and politics for planning-led growth, all of which amounted to a form of neoliberal spatial governance. Ultimately, like other eras of neoliberal spatial governance, localism and its associated elements will 'fail' and be replaced with a new constellation of ethos, spaces, scales and politics.

10 Conclusions

Introduction

This book is an attempt to understand the seemingly restless changes within English planning and its evolution over the past three decades or so. My argument is that planning, in the traditional post-war sense of land use regulation, has been incrementally replaced by what I term neoliberal spatial governance, a market- and growth-supportive approach that is unstable, fast-evolving and experimental. Yet this transformation sits behind the outward appearance of continuity. Planning and planners maintain a fiction that planning is an apolitical transparent process of mediating change in the public interest. This deceit is sustained by a combination of familiar language and terms used in planning, e.g. local plan combined with newer, positive notions such as sustainability. Behind this recognizable façade the purpose of planning, in the eyes of successive governments, is clearly linked to economic competitiveness. This chapter explores some of the implications of this argument and the future of English planning. Before doing so, however, it is important to acknowledge and discuss other ways of interpreting recent changes.

Alternative interpretations

There is always a danger of viewing the twists and turns of planning as being directed by some 'invisible hand' of neoliberalism even when the changes do not obviously match up to this. There is also a trap of confirmation bias whereby everything and anything can be seen as linked to some overarching structural drivers of change. The reality is that the reforms to English planning over the past three decades or so under the auspices of different political parties, leaders and ministers have been driven by a combination of (sometimes contradictory) neoliberal logic melded by two main factors. The first involves the scope of and necessity for autonomous local politics and professional doctrine to 'make sense' of and roll out this broader logic. The second is the impact of 'events', by which I mean the ways in which planning was charged with addressing issues of the day, such as terrorism, childhood obesity or climate change. This mix of influences has led to a range of approaches, some of which have worked better than others in terms of facilitating growth and change. There was no recipe for planning but neoliberalism provided the broad parameters and ingredients for its reform. There was and can never be a clear neoliberal end game for planning.

There is, however, another way of looking at the changes to planning that needs to be acknowledged. If neoliberalism is experimental, temporary and fickle then so too are its hosts, the parties of government. Are the Conservatives a market-driven deregulatory party or one that believes in a centralizing and top-down approach? The evidence from the changes to planning since the early 1980s points both ways. Did Labour attempt to outflank the Conservatives in the 2000s and become the party of growth or was Labour using the planning system and growth as a means to deliver social and environmental objectives? Discussions about neoliberal change tend to assume consistency, even stability, on the part of governments of the same party but that is not the case. There is an element of 'action-reaction' at work that also needs to be accounted for – neoliberalism has an impact upon and is in turn influenced by the nature of politics and party-based government. One can see this through the shift to localism under the coalition government from 2010. As discussed in Chapter 9 localism was as much a reaction against what the Conservatives portrayed as the centralizing elements of Labour's spatial planning as a commitment to local involvement and bottom-up decision making. As an ethos it also played an important role in countering the claim that the Conservatives were the 'nasty party'. This example again emphasizes the choices and wide scope of neoliberalism as well as how market-based government can take many forms. The point here is that even when there is an approach that is delivering growth and development, as spatial planning was before it was replaced by localism, it can still be open to change, criticism and revision. Neoliberalism always needs to be both legitimate and effective.

This means that there were choices for planning change that would have achieved better and more effective outcomes. In other words, some approaches work better than others. For example, there is no doubt that New Labour's approach to planning and other areas of public policy showed an alarming misunderstanding if not naivety about public policy and implementation. The constant, restless desire to reform and modernize led to an environment of 'fast policy' whereby insufficient time was given for change to make an impact leading to dissatisfaction and further reform and confusion. Similarly, the constant perceived need to deregulate planning by successive Conservative governments caused uncertainty and disruption. Even if one accepted that neoliberal planning and spatial governance were, on the whole, a 'good thing' there exist other reforms, some more and some less effective. This leads me to a further point concerning the emergence of multiple, often competing policy objectives or themes. At one level there was a deliberate attempt through spatial planning to create all-encompassing, neutral policy repositories through which the aspirations of different stakeholders and interests could be superficially reconciled. This was a conscious tool to displace and defer antagonism and conflict over growth as I discussed in Chapter 7. However, layered onto this deliberate attempt to obfuscate and displace the political was the less than deliberate lack of coherence and clarity about what planning was supposed to achieve and how it should respond to issues. The clear tensions between localism and the centralizing presumption in favour of development from 2010 is an example. Such tensions may have been within the bounds and logic of neoliberalism but actually worked against growth-led planning through the instilling of conflict and confusion that hindered rather than facilitated effective spatial governance. These tensions arose, in part, because of the need to garner support from different constituencies; in the case of localism these included the development industry and local Conservative party activists and communities. However, there were champions for such different perspectives from the variety of ministers, often within the same department but also within different government departments.

There are a variety of views and interpretations about the changes to planning that reflect the emphasis placed upon different elements and the time horizon of any analysis. What some see as the reorientation of planning to favour market-based governance could be interpreted in other ways, as the then opposition argued when contemplating spatial planning in the mid-2000s. In particular, there are three counter-interpretations of the changes to planning over the past three decades that potentially point to alternative analyses.

The suppression of opposition and the political or the facilitation of change?

Growth and development are not, in themselves, exclusive features or ends of neoliberal planning. Society needs more homes and jobs, and different governments have pursued these objectives prior to the more recent era of growth-led planning. So the general pro-development and growth agenda is not a new issue for or a characteristic of planning per se. The main aim of this book is to show the reorientation of planning towards growth at the expense of other objectives and the means through which growth is achieved. My focus upon three elements – space/scale, ethos and politics – highlights how planning has changed and has helped to facilitate neoliberal spatial governance. Yet there remains a value judgement of if and why this shift is damaging or undesirable and the answer to this is by no means equivocal. The rise in the use of soft spaces and fuzzy boundaries, for example, can also be seen to be driven by the need for 'creative moments' to deal with functional planning needs, crisis experimentation and delivery. It is notable that some soft spaces of planning are related to environmental protection or other non-growth-related phenomena such as river management or transport coordination. In other words soft spaces do not necessarily or even automatically arise in order to displace or defer the political through politics thereby avoiding antagonism and conflict.

As a number of authors have pointed out post-war planning emerged as a 'child of consensus' (Thornley, 1991) built upon a perception among planners that there was a commonality of interests. As Cooke puts it: 'It was ... assumed that there were no serious disagreements between the main social groupings in liberal democracies, all sharing the belief that there were substantial welfare gains to be achieved from social democratic planning' (1983: 87).

There is therefore a case to be made that planning has always assumed and been based upon the post-political notion that conflict has 'disappeared'. Whether planning was an early adaptor of the post-political, whether the post-political has a longer history and precedes the fall of state socialism in 1989 or whether the post-political is an empty, unhelpful notion is for another discussion. The point here is that since its modern inception planning practice has long uncritically assumed an unproblematic commonality of interests. This assumption has been necessary in order to sustain the myth of both a common public interest and the 'art and science' justification of planning.

There is also a counter-narrative around post-politics itself. While there is a dominant and critical academic literature on the causes and consequences of the post-political era Hay (2007) points out that there are other, more sanguine perspectives. For some, depoliticization is not a threat to democracy but a necessary consequence of an increasingly complex, informed and global society in which collective decisions on intractable problems do not easily translate into politics or political debate. According to this view post-politics is to be welcomed as a way forward in addressing deeply intractable and antagonistic public issues through taking 'political' questions away from politics and placing them in the hands of 'experts'.

Part of the justification for depoliticization as a conscious strategy is the claim that the collapse of competing systems of government in the late 1980s and early 1990s led to a loss of conflict. However, there is also the view that rather than a loss of conflict we are now experiencing a deepening of conflict and that depoliticization is actually necessary to govern in such times. The promise of an information revolution facilitating greater and more open communication has given way to a Balkanization of information as people look for affirmation or reinforcement of views rather than perspectives that challenge them. The discursive and reflective understanding of social practices holds but not in the ways understood by Giddens and Habermas. Rather than an open and respectful debate we have a series of ideologically determined stances that have little intention of learning or even trying to understand the other. Even if preferences and opinions are mutable and open to change in the face of alternative views as suggested by collaborative planners, there is little evidence of such changes taking place.

Rather than the view of depoliticization as a threat to democracy, accountability and transparency is it actually to be welcomed? Putting aside the argument that planning is founded upon depoliticization there are pragmatic and more fundamental views on this. On the one hand some argue that there are few alternatives to such moments and shifts: 'Egalitarians cannot reverse the arrival of post-democracy, but we must learn to cope with it – softening, amending, sometimes challenging it – rather than simply accepting it' (Crouch, 2004: 12). On the other hand there are those who argue for a return to more open and explicit conflict: 'There remains a need to legitimate conflict at times, or else these alternative ideas and visions for the area can simply be submerged by the more powerful' (McClymont, 2011: 252).

What cannot be ignored is the return of antagonism and conflict. In Chapter 9 I discussed experiences regarding the NPPF. More recently the general election of 2015 highlighted a debate between the main parties over housing affordability. The 'big issues' have not been managed away in some kind of technocratic shift in governance. Planning remains an arena for deep-seated conflict and yet it has been, consciously or not, attempting to take such issues out of the democratic arena. One could, perhaps, forgive this if planning as neoliberal spatial governance had actually delivered but the evidence is that the intractable problems remain as familiar now as they have for some time. A more pertinent response might be that the idea of the post-political is itself a distraction as planning has always assumed that conflicts did not exist. Planning should introduce rather than *re*introduce the political back into politics.

A *new ethos for planning or more of the same?*

Since the mid-1940s planning has justified its activities through the façade of 'public interest' and professional judgement while working to legitimize and facilitate change and growth. The public interest was presented as neutral and apolitical while, as many have argued, the reality was that planning favoured certain groups and values over others (e.g. Healey *et al.*, 1988; Reade 1987). From this perspective it could be argued that neoliberalism and the associated narratives of spatial planning, such as localism, are merely part of this tradition, providing for and facilitating growth behind positive, apolitical narratives. Yet underpinning these notions are the more fundamental, long-standing and uncritical beliefs held by planners, specifically that planning is progressive and reformist.

There is nothing intrinsically wrong or harmful with planning having an ethos. On the contrary, there are very good reasons for helping to shape decisions and policy at the local level, and providing guidance to 'fill the gaps' where national objectives meet local circumstances. An ethos for planning helps to answer the question of 'what is planning for?' when facing choices. Again, the point is not that neoliberalism is unique or can be distinguished through providing an ethos for planning but that the nature of the purposes for planning were multiple and contradictory. Whether this situation arose deliberately or not is open to question, though the impact of multiple competing and misleading narratives concerning the purpose of planning includes the continued uncritical belief on the part of planners that the world is a better place because of them. Such a continued belief has been in sharp contrast to the growing disillusionment on the part of communities and the public that has arisen from the mismatch between rhetoric about notions such as sustainable development and the reality of change on the ground.

The complicity of planners or business as usual?

Putting aside the view that, to greater or lesser degrees, planning has always fulfilled a market-supportive role what are the implications if planning becomes a tool of neoliberalism rather than, as previously, an arena for contestation in the general public good? At one level there is a clear need for planning and planners to ensure that neoliberalism 'works': neoliberal spatial governance has inherent tensions and contradictions that need to be resolved and mediated, particularly when local circumstances are factored into growth. There is also another driver and motivation for planners to make neoliberalism 'work' which is the extent to which wider policy objectives are increasingly linked to development activity. In a system whereby affordable housing, for example, is mainly delivered through new development any 'failure of planning' has serious consequences for those in need. Policy objectives such as greater amounts of affordable housing require more development, e.g. growth and improvements in infrastructure, and open space. This link provides a pro-development logic or sensibility even in those areas where growth may not be either desirable (e.g. from an environmental perspective) or possible (e.g. there is little or no market demand). Yet the pro-growth necessity and logic of neoliberal spatial governance dominates and requires planners to promote and facilitate development. Such implicit incentives are backed up by more explicit measures. Policies such as the New Homes Bonus, which rewarded areas according to how much housing was built, further emphasize the pro-growth agenda and logic of contemporary planning through pro-rata cash incentives for local planning authorities linked to development activity.

Making neoliberalism 'work' is part and parcel of planning. At one level planners are required to reconcile the differences between competing narratives, such as localism and deregulation. At another level planners also seek to resolve more natural and inherent tensions of national policy objectives and local circumstances, e.g. what does sustainable development 'look like' on the ground for a particular locality or community? The latter is a more traditional role for planners, acting in the public interest against a backdrop of professional values and doctrine. Yet the era of neoliberalism has required a more active and facilitative role of planners, one that is more biased towards the roll-out of growth and development. To achieve this planners have worked with their professional skills, imagining what tools (spaces, scales, techniques, etc.) would make the system 'work'. To some extent this active role is understandable, particularly after the atmosphere of repeated criticisms which characterized the 1980s and 1990s that planning was 'negative' and anti-growth. It is also worth remembering that planners have been urged to embrace this role. The then Deputy Prime Minister, John Prescott, spearheaded a 'culture change' in planning in the 2000s combining exhortation, incentives and investment against a background threat of more fundamental reform. The government put substantial investment behind its desire to improve the process of planning through the Planning Delivery Grant (PDG), linking achievements across a basket of performance indicators to cash. League tables of performance were also published in an attempt to 'shame' dilatory authorities. In later rounds of PDG the emphasis shifted from speed of processing to actual delivery of development. The impact of such incentives upon local authorities was as intended: planning was prioritized as a function though authorities could use the PDG to invest in planning or other areas. Speeding up planning and delivering development provided a general and useful source of income.

Planners have therefore been complicit in the roll-out of neoliberal spatial governance but what was the alternative? There was a pragmatic approach to means and ends, particularly under New Labour. Ministers had made it clear that if planners and planning did not deliver or reform them further, more substantial change was a distinct possibility. Like the Conservatives there was no particular loyalty towards planning. According to the New Labour mantra of the time, what counts is what works (Allmendinger, 2011).

What have been the implications of this shift? Two issues arise. First, can planning hold on to its long-cherished, 'apolitical' position any longer? While there are strong arguments that planning has never been apolitical recent changes have further undermined the notion that it stood apart from a particular agenda. More fundamentally there is also the related question of trust. If planning is no longer (if it ever was) a neutral arbiter of competing objectives and values then what is its position and how should different interests understand this? One response from the wider public whom planning is supposed to represent has been to shift the focus of debate on future development from the planning to the legal arena, appealing to the courts through judicial and statutory review. The number of planning-related judicial reviews over the past two decades has increased significantly as environmental groups and other actors have sought to challenge planning decisions through the courts. There is a direct link between the increase in the incidence of judicial review and the pro-growth agenda of planning. However, challenges to planning decisions are not uniform. As planning and planners have moved in one direction, facilitating and helping to deliver growth, general public opinion has bifurcated between urban and rural areas and owner-occupiers and renters (DCLG, 2014). Those who live in urban areas and rent rather than own their homes are, understandably, more inclined to accept new development than those who are homeowners in rural areas. Furthermore, research for the CPRE found an age split on attitudes towards new development (CPRE, 2013). An Ipsos-Mori poll found that 53 per cent of those aged over 55 years were strongly pro-retention of the green belt, whereas only 31 per cent of those aged between 35 and 44 years felt that the green belt was important enough to preserve. Even if planning and planners were to determine future development in the public interest it is far from clear that there is a single public interest.

Is neoliberal spatial governance the inevitable future?

When Margaret Thatcher was Prime Minister she was renowned if not infamous for her phrase that 'there is no alternative'. During the early 1980s her government embarked upon severe public expenditure cuts, privatization of state-owned assets and deregulation. There was significant opposition in the form of strikes and protests. There was also a sense of division that led some to speculate that the long post-war consensus had given way to strife and a re-emergence of class conflict. Yet, due in part to the outcome of the Falklands conflict and an ineffective opposition, the government increased its majority at the 1983 general election. A quarter of a century later, during the height of the financial crisis involving the nationalization of some UK banks in 2008, there was a similar *fin de siècle* feeling about crisis and change. Yet nearly a decade later those banks remain in business and, despite persistent national debt and austerity in some countries, the system survives and once more there is relative stability in the economy and society. The situations and reactions of the early 1980s and late 2000s were part of the market-led neoliberal strategies and governance though the earlier era involved state contraction and the later era state expansion. The point to underline here is the robustness, resilience and opportunism of neoliberalism in the face of (inevitable) crisis. According to Peck, neoliberalism will not collapse for the simple reason that it was never a monolithic structure in the first place. Instead, it is evolving and embedded:

> Neoliberalism ... is not what it used to be (and it can *never* be what it used to be). From dogmatic deregulation to market friendly reregulation, from structural adjustment to good governance, from budget cuts to regulation by audit, from welfare retrenchment to active social policy, from privatization to public-private partnership, from greed is good to markets with morals ... the variegated face of 'roll out' neoliberalism represents, at the same time, a deeply consolidated *and* a crisis driven form of market rule.
>
> (Peck, 2010: 106, emphasis in the original)

As for alternatives Peck is equally clear: neoliberalism may be 'dead' but it remains dominant, driving and helping to structure change and reform. Facilitating that process is a wide range of right-leaning proposals or 'next steps', including many for planning. However, it is somewhat surprising that the left, given its social, environmental not to mention socialist origins, offers few alternatives to the neoliberalization of planning. It is as though the inevitability and dominance of neoliberalism has been accepted. Where such left of centre analyses and proposals do exist they tend towards risk-averse pragmatism and lack radical or fundamental suggestions. Labour's 2015 general election manifesto contained two proposals for planning; the first sought to protect more green spaces and the second to provide greater powers to allow communities to restrict the change of use of shops to pay day lenders and betting shops. There was a commitment to increase housing supply more generally that would have been achieved through allowing local authorities to build more homes. The Conservatives' manifesto in 2015 talked of the further roll-out of neighbourhood planning and green belt protection while also claiming to have 'unblocked planning' through deregulation. One might expect such documents to be vague and non-committal though there is lack of vision for planning and what it might contribute towards improving housing affordability and mitigating the impact of climate change, for example,. Instead, there are mixed messages to different audiences about 'more *and* less' planning combined with a pragmatic, knee-jerk approach to reform more reminiscent of the New Labour era. During the 2000s a typical response to any issue of public concern that arose was to add it to the list of objectives for planning.

Notwithstanding the source and political leaning there are broadly two common elements to the current post-2015 era for planning across the major political parties and think tanks. The first common element concerns the attitude towards planning. Planning as a distinct area of public policy is seldom discussed (as opposed to, say, housing). Instead, planning comes within the broad analysis of the state and public sector more generally. This broad analysis tends to take a schizophrenic shape. On the one hand planning is held up as some kind of bulwark against progress in the form of a rapacious concreting of the England's 'green and pleasant land'. On the other hand planning is also often portrayed as a barrier to progress and growth, impacting upon individuals through higher house prices as a result on the restrictions upon new development. This 'feast or famine' attitude neatly echoes the desire for simple, binary, easy to digest messages and narratives around issues and solutions, particularly at the time of general elections. The lack of nuance in these debates also echoes the pattern of portraying a 'crisis' that urgently needs to be addressed, usually in the form of change. Such 'crises' largely go unchallenged as there are few defenders or champions of planning compared to business or finance interests and umbrella groups, for example. There has been an absence of argument or debate that makes a positive case for planning in economic growth, climate change mitigation and infrastructure coordination, for example.

The second common dimension to debates on the future of planning is a view that the system us flawed and in need of reform en bloc. The experiences of planning over the past three decades or so discussed in this book highlight that one system or approach cannot balance different needs and aspirations without the kind of sophistry, politics, multiple and overlapping spaces and scales that guarantee dissatisfaction and further reform. The common assumption of a 'one size fits all' approach that privileges growth provides a unified and, in places, inappropriate model and purpose for planning. Many of the issues that have discredited planning and planners in the eyes of the public in recent years have come about because of the need to deploy techniques and tools either to facilitate or resist the 'growth ethos' of planning. Nevertheless, there is also another argument against a unified, homogenous planning. Even in less contested environments dissatisfaction with planning is inherent in the pluralist, governance-based approaches and institutional framework that currently dominate. Rydin (2013) argues that the notion of governance and collaborative planning inevitably leads to compromise regarding the level of growth rather than the more fundamental question of whether growth is actually appropriate. As she goes on to argue, 'growth-dependent planning is never going to be able to achieve desirable change in all locations at all times and meet the needs of all groups in society' (ibid., 2013: 9). Trying to achieve a balance between competing demands is further necessitated by the link between improvements in infrastructure, affordable housing, environmental protection, schools and new development. Yes, your community can have necessary investment in public goods and services but this will be dependent upon and, in part, paid for by the acceptance of new development. Such a situation amounts to a 'double bind' of an ethos of growth backed up by a link between development and societal improvements.

So how can we go about rethinking planning? The analysis thus far has sought to highlight that it is not neoliberal spatial governance and growth-led planning per se that has been the problem, but the 'one size fits all' homogeneity, the restless churn of reform and approaches inherent in such an approach that undermines long-term strategic planning combined with the dishonesty and duplicity in the way in which neoliberalism has been achieved and rolled out and, in places, resisted. The promulgation of the view that there is no alternative or that we are 'all liberals now' in the words of Fukuyama has somehow been taken to mean that growth and economic development are an orthodoxy to which society needs to be orientated. Economic globalization has helped to drive this mantra with the notion that free competition and the reduction in supply-side constraints such as planning will help to attract investment and jobs, scaring politicians and communities into accepting development and pro-growth policies.

This view ignores the fact that markets and investors value certainty and high-quality environments as much as flexibility and speed of decision making. Indeed, the development and evolution of neoliberalism highlights the tension between deregulation and the need for long-term planning and environmental protection not to mention the necessary active role played by the national and local state in promoting and facilitating change and growth in areas of market failure. Yet such different roles are largely lost or downplayed in the rhetoric of planning controls that portrays them as a burden on business. It is largely because of the need for multiple models and approaches that tensions and dissatisfaction arise. So a rethought planning needs to recognize and be based around a plurality of approaches and models. Constant reform and the duplicity of planners in deploying new spaces, scales and politics arise from forcing a growth-led approach upon all areas. Moving away from this and recognizing the multiplicity of models is the first and main step in rethinking planning and working with spaces, scales and politics that reflect the needs and desires of different areas. This is not to say that there are no overarching policy objectives: a key question and tension within any system is how do we ensure consistency and think strategically while allowing for differentiation and a move away from one approach? More specifically, how do we reconcile national priorities such as climate change mitigation and adaptation with local circumstances? Such tensions are not immutable – there is no contradiction between having supra-national priorities or policies and a varied, locality-sensitive approach to planning. On the contrary, allowing different approaches to emerge that have scales, spaces and politics may well better achieve national priorities.

One could foresee growth-restraining and growth-stimulating systems sitting alongside the current ethos of growth-led planning, each with their own characteristics and each seeking to interpret and realize national issues in different ways. With such a diversity of approaches there could be a conflict between a national presumption in favour of development and the underlying notion that planning exists to facilitate development.

The future: where next for planning?

Sadly, as shown above the plurality of planning is being discredited through the current emphasis and focus upon localism and neighbourhood planning. The spirit if not the promise of localism is founded upon diversity and tailored approaches though these are tightly circumscribed if not frustrated by other initiatives, particularly the presumption in favour of sustainable development, deregulation and national infrastructure proposals. In its current form localism will become discredited as the gap between rhetoric of local control and the reality of centralization and deregulation becomes apparent.

At the time of writing there are two clear narratives for English planning post-2015. The first involves localism in the form of an acceleration of neighbourhood planning and devolution of powers to cities and local government. Considered rather gimmicky when first floated, neighbourhood plans and planning have emerged as an unexpected success in the eyes of the Conservatives though their impact on the ground has been less than clear. As of April 2014 there were thirteen adopted and eighty draft plans. A Business Neighbourhood Plan in Milton Keynes has also been adopted. Most of these plans were supported financially by the government with a fund of around £10m. over two years. Parish councils will receive up to 25 per cent of the Community Infrastructure Levy associated with development in the area. Yet despite a rather marginal impact in terms of numbers the Conservative government elected in 2015 has pledged to accelerate and expand the roll-out of neighbourhood planning.

The devolution agenda is of significance for planning in that the combination of authorities are incentivized to create, in effect, a single-tier planning body as with the Growth/City Deals under the coalition from 2010–15. In 2015 a Cities and Local Government Devolution Bill was introduced to expand devolution further, particularly to those areas that agreed to form a combined authority. Combined authorities are corporate bodies that allow local authorities to work together on economic development, regeneration and transport. They are, in effect, functional planning areas. The five combined authorities approved after 2009 were large metropolitan areas, e.g. Greater Manchester or West Yorkshire. A further wave of combined authorities under the post-2015 proposals could include a much wider range of local authority functions and the possibility of an elected mayor for the authority.

A significant question given the purpose of this book is why have these two initiatives – localism and City/Growth Deals and devolution through combined authorities – survived and indeed prospered while others have fallen away?

Within central government both are regarded as successful for a range of reasons. First, they are growth-based initiatives that seek to deliver development through locally agreed schemes. As the Chancellor put it:

> Here's the deal: We will hand power from the centre to cities to give you greater control over your local transport, housing, skills and healthcare. And we'll give the levers you need to grow your local economy and make sure local people keep the rewards. But it's right people have a single point of accountability: someone they elect, who takes the decisions and carries the can. So with these new powers for cities must come new city-wide elected mayors who work with local councils. I will not impose this model on anyone. But nor will I settle for less.
>
> (George Osborne, speech on the Northern Powerhouse, 14 May 2015)

There are incentives for localities and cities to participate though the overall effect is to neutralize opposition and create a coalition for growth. Second, they are largely uncontentious and low cost. A significant amount of community activity has been generated for relatively little cost. The devolution or localism agenda provides a ready response to communities, including business groups, who wish to engage more in planning, either in a positive way (i.e. wanting more growth) or negative wat (i.e. resisting more growth). However, as the Government points out, neighbourhood plans give communities a say in where new housing and offices should be located and what they should look like. Neighbourhood plans must still meet the needs of the wider area, including housing and employment demands. The City Deals do include some significant resources though these are in return for other, growth-linked public and private investment. The devolution of powers is also conditional upon a range of joint authority measures around planning and transport, etc. which may create efficiencies in provision and refocus areas on growth delivery. Third, they achieve a wider impact by helping to portray the government in a positive, collaborative light very from to the prevailing public sector cutting, anti-European and immigrant controversies. Neighbourhood plans and growth strategies are positive initiatives that provide a useful counter to the deregulatory narrative and image of government.

The second clear narrative for English planning post-2015 is a continuation of deregulation and the view of planning as a 'brake on business'. In July 2015 the Chancellor published his Productivity Plan that included a number of initiatives to speed up and deregulate planning, including the introduction of a zoning-based system and targets for the preparation of local plans (HMG, 2015). Once again, the deregulation of planning is being emphasized as the key to addressing a range of issues, including economic competitiveness and housing affordability. Localism, devolution and deregulation exhibit a form of schizophrenia that creates uncertainty and confusion that makes it possible to construct arguments that support a proposal based upon either view. For those who wish to promote development there is the language and evidence to support the view that planning should 'get out of the way' and not impose costs and delays. For others who wish to resist change there is the ethos of localism and bottom-up planning. Ironically, it is this disputatious underpinning that creates the need for political displacement and deferral through raising expectations that planning can be both pro- and anti-growth.

There are some longer-term strategic consequences for planning of further devolution and deregulation that are worth reflecting upon. One issue is the diminishing role of local authorities. As neighbourhood plans are further rolled out, Growth/City Deals with associated, conditional unitary, strategic planning are extended and the influence of LEPs in planning, housing and infrastructure increases the local authority as a territorial unit of planning and the main vehicle for democratic accountability will be diminished. Further expected extensions to the General Permitted Development Order will also bypass planning authorities through deregulation. One consequence of any such shift will be that the local plan will become less significant as an influence upon development and one wonders if local authorities will continue to prepare them.

Another possible longer-term consequence concerns the potential reaction against increased devolution and fragmentation from businesses. The aggressive deregulation of the successive Thatcher governments in the 1980s was reversed when it became clear to the government that it threatened growth and business interests. The outcome was a centralization of control.

Conclusions

There is a commonly used image of change in planning that is based on reaching a crossroads where there are definite and clear though difficult decisions to be made about the way forward. The underlying point is that reform is a regular and permanent feature of planning. Two examples help to back up this perception. The first is from an inquiry set up in the mid-1970s, not long after a major reform of planning in the 1960s:

> When the recommendations of the 1965 report of the Planning Advisory Group (PAG) were enacted by Parliament in the 1968 Town and Country Planning Act, many felt that Britain had created a planning system that could cope with the dynamic and unpredictable society of the late twentieth century. But even before the new system has been fully established – a process that has taken the best part of a decade – it is coming under fire. As the first of the new Structure Plans begin to appear, we are told by the general and technical press that the system is too slow and too unwieldy; that it is ineffectual in achieving concrete results; that it is insufficiently relevant to those who are planned; that it is imperfectly related to other areas of local government activity, such as housing or social services or health; and that it does not promote a rational allocation of limited local resources.
>
> (RTPI, 1976: 5)

Planning and the Future was published in 1975 by the RTPI to rethink planning against a backdrop of growing criticism and dissatisfaction with the system despite recent changes and reforms. The analysis and recommendations pointed to the need to rethink the purpose and tools of planning in order to reflect the changed circumstances of the 1970s, particularly concerns about the stalling national economic situation and growing environmental awareness of our finite resources following the oil crisis in the early 1970s.

Despite being multidisciplinary and taking evidence from a wide range of interests the report was largely ignored and overtaken by events: by the mid-1970s the national discourse was becoming one of 'state overload' and the need for less not more state regulatory functions. As a result planning continued to be a source of frustration for business interests and environmentalists. And so it was that a few years later in 1983 the Nuffield Foundation set up its own enquiry into planning against the continued backdrop of dissatisfaction. As the report noted:

> Critics find the planning system unsatisfactory because of the persistent failure of successive governments to make clear statements of national policy as a framework for local plan making. Nor is there an adequate means to deal with regional. The structure is inappropriate because of the division of functions between counties and districts, the location of boundaries and the proliferation of special agencies. Present regulations and procedures are an obstacle to good planning: too much detail is pre-scribed by central government, the preparation of development plans takes too long, likewise their approval, plans are more like blueprints than guidelines and there are too many regulations. Public participation is ineffective and the public inquiry favours the strong at the expense of the weak. The planning profession finds itself in a position of increasing political exposure for which it is ill prepared.
>
> (1986: 2–3)

The analysis and recommendations from the Nuffield Foundation also high-lighted the mismatch between the system as established in 1947 but largely still in operation and the contemporary needs and demands of society. However, the inquiry identified two significant issues that it considered key to any reform of planning. The first was the assumption of a consensus that planning was a 'good thing'. The second was a reluctance to tackle the fundamental question of what planning was for in case the fragile consensus around it dissolved. The report found that there was fundamental disagreement around a wide range of issues and aspects of planning though reform should start by recognizing that the consensus around the need for planning in the immediate post-war years had evaporated. Like the RTPI's inquiry the report was largely ignored or overtaken by events. The questions posed by Nuffield about the purpose of planning in 1986 were answered by the ideological determination of the Thatcher administration in the Housing and Planning Act of the same year, an Act that further deregulated planning.

Such reflections, like reform itself, are a regular characteristic of planning in the UK, as has been chronicled in this book. What is interesting about the analysis of RTPI and Nuffield inquiries is that, give or take a few issues relating to climate change and globalization, both could have been written at any time subsequently. Indeed, many of the same concerns and issues were discussed in the Barker Review (2004). The broad thrust of these analyses would not look out of place if published tomorrow. However, the image of planning at a regular crossroads does. Keeping to the theme of traffic, a more accurate image is of a roundabout, given that each reform focuses upon the same issues and grapples with the same tensions and options – the demands for more planning *and* less planning. When major reforms to planning are introduced, as in 1979, 1986, 1990/1991, 2004 and 2010, they tend to sway one way and then the other, seeking to reduce planning and then subsequently expand it, each change establishing a different approach for a few years that is inevitably reformed again a short time later.

The argument of this book is that instability is both inherent and damaging to longer-term strategic planning and consequently to the broader objectives of planning including sustainable development. More significantly, the regularity of reform and the flexibility of planning to accommodate change has lately had a specific driver, namely pro-growth, market-supportive governance. Underlying the inherent contradictions of neoliberalism is a set of more fundamental and inherent tensions within planning itself, as highlighted in the RTPI study above. This layer cake of stresses and interactions that the RTPI and Nuffield highlighted, combined with the tensions and experimental nature of neoliberalism, makes it difficult to pinpoint or even resolve the problems and issues that beset planning and spatial governance. However, one could start by attempting to remove the top layer of tensions, the pro-growth 'one size fits all' neoliberalism that has dominated planning for the past three decades. Without this separation of inherent tensions and those of the neoliberal objectives for planning, any reflection upon the more fundamental issues concerning planning and its purpose in the twenty-first century will be problematic.

Bibliography

Adam Smith Institute (2012) *Planning in a Free Society. London as a Case Study for a Spontaneously Planned Future.* London: Adam Smith Institute.

Allen, J. and Cochrane, A. (2010) Assemblages of State Power: Topological Shifts in the Organization of Government and Politics. *Antipode* 42(5): 1071–1089.

Allmendinger, P. (1997) *Thatcherism and Planning. The Case of Simplified Planning Zones.* Aldershot: Avebury.

Allmendinger, P. (1998) Planning Practice and the Postmodern Debate. *International Planning Studies* 3(2): 227–248.

Allmendinger, P. (2000) *Planning in Postmodern Times.* London: Routledge.

Allmendinger, P. (2006) Zoning by Stealth? The Diminution of Discretionary Planning. *International Planning Studies* 11(2): 137–143.

Allmendinger, P. (2009) Explaining the Paradox of Performance Improvements and Delay in Development Control. *Urban Design and Planning* 162(2): 79–86.

Allmendinger, P. (2010) *Transaction Costs, Planning and Housing Supply.* London: Royal Institute of Chartered Surveyors.

Allmendinger, P. (2011) *New Labour and Planning: From New Right to New Left.* London: Routledge.

Allmendinger, P. (2013) Non-plan. In M. Tewdwr-Jones, N. Phelps and R. Freestone (eds) *Planning Imagination: Peter Hall and the Study of Urban and Regional Planning.* London: Routledge.

Allmendinger, P. and Haughton, G. (2009) Critical Reflection on Spatial Planning. *Environment and Planning A*, 41: 2544–2549.

Allmendinger, P. and Haughton, G. (2011a) Post-Political Planning: The End of Consensus? Stockholm: KTH University, May.

Allmendinger, P. and Haughton, G. (2011b) Moving On: From Spatial Planning to Localism and Beyond. *Town and Country Planning* (April): 184–187.

Allmendinger, P. and Haughton, G. (2012) Post-political Spatial Planning in England: A Crisis of Consensus? *Transactions of the Institute of British Geographers* 37(1): 89–103.

Allmendinger, P. and Haughton, G. (2013) The Evolution and Trajectories of Neoliberal Spatial Governance: 'Neoliberal' Episodes in Planning. *Planning Practice and Research* 28(1): 6–26.

Allmendinger, P. and Haughton, G. (2015) Post-political Regimes in English Planning: From Third Way to Big Society. In J. Metzger, P. Allmendinger and S. Oosterlynck (eds) *Planning Against the Political: Democratic Deficits in European Territorial Governance.* London: Routledge.

Allmendinger, P. and Tewdwr-Jones, M. (1997a) A Mile or a Millimetre? Measuring the 'Planning Theory-Practice Gap'. *Environment and Planning B* 24(6): 802–806.

Allmendinger, P., and Tewdwr-Jones, M. (1997b) Post-Thatcherite Urban Planning and Politics: A Major Change? *International Journal of Urban and Regional Research* 21(1): 100–116.

Allmendinger, P. and Thomas, H. (1998) (eds) *Urban Planning and the British New Right*. London: Routledge.

Allmendinger, P., Haughton, G., Knieling, J. and Othengrafen, F. (2015) *Soft Spaces of Governance in Europe: A Comparative Perspective*. London: Routledge.

Altvater, E. (2009) Postneoliberalism Or Postcapitalism? The Failure of Neoliberalism in the Financial Market Crisis. *Development Dialogue* 51: 73–86.

Ambrose, P. (1986) *Whatever Happened to Planning?* London: Methuen.

Amin, A. (2004) Regions Unbound: Towards a New Politics of Space. *Geografiska Annaler* 86B: 33–44.

Amin, A. and Thrift, N. (2002) *Cities: Reimagining the Urban*. Cambridge: Polity.

Andersen, J. and Pløger, J. (2007): The Dualism of Urban Governance in Denmark. *European Planning Studies* 15(10): 1350–1367.

Badiou, A. (2009) *Theory of the Subject*. London: Continuum International Publishing.

Baeten, G. (2007) The Uses of Deprivation in the Neoliberal City. In BAVO (ed.) *Urban Politics Now: Reimagining Democracy in the Neoliberal City*. Rotterdam: NAi Publishers, pp. 44–56.

Banham, R., Barker, P., Hall, P. and Price, C. (1969) Non-plan: An Experiment in Freedom. *New Society*, 20 March.

Banfield, E. (1974) *Unheavenly Cities Revisited*. Long Grove, Il: Waveland Press.

Barker, K. (2003) *Barker Review of Housing Supply: Interim Report Analysis*. London: HMT.

Barker, K. (2004) *Barker Review of Housing Supply: Final Report*. London: HMT.

Barker, K. (2006) *Barker Review of Land Use Planning: Final Report*. London: HMT.

Barker, P. (2000) Thinking the Unthinkable. In J. Hughes and S. Sadler (eds) *Non-Plan: Essays on Freedom, Participation and Change in Modern Architecture and Urbanism*. Oxford: Architectural Press.

Barlow, M. (1940) *Report of the Royal Commission on the Distribution of the Industrial Population. Barlow Report*. Cmd 6153. London: HMSO.

Baudrillard, J. (1970) *The Consumer Society: Myths and Structures*. London: Sage.

Baudrillard, J. (1972) *For a Critique of the Political Economy of the Sign*. Candor, NY: Telos Press.

Baudrillard, J. (1987) *Forget Foucault*. New York: Semiotext(e).

Baudrillard, J. (1992) *The Illusion of the End*. Cambridge: Polity.

Baum, H. S. (1983) *Planners and Public Expectations*. New York: Schenkman.

Beauregard, R. (1989) Between Modernity and Postmodernity: The Ambiguous Position of US Planning. *Environment and Planning D: Society and Space* 7: 381–395.

Beck, U. (1995) *Ecological Politics in an Age of Risk*. Cambridge: Polity.

Beck, U. (1996) *The Reinvention of Politics: Rethinking Modernity in the Global Social Order*. Cambridge: Polity.

Beck, U. (1998a) *Democracy without Enemies*. Cambridge: Polity.

Beck, U. (1998b) *World Risk Society*. Cambridge: Polity.

Bell, D. (1973) *The Coming of the Post-industrial Society*. New York: Basic Books.

Bell, D. (1980) The Social Framework of the Information Society. In T. Forester (ed.) *The Microelectronics Revolution*. Oxford: Basil Blackwell.

Bengs, C. (2005) Planning Theory for the Naïve? *European Journal of Spatial Development*, 1650–9544. Available at: http://www.nordregio.se/EJSD/-ISSN.

Best, S. and Kellner, D. ([1991] 1997) *Postmodern Theory*. London: Macmillan.

Better Regulation Task Force (2000) *Tackling the Impact of Increasing Regulation: A Case Study of Hotels and Restaurants*. London: Cabinet Office.

Beveridge, W. (1942) *Social Insurance and Allied Services, Beveridge Report*, Cmd 6404. London: HMSO.

Bow Group (2009) *Our Towns, Our Cities: The Next Steps for Planning Reform*. London: Bow Group.

Bracewell-Milnes, B. (1974) *Is Capital Taxation Fair?* Sydney: The Sydney Press.

Brenner, N. and Theodore, N. (2002) *Spaces of Neoliberalism: Urban Restructuring in North America and Western Europe*. Oxford: Blackwell.

Brenner, N., Peck, J. and Theodore, N. (2010) After Neoliberalization? *Globalizations* 7(3): 327–345.

British Chambers of Commerce (2009) *Planning for Recovery*. London: British Chambers of Commerce.

British Property Federation (BPF) (2008a) *Planning Manifesto: Making Planning Work*. London: BPF.

British Property Federation (BPF) (2008b) *Tax Increment Finance: A New Tool for Funding Regeneration in the UK?*London: BPF.

British Property Federation (BPF) (2011) *Briefing on Second Reading of Localism Bill*. London: BPF.

Buller, J. and Flinders, M. (2005) The Domestic Origins of Depoliticisation in the Area of British Economic Policy. *British Journal of Politics and International Relations* 7(4): 526–544.

Burnham, P. (2001) New Labour and the Politics of Depoliticisation. *British Journal of Politics and International Relations* 3(2): 127–149.

Cabinet Office (2010) *The Coalition: Our Programme for Government*. London: HMSO.

Callinicos, A. (2002) *Against the Third Way*. Cambridge: Polity.

Camhis, M. (1979) *Planning Theory and Philosophy*. London: Tavistock.

Campbell, J. L. and Pederson, O. K. (eds) (2001) *The Rise of Neoliberalism and Institutional Analysis*. Princeton, NJ: Princeton University Press.

Campaign to Protect Rural England (CPRE) (2006) *Policy-Based Evidence Making: The Policy Exchange's War against Planning*. London: CPRE.

Campaign to Protect Rural England (CPRE) (2013) *Countryside Promises, Planning Realities*. London: CPRE.

Campaign to Protect Rural England (CPRE), Royal Society for the Protection of Birds, World Wildlife Foundation, Town and Country Planning Association, Civic Trust, Roomfor Housing and Planning, Friends of the Earth, Environmental Law Foundation (2002) *Third Party Rights of Appeal of Planning*. London: CPRE*et al.*

Castells, M. (1978) *The Urban Question: A Marxist Approach*. London: Edward Arnold.

Castells, M. (2000) *The Rise of the Network Society: The Information Age: Economy, Society and Culture*, Vol. 1. Oxford: Blackwell.

Castoriadis, C. ([1975] 1998) *The Imaginary Institution of Society*. Trans. Kathleen Blamey. Cambridge, MA: MIT Press.

Centre for Cities (2010) *Arrested Development: Are We Building Houses in the Right Places?* London: Centre for Cities.

Chadwick, G. (1971) *A Systems View of Planning: Towards a Theory of the Urban and Regional Planning Process*. Oxford: Pergamon.

Cherry, G. E. (1996) *Town Planning in Britain since 1900: The Rise and Fall of the Planning Ideal*. Oxford: Blackwell.

Cochrane, A. (2012) Making Up a Region: The Rise and Fall of the 'South East of England' as a Political Territory. *Environment and Planning C: Government and Policy* 30: 95–108.

Colomb, C. (2007) Unpacking New Labour's 'Urban Renaissance' Agenda: Towards a Socially Sustainable Reurbanization of British Cities? *Planning Practice and Research* 22(1): 1–24.

Confederation of British Industry (CBI) (2001) *Planning for Productivity: A 10-Point Action Plan*. London: CBI.

Confederation of British Industry (CBI) (2011) *CBI Response to the Government's Growth Review*. London: CBI.

Conservative Party (2010a) *An Invitation to Join the Government of Britain*. London: Conservative Party.

Conservative Party (2010b) *Open Source Planning Green Paper*. London: Conservative Party.

Cooke, P. (1983) *Theories of Planning and Spatial Development*. London: Hutchinson.

Cowell, R. (2013) The Greenest Movement Ever? Planning and Sustainability in England after the May 2010 Elections. In G, Haughton and P. Allmendinger (eds) *Spatial Planning and the New Localism*. London: Routledge.

Crouch, C. (2004) *Post-democracy*. Cambridge: Polity.

Davies, J. G. (1972) *The Evangelistic Bureaucrat*. London: Tavistock.

Davoudi, S. and Strange, I. (eds) (2009) *Conceptions of Space and Place in Strategic Spatial Planning*. London: Routledge.

Dear, M. (1986) Postmodernism and Planning. *Environment and Planning D: Society and Space* 4: 367–384.

Dear, M. (2000) *The Postmodern Urban Condition*. Oxford: Blackwell.

Dear, M. and Scott, A. (1981) *Urbanization and Urban Planning in Capitalist Society*. London: Methuen.

Deas, I. (2013) Towards Post-Political Consensus in Urban Policy? Localism and the Emerging Agenda for Regeneration under the Cameron Government. In G. Haughton and P. Allmendinger *Spatial Planning and the New Localism*. London: Routledge.

Dembski, S. (2012). Symbolic Markers and Institutional Innovation in Transforming Urban Spaces. Unpublished PhD, University of Amsterdam.

Department for Environment, Food and Rural Affairs (DEFRA) (2005) *Securing the Future: UK Government Sustainable Development Strategy*. London: HMSO.

Deleuze, G. and Guattari, F. (1972). *Anti-Oedipus*. English trans. 2004. London and New York: Continuum.

Department of Communities and Local Government (DCLG) (2006a) *Achieving Successful Participation: Spatial Plans in Practice*, London: HMSO.

Department of Communities and Local Government (DCLG) (2006b) *Preparing Core Strategies: Spatial Plans in Practice*, London: HMSO.

Department of Communities and Local Government (DCLG) (2011) *Draft National Planning Policy Framework*. London: HMSO.

Department of Communities and Local Government (DCLG) (2014) *Public Attitudes to New House Building: Findings from the 2013 British Social Attitudes Survey*. London: HMSO.

Department of the Environment, Transport and the Regions(DETR) (1998) *Modernising Planning: A White Paper*. London: DETR.

Department of the Environment, Transport and the Regions (DETR) (2000a) *Planning Policy Guidance Note 3: Housing*. London: HMSO.

Department of the Environment, Transport and the Regions (DETR) (2000b) *Our Towns and Cities: The Future – Delivering an Urban Renaissance*. London: HMSO.

Department of the Environment, Transport and the Regions (DETR) (2001) *Planning: Delivering a Fundamental Change*. London: HMSO.

Department of the Environment (DoE) (1986) *The Future of Development Plans*. London: HMSO.

Department of Trade and Industry (DTI) (1999) *Biotechnology Clusters*. Report of a Team led by Lord Sainsbury, Minister for Science. London: DTI.

Department of Transport, Local Government and the Regions (DTLR) (2001) *Planning: Delivering a Fundamental Change*. London: HMSO.

Dikeç, M. (2005) Space, Politics, and the Political. *Environment and Planning D: Society and Space* 23(2): 171–188.

Dikeç, M. (2012) Space as a Mode of Political Thinking. *Geoforum* 43: 669–676.

Drucker, P. (1969) *The Age of Discontinuity*. London: Heinemann.

Dryzek, J. (1990) *Discursive Democracy. Politics, Policy and Political Science*. Cambridge: Cambridge University Press.

Duncan, S. and Savage, M. (1991) New Perspectives on the Locality Debate. *Environment and Planning A* 23: 155–164.

Evans, B. (1997) Town Planning to Environmental Planning. In A. Blowers and B. Evans (eds) *Town Planning into the 21st Century*. London: Routledge.

Evans, A. (1991) Rabbit Hutches on Postage Stamps: Planning Development and Political Economy. *Urban Studies* 28(6) 853–870.

Evans, A. and Hartwich, O. (2006) *Better Homes, Greener Cities*. London: Policy Exchange.

Faludi, A. (1973) *Planning Theory*. Oxford: Pergamon.

Fischer, F. and Forester, J. (eds) (1993) *The Argumentative Turn in Policy Analysis and Planning*. London: UCL Press.

Flinders, M. (2004) Delegated Governance in the European Union. *Journal of European Public Policy* 11(3): 520–544.

Flyvbjerg, B. (1998) *Rationality and Power: Democracy in Practice*. Chicago: University of Chicago Press.

Foley, D. (1960) British Town Planning: One Ideology or Three? *British Journal of Sociology* 11(3): 211–231.

Forester, J. (1989) *Planning in the Face of Power*. Berkeley, CA: University of California Press.

Foucault, M. (1976) *Discipline and Punish: The Birth of the Prison*. London: Allen Lane.

Foucault, M. (1980) *The History of Sexuality*. New York: Vintage Books.

Friedman, M. (1962) *Capitalism and Freedom*. Chicago: University of Chicago Press.

Friedmann, J. (1987) *Planning in the Public Domain: From Knowledge to Action*. Princeton, NJ: Princeton University Press.

Fukuyama, F. (1989) The End of History, *The National Interest* 16 (Summer): 3–18.

Gamble, A. (1988) *The Free Economy and the Strong State*. London: Macmillan.

Gamble, A. (2009) *The Spectre at the Feast. Capitalist Crisis and the Politics of Recession*. London: Palgrave Macmillan.

Geddes, M. (2006): Partnership and the Limits to Local Governance in England: Institutionalist Analysis and Neoliberalism, *International Journal of Urban and Regional Research* 30(1): 76–97.

Gibson-Graham, J. K. (2008) Diverse Economies: Performative Practices for 'Other Worlds'. *Progress in Human Geography* 32(5): 613–632.

Giddens, A. (1984) *The Constitution of Society.* Cambridge: Polity.

Giddens, A. (1990) *The Consequences of Modernity.* Oxford: Polity.

Giddens, A. (1991) *Modernity and Self-Identity.* Cambridge: Polity.

Giddens, A. (1994) *Beyond Left and Right. The Future of Radical Politics.* Cambridge: Polity.

Giddens, A. (1999) *Runaway World.* London: Profile Books.

Glass, R. ([1959] 1973) The Evaluation of Planning: Some Sociological Considerations. In A. Faludi (ed.) *A Reader in Planning Theory.* Oxford: Pergamon.

Goodstadt, V. (2009) Working across Boundaries. *Town and Country Planning* 78(3): 8.

Gough, J. (2002) Neoliberalism and Socialization in the Contemporary City: Opposites, Complements and Instabilities. *Antipode* 34(3): 405–426.

Gunder, M. (2010) Planning as the Ideology of (Neoliberal) Space. *Planning Theory* 9(4): 298–314.

Habermas, J. (1984) *The Theory of Communicative Action,* Vol. 1: *Reason and the Rationalisation of Society.* Cambridge: Polity.

Habermas, J. (1987) *The Philosophical Discourse of Modernity.* Cambridge: Polity.

Habermas, J. (1999) The European Nation State and the Pressures of Globalisation. *New Left Review* 1(235): 54.

Hackworth, J. and Moriah, A. (2006) Neoliberalism, Contingency and Urban Policy: The Case of Social Housing in Ontario. *International Journal of Urban and Regional Research* 30(3): 510–527.

Hall, P. (1977a) The Inner Cities Dilemma. *New Society,* 3 February.

Hall, P. (1977b) Green Fields and Grey Areas, Speech to the RTPI Annual Conference, Chester, 15 June.

Hall, P. (1998) *Cities in Civilization: Culture, Technology, and Urban Order.* London: Weidenfeld & Nicolson; New York: Pantheon Books.

Hall, P. (1983) *Cities of Tomorrow.* London: Blackwell.

Hall, P. (1980) *Great Planning Disasters.* Berkeley, CA: University of California Press.

Hall, P., Gracey, H., Drewett, R. and Thomas, R. (1973) *The Containment of Urban England.* London: Allen and Unwin.

Hall, P. with Tewdwr-Jones, M. (2011) *Urban and Regional Planning.* London: Routledge.

Harper, T. L. and Stein, S. M. (1995) Out of the Postmodern Abyss: Preserving the Rationale for Liberal Planning. *Journal of Planning Education and Research* 14: 233–244.

Hart, G. (2010) D/developments after the Meltdown. *Antipode* 41: 117–141.

Harvey, D. (1973) *Social Justice and the City.* London: Arnold.

Harvey, D. (1978) On Planning the Ideology of Planning. In R. Burchell and G. Sternlieb (eds) *Planning Theory in the 1980s.* New Brunswick, NJ: CUPR, 213–233.

Harvey, D. (1982) *The Limits to Capital.* London: Arnold.

Harvey, D. (1985) *The Urbanization of Capital.* Baltimore, MD: Johns Hopkins University Press.

Harvey, D. (1989) *The Condition of Postmodernity.* London: Blackwell.

Harvey, D. (2006) Neoliberalism and the Restoration of Class Power. In *Spaces of Global Capitalism. Towards a Theory of Uneven Geographical Development.* London: Verso.

Hassan, I. (1985) The Culture of Postmodernism. *Theory, Culture and Society* 2(3): 119–132.

Haughton, G. (2012) Planning and Growth. *Town and Country Planning* 81(3): 121–125.

Haughton, G. and Allmendinger, P. (2010) Spatial Planning, Devolution and New Planning Spaces. *Environment and Planning C, Government and Policy* 28(5): 803–818.

Haughton, G. and Allmendinger, P. (2013) Spatial Planning and the New Localism. *Planning Practice and Research* 28(1): 1–5.

Haughton, G. and Allmendinger, P. (forthcoming) Fluid Spatial Imaginaries: Evolving Estuarial City-Regional Spaces. *International Journal of Urban and Regional Research*.

Haughton, G., Allmendinger, P. and Oosterlynck, S. (2015) Spaces of Neoliberal Experimentation: Soft Spaces, Post-Politics and Neoliberal Governmentality. *Environment and Planning A* 45: 217–234.

Haughton, G., Allmendinger, P., Counsell, D. and Vigar, G. (2010) *The New Spatial Planning: Soft Spaces, Fuzzy Boundaries and Territorial Management*. London: Routledge.

Hay, C. (1996) *Re-stating Social and Political Change*. Milton Keynes: Open University Press.

Hay, C. (2007) *Why We Hate Politics*. Cambridge: Polity.

Hay, C. and Farrall, S. (2011) Establishing the Ontological Status of Thatcherism by Gauging Its 'Periodisability': Towards a 'Cascade Theory' of Public Policy Radicalism, *British Journal of Politics and International Relations* 13(4): 439–458 .

Hayek, F. A. (1944) *The Road to Serfdom*. Chicago: University of Chicago Press.

Hayek, F.A. (1960) *The Constitution of Liberty*. Chicago: University of Chicago Press.

Healey, P. (1992) A Planner's Day: Knowledge and Action in Communicative Practice, *Journal of the American Planning Association* 58(1): 157–182.

Healey, P. (1993a) The Communicative Work of Development Plans, *Environment and Planning B: Planning and Design* 20: 83–104.

Healey, P. (1993b) Planning through Debate: The Communicative Turn in Planning Theory, in F. Fischer and J. Forester (eds) *The Argumentative Turn in Policy Analysis and Planning*. London: UCL Press.

Healey, P. (1996) *Collaborative Planning: Shaping Places in Fragmented Societies*. Basingstoke: Palgrave Macmillan.

Healey, P. (1997) *Collaborative Planning: Shaping Places in Fragmented Societies*. London: Macmillan.

Healey, P. (2006a) Transforming Governance: Challenges of Institutional Adaptation and a New Politics of Space. *European Planning Studies* 14(3): 299–320.

Healey, P. (2006b) Relational Complexity and the Imaginative Power of Strategic Spatial Planning. *European Planning Studies* 14(4): 525–546.

Healey, P. (2007) *Urban Complexity and Spatial Strategies: Towards a Relational Planning for Our Times*. London: Routledge.

Healey, P., McNamara, P., Elson, M. and Doak, A. (1988) *Land Use Planning and the Mediation of Urban Change*. Cambridge: Cambridge University Press.

Hebdige, D. (1988) *Hiding in the Light: On Images and Things*. London: Routledge.

Heley, J. (2013) Soft Spaces, Fuzzy Boundaries and Spatial Governance in Post-Devolution Wales. *International Journal of Urban and Regional Research* 37: 1325–1348.

Her Majesty's Government (HMG) (2015) *Fixing the Foundations: Creating a More Prosperous Nation*. London: HMSO.

Her Majesty's Treasury (HMT) (2003) UK Membership of the Single Currency: An Assessment of the Five Economic Tests, Cm 5776. London: HMSO.

Her Majesty's Treasury (HMT) (2007) *Review of Sub-national Economic Development and Regeneration*. London: HMT.

Her Majesty's Treasury (HMT) (2011) *National Infrastructure Plan*. London: HMSO.

Heseltine, M. (2012) *No Stone Unturned*. London: BIS.

Higgins, M. and Allmendinger, P. (1999) The Changing Nature of Public Planning Practice under the New Right: The Legacies and Implications of Privatisation. *Planning Practice and Research* 14(1): 39–67.

Hillier, J. (2002) *Shadows of Power: An Allegory of Prudence in Land Use Planning*. London: Routledge.

Hillier, J. and Healey, P. (2008) Introduction to Part 1. In J. Hillier and P. Healey (eds) *Critical Essays in Planning Theory*. Vol. 3*Contemporary Movements in Planning Theory*Aldershot: Ashgate..

Hirsh, A. (1981) *The French New Left: An Intellectual History from Sartre to Gorz*. Boston: South End Press.

House of Commons (HoC) (2002) Third Party Rights of Appeal, Paper 2/38. 22 May. London: House of Commons.

House of Commons Communities and Local Government Committee (HoC CLG) (2011) The National Planning Policy Framework. Eighth Report of Session 2010–2012. London: HMSO.

House of Commons Communities and Local Government Committee (HoC CLG) (2012) *Financing of New Housing Supply*. London: HMSO.

House of Commons Environmental Audit Committee (HoC EAC) (2011) Sustainable Development and the Localism Bill. Third Report of Session, London: HMSO.

House of Commons (Office of the Deputy Prime Minister) Housing, Planning, Local Government and the Regions Committee (HoC ODPM) (2003) Planning for Sustainable Housing and Communities: Sustainable Communities in the South East. Eighth Report of Session. London: HMSO.

House of CommonsTransport, Local Government and the Regions Committee (HoC TLGR) (2002) Thirteenth Report: Planning Green Paper. London: HMSO.

Hodkinson, S. (2011) Housing Regeneration and the Private Finance Initiative in England: Unstitching the Neoliberal Urban Straightjacket. *Antipode* 43(2): 358–383.

Home Builders Federation (HBF) (2010) *Let's Start at Home. Building Out of Recession*. London: HBF.

Howard, M. C. and King, J. E. (2008) *The Rise of Neoliberalism in Advanced Capitalist Economies: A Materialist Analysis*. Basingstoke: Palgrave Macmillan.

Imrie, R. and Raco, M. (eds) (2003) *Urban Renaissance? New Labour, Community and Urban Policy*. Bristol: Policy Press.

Imrie, R. and Thomas, H. (1999) (eds) *British Urban Policy: An Evaluation of the Urban Development Corporations*. 2nd edn. London: Sage.

Imrie, R. and Thomas, H. (2003) (eds) *Urban Renaissance?: New Labour, Community and Urban Policy*. Bristol: Policy Press.

Imrie, R., Lees, L. and Raco, M. (eds) (2009) *Regenerating London: Governance, Sustainability and Community in a Global City*. London: Routledge.

Inch, A. (2012) Deconstructing Spatial Planning: Reinterpreting the Articulation of a New Ethos for English Local Planning. *European Planning Studies* 20(6) 1039–1057.

Innes, J. E. (1995) Planning Theory's Emerging Paradigm: Communicative Action and Interactive Practice. *Journal of Planning Education and Research* 14(3): 183–190.

Innes, J. E. and Booher, D. E. (2010) *Planning with Complexity: An Introduction to Collaborative Rationality for Public Policy*. London: Routledge.

Jacobs, J. (1961) *The Death and Life of Great American Cities*. London: Penguin.

Jameson, F. (1991) *Postmodernism or the Cultural Logic of Late Capitalism*. London: Duke University Press.

Jessop, B. (1990) *State Theory*. Cambridge: Polity.

Jessop, B. (2002) Liberalism, Neoliberalism and Urban Governance: A State-Theoretical Perspective. In N. Brenner and N. Theodore (eds) *Spaces of Neoliberalism: Urban Restructuring in North America and Western Europe*. Oxford: Blackwell.

Jessop, B. (1997) The Entrepreneurial City. Re-imaging Localities, Redesigning Economic Governance, or Restructuring Capital? In N. Jewson and S. MacGregor (eds) *Transforming Cities: Contested Governance and New Spatial Divisions*. London: Routledge, pp. 28–41.

Jessop, B. and Peck, J. (1998) *Fast Policy/Local Discipline: The Politics of Time and Scale and the Neoliberal Workfare Offensive*. Mimeograph. Lancaster: Department of Sociology, University of Lancaster.

Jones, M. (2001) The Rise of the Regional State in Economic Governance: Partnerships for Prosperity or New Scale of State Power? *Environment and Planning A* 33: 1185–1211.

Jones, M. (2009) Phase Space: Geography, Relational Thinking, and Beyond. *Progress in Human Geography* 33(4): 487–506.

Jones, R. (1982) *Town and Country Chaos*. London: Adam Smith Institute.

Joseph, K. (1976) *Monetarism Is Not Enough*. London: Centre for Policy Studies.

Keeble, L. (1969) *Principles and Practice of Town and Country Planning*. London: Estates Gazette.

Killian, J., and Pretty, D. (2008) *Planning Applications: A Faster and More Responsive System: Final Report*. London: DCLG.

Labour Party (1997) *New Labour, New Life for Britain*. London: Labour Party.

Lash, S. and Urry, J. (1987) *The End of Organized Capitalism*. Cambridge: Polity.

Lash, S. and Urry, J. (1994) *Economies of Signs and Space*. London: Sage.

Lee, D. (1973) Requiem for Large Scale Planning Models. *Journal of the American Institute of Planners* 39: 117–142.

Lees, L. (2014) The Urban Injustices of New Labour's 'New Urban Renewal': The Case of the Aylesbury Estate in London. *Antipode* 46(4): 921–947.

Le-Las, W. and Shirley, E. (2012) Does the Planning System Need a Tea Party? *Journal of Planning Law* 3: 239–243.

Lefebvre, H. (1946) *L'Existentialisme*. Paris: Éditions du sagittaire.

Lefebvre, H. (1962) *Introduction à la modernité*. Paris: L'Arche.

Lefebvre, H. (1969) *The Sociology of Marx*. New York: Pantheon Books.

Lefebvre, H. (1974) *La production de l'espace*. English trans. 1991. Paris: Anthropos.

Lloyd, M. G., McCarthy, J., McGreal, S. and Berry, J. (2003) Business Improvement Districts, Planning and Urban Regeneration. *International Planning Studies* 8(4): 295–321.

Lowndes, V. (1996) Varieties of New Institutionalism: A Critical Appraisal. *Public Administration* 74: 181–197.

Lowndes, V. (2005) Something Old, Something New, Something Borrowed ...: How Institutions Change (and Stay the Same) in Local Governance. *Policy Studies* 26(3): 291–309.

Lyotard, J.-F. ([1979] 1984) *The Postmodern Condition: A Report on Knowledge*. Minneapolis, MN: University of Minnesota Press.

Lyotard, J.-F. ([1983] 1988) *The Differend: Phrases in Dispute*. Minneapolis, MN: University of Minnesota Press.

Macartney, H. (2011) *Variegated Neoliberalism. EU Varieties of Capitalism and International Political Economy*. London: Routledge.

McAuslan, P. (1981) *The Ideologies of Planning Law*. Oxford: Pergamon Press.

McCann, E. and Ward, K. (2011) *Mobile Urbanism: Cities and Policy Making in the Global Age*. Minneapolis, MN: University of Minnesota Press.

McClymont, K. (2011) Revitalising the Political: Development Control and Agonism in Planning Practice. *Planning Theory* 10(3): 230–256.

McCormick, J. (1991) *British Politics and the Environment*. London: Earthscan.

McGuirk, P. M. (2005) Neoliberalist Planning? Re-thinking And Re-casting Sydney's Metropolitan Planning. *Geographical Research* 43(1); 59–70.

McKinsey Global Institute (1998) *Driving Productivity and Growth in the UK Economy*. London: McKinsey Global Institute.

McLoughlin, B. (1969) *Urban and Regional Planning: A Systems Approach*. London: Faber and Faber.

McNay, L. (1994) *Foucault: A Critical Introduction*. Cambridge: Polity.

Mannheim, K. ([1940] 1980) *Man and Society in an Age of Reconstruction*. London: Routledge and Kegan Paul.

Marchart, O. (2007). *Post-Foundational Thought: Political Difference in Nancy, Lefort, Badiou and Laclau*. Edinburgh: Edinburgh University Press.

Marquand, D. (2004) *The Decline of the Public: The Hollowing Out of Citizenship*. Cambridge: Polity.

Marsh, D., and Rhodes, R. A. W. (1992) *Implementing Thatcherite Policies: Audit of an Era*. Buckingham: Open University Press.

Massey, D. (2005) *For Space*. London: Sage.

Massey, D. (2011) A Counterhegemonic Relationality of Place. In E. McCann and K. Ward (eds) *Mobile Urbanism: Cities and Policymaking in the Global Age*. Minneapolis, MN: University of Minnesota Press.

Massey, A. and Pyper, R. (2005) *Public Management and Modernisation in Britain*. Basingstoke: Palgrave Macmillan.

Merrifield, A. (2002) *Metromarxism*. London: Routledge.

Metzger, J. and Schmitt, P. (2012). When Soft Spaces Harden: The EU Strategy for the Baltic Sea Region. *Environment and Planning A*. 44: 263–280.

Metzger, J., Allmendinger, P. and Oosterlynck, S. (2015) *Displacing the Political: Democratic Deficits in Contemporary European Territorial Governance*. London: Routledge.

Moore-Milroy, B. (1991) Into Postmodern Weightlessness. *Journal of Planning Education and Research* 10(3): 181–187.

Morphet, J. (2011) *Effective Practice in Spatial Planning*. London: Routledge.

Mouffe, C. (2005) *On the Political*. London: Routledge.

Nathanial Lichfield and Partners (NLP) (2013) *Objectively Speaking. 12 Months of Applying the NPPF to Housing Targets in Local Plans: A Review of Examinations*. London: NLP.

National Audit Office (NAO) (2007) *The Thames Gateway: Laying the Foundations*. London: HMSO.

National Audit Office (NAO) (2008) *Planning for Homes: Speeding up Planning Applications for Major Housing Developments in England*. London: HMSO.

National Housing and Planning and Advisory Unit (NHPAU) (2009) *Attitudes towards Housing*. London: HMSO.

National Housing and Planning Advisory Unit (NHPAU) (2010) *Public Attitudes to Housing*. London: HMSO.

Newman, P. and A. Thornley (1997) Fragmentation and Centralisation in the Governance of London: Influencing the Urban Policy and Planning Agenda. *Urban Studies* 34(7): 967–988.

Norman, J. (2010) *The Big Society: The Anatomy of the New Politics*. Buckingham: University of Buckingham Press.

Nuffield Foundation (1983) *Town and Country Planning: The Report of a Committee of Inquiry Appointed by the Nuffield Foundation*. London: Nuffield Foundation.

Offe, C. (1984) Contradictions of the Welfare State. Cambridge, MA: MIT Press.

Office of the Deputy Prime Minister (ODPM) (2002) *Sustainable Communities: Delivering through Planning*. London: ODPM.

Office of the Deputy Prime Minister (ODPM) (2003) *Housing Planning Local Government and the Regions Committee, Planning, Competitiveness and Productivity*, Fourth Report of Session 2002–2003. London: HMSO.

Office of the Deputy Prime Minister (ODPM) (2004) *The Egan Review: Skills for Sustainable Communities*. London: HMSO.

Office of the Deputy Prime Minister (ODPM) (2005) *Sustainable Communities: Homes for All*. London: HMSO.

Oosterlynck, S. and Swyngedouw, E. (2010) Noise Reduction: The Post-political Quandary of Night Flights at Brussels Airport. *Environment and Planning A* 42(7): 1577.

Orwell, G. (1949) *Nineteen Eighty-Four*. London: Secker and Warburg.

Pain, T. (2015) It's Planning, Captain, but Not as We Know It. *Town and Country Planning*. (June/July): 262–263.

Painter, J. (2010) Rethinking Territory. *Antipode* 42: 1090–1118.

Paris, C. (ed.) (1982) *Critical Readings in Planning Theory*. Oxford: Pergamon.

Pearce, L. (2010) Tory Planning Green Paper Has Industry Up in Arms. *Construction Magazine*, 26 February.

Peck, J. (2010) *Constructions of Neoliberal Reason*. Oxford: Oxford University Press.

Peck, J. and Tickell, A. (2002) Neoliberalizing Space. *Antipode* 34(3): 380–404.

Peel, D. and Lloyd, M. G. (2007) Neo-Traditional Planning: Towards a New Ethos for Land Use Planning? *Land Use Policy* 24: 396–403.

Pennington, M. (2000) *Planning and the Political Market*. London: Athlone Press.

Pickvance, C. (1982) Physical Planning and Market Forces in Urban Development. In C. Paris (ed.) *Critical Readings in Planning Theory*. Oxford: Pergamon.

Planning Advisory Group (PAG) (1965) *The Future of Development Plans*. London: HMSO.

Planning Officers Society (2005) *Policies for Spatial Plans: A Guide to Writing the Policy Content of Local Development Documents*. London: POS.

Ploger, J. (2004) Strife: Urban Planning and Agonism. *Planning Theory*. 3: 71–92.

Polanyi, K. (1944) *The Great Transformation: The Political and Economic Origins of Our Time*. Boston: Beacon Press.

Policy Exchange (2007) *The Best Laid Plans: How Planning Prevents Economic Growth*. London: Policy Exchange.

Policy Exchange (2012) *Planning for Less: The Impact of Abolishing Regional Planning*. London: Policy Exchange.

Popper, K. (1945) *The Open Society and Its Enemies*. London: Routledge.

Purcell, M. (2009) Resisting Neoliberalisation: Communicative Planning or Counter-Hegemonic Moments? *Planning Theory* 8(2): 140–165.

Rabinow, P. (1984) *The Foucault Reader*. London: Penguin Books.

Raco, M. (2005) Sustainable Development, Rolled-out Neoliberalism and Sustainable Communities. *Antipode* 37(2): 324–347.

Raco, M. (2011) Conflict Management, Democratic Demands, and the Post-Politics of Privatisation. Paper presented at the symposium Post-Political Planning: The End of Consensus?KTH University, Stockholm, May.

Raco, M. (2013) *State-led Privatisation and the Demise of the Democratic State: Welfare Reform and Localism in an Era of Regualtory Capitalism.* Aldershot: Ashgate.

Raco, M. (2014) Conflict Management, Democratic Demands and the Post-Politics of Privatization. In J. Metzger, P. Allmendinger and S. Oosterlynck (eds) *Planning Against the Political: Democratic Deficits in European Territorial Governance.* London: Routledge.

Rancière, J. (1983) The Myth of the Artisan: Critical Reflections on a Category of Social History. *International Labour and Working Class History.* 24(Fall): 10

Rancière, J. (1999) *Disagreement: Politics and Philosophy.* Minneapolis, MN: University of Minnesota Press.

Rancière, J. (2001) Ten Theses on Politics. *Theory and Event* 5(3): 14–29.

Rancière, J. (2004) *Malais dans l'esthétique.* Paris: Éditions Galilée.

Rancière, J. (2006) *Hatred of Democracy.* London: Verso.

Ravetz, A. (1980) *Remaking Cities: Contradictions of the Recent Urban Environment.* London: Croom Helm.

Reade, E. J. (1987) *British Town and Country Planning.* Milton Keynes: Open University Press.

Rhodes, J., Tyler, P. and Brenna, A. (2002) *The Single Regeneration Budget: Final Evaluation.* London: HMSO.

Robison, R. (2006) Introduction. In R. Robison (ed.) *The Neo-Liberal Revolution: Forging the Market State.* Basingstoke: Palgrave Macmillan.

Royal Commission on Environmental Pollution (RCEP) (2002) *Environmental Planning.* London: HMSO.

Royal Town Planning Institute (RTPI) (1976) *Planning and the Future.* London: RTPI.

Royal Town Planning Institute (RTPI) (2001) *A New Vision for Planning.* London: RTPI.

Royal Town Planning Institute (RTPI) (2007) *Shaping and Delivering Tomorrow's Places: Effective Practice in Spatial Planning.* London: RTPI.

Rydin, Y. (1993) *Urban and Environmental Planning in the UK.* Basingstoke: Palgrave Macmillan.

Rydin, Y. (2013) *The Future of Planning: Beyond Growth Dependence.* Bristol: Policy Press.

Saint UK Index (2012) *Annual Barometer of Public Attitudes towards Development.*

Sager, T. (1994) *Communicative Planning Theory.* Aldershot: Avebury.

Sager, T. (2013) *Reviving Critical Planning Theory: Dealing with Pressure, Neo-liberalism, and Responsibility in Communicative Planning.* London: Routledge.

Sandercock, L. (1998) *Towards Cosmopolis.* Chichester: John Wiley.

Schon, D. A. (1983) *The Reflective Practitioner.* New York: Basic Books.

Schiller, D. (2000) *Digital Capitalism.* Cambridge, MA: MIT Press.

Schmidt, V. (2008) Discursive Institutionalism: The Explanatory Power of Ideas and Discourse. *Annual Review of Political Science* 11: 303–326.

Scott, L. F. (chair) (1942) *Report of the Committee on Land Utilisation in Rural Areas, Scott Report.* Cmd 6378. London: HMSO.

Scott, A. J. and Roweis, S. T. (1977) Urban Planning Theory in Practice: A Reappraisal. *Environment and Planning A* 9: 1097–1119.

Sharpe, M. and Boucher, G. (2010) *Žižek and Politics: A Critical Introduction.* Edinburgh: Edinburgh University Press.

Sharpe, T. ([1940] 1945) *Town Planning.* Harmondsworth: Penguin.

Siegan, B. (1972) *Land Use without Zoning.* Lanham, MD: Lexington Books.

Skeffington, A. (1969) *People and Planning.* London: HSMO.

Sorenson, A. D. and Day, R. A. (1981) Libertarian Planning. *Town Planning Review* 52:166–178.

Stiglitz, J. (2010) *Freefall: Free Markets and the Sinking of the Global Economy.* London: Penguin.

Storper, M. 1997: *The Regional World: Territorial Development in a Global Economy.* New York: Guilford.

Swyngedouw, E. (2009) The Antimonies of the Post-Political City: In Search of a Democratic Politics of Environmental Production. *International Journal of Urban and Regional Research* 33: 601–620.

Swyngedouw, E. (2011) Interrogating Post-Democratisation: Reclaiming Egalitarian Political Spaces. *Political Geography* 30: 370–380.

Thomas, M. J. (1982) *The Procedural Planning Theory of A. Faludi.* In C. Paris (ed.) *Critical Readings in Planning Theory.* Oxford: Pergamon.

Thorne, M. (1986) Pressure on Development Control. *Planning Practice and Research* 1(1): 28–30.

Thornley, A. (1991) *Urban Planning under Thatcherism. The Challenge of the Market.* London: Routledge.

Toffler, A. (1970) *Future Shock.* New York: Random House.

Toffler, A. (1981) *The Third Wave.* New York: Bantam Books.

Touraine, A. (1988) *Return of the Actor.* Minnesota, MN: University of Minnesota Press.

Town and Country Planning Association (TCPA) (2015) *The Future of Planning and Placemaking.* London: TCPA.

University College London (UCL) and Deloitte (2007) *Shaping and Delivering Tomorrow's Places: Effective Practice in Spatial Planning.* London: RTPI.

Uthwatt Committee (Expert Committee on Compensation and Betterment) (1942) *Final Report,* Cmd 6386. London: HMSO.

Vivid Economics (2012) *Inexpensive Progress? A Framework for Assessing the Costs and Benefits of Planning Reform.* London: Vivid Economics.

Ward, S. V. (1994) *Planning and Urban Change.* London: Spon.

Watson, J., and Crook, M. (2009) Fewer Plans, More Planning? *Town and Country Planning.* 78(3): 123–124.

Webster, F. (2006) *Theories of the Information Society.* 3rd edn. London: Routledge.

Wilks-Heeg, S. (1996) Urban Experiments Limited Revisited: Urban Policy Comes Full Circle? *Urban Studies* 33(8): 1263–1279.

Žižek, S. (1989) *The Sublime Object of Ideology.* London: Verso.

Žižek, S. (1994) The Spectre of Ideology. In S. Žižek (ed.) *Mapping Ideology.* London: Verso.

Žižek, S. (1999) *The Ticklish Subject: The Absent Centre of Political Ontology.* London: Verso.

Žižek, S. (2002a) *Welcome to the Desert of the Real.* London: Verso.

Žižek, S. (2002b) Holding the Place. In J. Butler, E. Laclau and S. Žižek, *Contingency, Hegemony and Universality.* London: Verso.

Index

Note: Page numbers followed by 'f' refer to figures and followed by 't' refer to tables.